THE ART SONG

MUSIC RESEARCH AND
INFORMATION GUIDES
(VOL. 6)

GARLAND REFERENCE LIBRARY
OF THE HUMANITIES
(VOL. 673)

MUSIC RESEARCH AND INFORMATION GUIDES

THE ART SONG
A Research and Information Guide

Douglass Seaton

GARLAND PUBLISHING, INC. • NEW YORK & LONDON
1987

Library of Congress Cataloging-in-Publication Data

Seaton, Douglass.
  The art song.

  (Music research and information guides ; vol.
6) (Garland reference library of the humanities ;
vol. 673)
    Bibliography: p.
    Discography: p.
    1. Songs—Bibliography. I. Title. II. Series.
III. Series: Garland reference library of the
humanities ; v. 673.
ML128.S3S33 1987   016.7843   86-33553
ISBN 0-8240-8554-X (alk. paper)

Printed on acid-free, 250-year-life paper
Manufactured in the United States of America

To Gayle

... like music on the waters
Is thy sweet voice to me: ...

                    Byron
                    "Stanzas for Music"

ACKNOWLEDGMENTS

The support of a Developing Scholar Award from The Florida State University for the year 1985-86 made the completion of this book possible. In addition, credit is due to the fine facilities of the libraries at The Florida State University and their hard-working and long-suffering librarians. Thanks are especially owed to the staff of the Warren D. Allen Music Library and to the Interlibrary Loan Office at the Robert Manning Strozier Library. I am also very grateful to my graduate assistants who helped to locate materials, Mark Knoll, J. Michael Cooper, Carla Copeland, and particularly Edmund Goehring who also assisted in the preparation of the typescript.

CONTENTS

x   **Contents**

PREFACE

It is hoped that this book will be helpful to a wide user-ship. Although it has been prepared by a musicologist, it includes materials that are believed to be useful to general music students and scholars, performers, and listeners.

The introduction begins by discussing the problem of defining the scope of the art song itself. There follow some basic indications of major artistic principles in the field of song, into which I have inserted a few thoughts on how these principles might affect the different users of this book. A brief historical overview of the history of the art song from about 1600 to the twentieth century then offers a general orientation to some major developments and issues in the genre, century by century.

The bibliography chapters contain items in English, German, and the major Romance languages. They include specific studies of art song published as books and monographs, selected articles in periodicals and collections, and some dissertations and theses. I have excluded obvious, general materials such as dictionaries, survey histories of music, and basic biographies of composers. Articles from periodicals addressed primarily to a pedagogical public were omitted. Most notable among these is the National Association of Teachers of Singing **Bulletin** (recently renamed **Journal**), which contains numerous articles of widely varying styles, degrees of technicality, and significance; merely to have indexed the **NATS Bulletin** would have made this book unwieldy. Dissertations were treated on a case-by-case basis; their inclusion depended partly on whether they themselves or their abstracts were accessible and partly on whether they appeared to fill gaps in the general literature.

Of several thousand items read and considered, only a small percentage could actually be listed. The literature grows continuously, and one of the most frustrating aspects of the preparation of such a book is the constant awareness of the inevitability that some valuable items will be overlooked. The bibliography is only a guide, not an omnibus that can deliver all and sundry; as a guide, it should point the reader in directions for further study.

Each entry includes standard bibliographic information on the item, which should permit the reader to locate it easily. As far as possible, the annotations are based on direct reading of the material. Where that has not been possible, I have relied on abstracts and have indicated what abstract was consulted. The annotations are intended to indicate the nature of the items in terms of both organization and content; they also list the presence of appendix material, bibliographies and work-lists, and indexes.

In organizing the bibliography, I have attempted to place items where they would be discovered most easily. In the several cases in which entries could logically have been located in more than one place, cross-references and the index will give access to them. Within each section or subsection of the bibliography, items are listed alphabetically.

INTRODUCTION

Definitions

The term "art song" generally implies a solo song with keyboard accompaniment. In the latter half of the twentieth century it belongs almost exclusively to the vocal recital. To define "art song" in a precise fashion is not by any means straightforward, however.

The performers required for the song are a significant criterion in defining the genre, but there is a considerable variety of possibilities that must be considered. The nineteenth-century, piano-accompanied song is only the most familiar type. It is also necessary to include the lute songs and the basso continuo songs of the seventeenth century. Songs with obbligato parts for solo instruments complicate the issue further. It is certainly usual to rule out pieces for more than one singer, though even here one runs up against such works as Schumann's **Spanisches Liederspiel,** which is comprised of not only solo songs but also duets and even a quartet. One might be inclined to include the English consort song of the early seventeenth century but wish to assign works for solo voices with instrumental ensembles from the present century to another genre. To rule out even orchestrally accompanied pieces is impossible, given the orchestrations of songs originally written for voice and piano, such as Berlioz's **Nuits d'été** and the direct evolution of orchestrally conceived songs from the piano Lied (e.g., Strauss, **Vier letzte Lieder**).

The intended performance milieu of a song might be considered a factor in classifying it as to genre. Yet on these grounds it would often be difficult to justify conceptually the usage of the term in practice. For example, it would be impossible to eliminate the domestic Lieder of eighteenth-century Germany from the category of art song, but English and American parlor songs of the nineteenth century are generally excluded, although sociologically these two repertoires are closer to each

xiii

other than either is to the late nineteenth-century concert Lied.

One might attempt to define the art song in negative terms, separating it from other types of song, but here, too, problems arise. First of all, art song is distinguished from popular or folk song; but many songs that belong in the recital repertoire are settings of folk songs. Haydn, Beethoven, and Brahms wrote numerous arrangements of folk songs, as have Aaron Copland and John Jacob Niles, to name only a few of the most obvious examples. The enormous influence of the folk style on the art song renders the distinction still hazier. It is even possible for art songs to become so absorbed into popular culture that they are known as folk songs; Schubert's "Der Lindenbaum" and Brahms's "Wiegenlied" would fall into this category.

Likewise, the art song may be distinguished from the dramatic song or operatic aria. In the case of the aria, a real contrast may be seen in the style of the music, for the art song generally requires less virtuosity and demands more intimate interaction between singer and accompanist. Arias, of course, cohabit the recital stage with art songs. In the cases of other kinds of dramatic songs, the line of demarcation is fuzzier. A setting of a song text from a play, intended for the theater, may become dissociated from its original context and become an art song. There also existed in the early nineteenth century the practice of performing independent songs in the context of informal dramas centered on the songs and played by amateurs in a domestic milieu.

Finally, one might make a distinction between art song and religious song. Here, however, the crucial point is the force of liturgical versus non-liturgical intention, not the sacred character of the texts. Schubert's "Ave Maria," based on Walter Scott, is an example of an art song that is far more likely today to be heard in a church setting than in a recital. Brahms's **Vier ernste Gesänge** are recital repertoire. Ives's "Serenity" is difficult to classify exclusively in either category.

Turning to the classifications of art songs in various languages, even those in the narrowest mainstream of the history of Western music, difficulties in definition become surprisingly and disconcertingly complex.

The German word "Lied" is casually thought of as an equivalent to the English term "art song." The German term is even used to refer to art songs in other languages. Ironically, an essential connotation of the word "Lied" is that the piece must be characterized by artlessness, and it has specific implications for style and form. To circumvent that connotation, the compound "Kunstlied" had to be invented. In German, moreover, one is more likely to find the indication of sub-genres such as "Gesang" for

a more sophisticated song or "Ballade" for a setting of a narrative poem. Hugo Wolf's employment of the term "Gedichte" for his
major collections of songs on poems of Mörike, Eichendorff, and
Goethe indicates not only his emphasis on the importance of the
poets and the poems, but also the sense that for his style the
word "Lied" seems inappropriate.

In French, the art song has been denominated differently
from century to century. During the seventeenth century the
common term was "air." Specific song types such as the vaude-
ville and brunette were also recognized. These gave way during
the eighteenth century to the "romance," at first denoting a
setting of a narrative text but later used quite broadly. This
term was widely adopted in Latin America, even in Germany, and in
Russia. In the Romantic period the more sophisticated, expressive, salon or concert song became known as "mélodie." The
French word "chanson," which foreigners probably learn as the
word for song, refers to the popular or cabaret song in modern
French usage, but may be encountered in reference to art songs as
well, as in Debussy's **Chansons de Bilitis**.

During the seventeenth century in Italy the song was referred to variously as "madrigal" or "aria," depending on style,
or, in the first part of the century, "cantata." In the eighteenth century the common term was "canzonetta," which has conno-
tations of simplicity of structure and lightness of mood. The
dominant modern usage for the sophisticated art song is "lirica."

Given such terminological flexibility, the delimitation of
the material for this book has been no easy matter. To a great
extent, the selection has been empirical, taking into consideration all the points outlined above. It has relied upon what the
author has believed to be common usage of the term "art song" and
in some cases on extensions of that usage to incorporate other
repertoire that seems logically or usefully to belong to the
genre.

Aesthetic Issues

The artistic principles that underlie the art song from the
Renaissance up to the twentieth century were formulated in the
sixteenth century. They rely on the general assumption that the
text is composed before the music and that the music then responds to the text. It is helpful to conceive a song as a
reading of the text, not unlike an oral reading but to some
extent more permanent. Whether or not the composer intends to
impose an interpretation on a poem, his way of reading it will
necessarily be evident from his music, even if that reading is

misguided or trivial. When the student approaches any musical
work, it ought to be with the idea of discovering how the composer thinks and provokes thought in music. In the case of a
song, the approach is appropriately directed to understanding how
one artist (the composer) reads the work of another (the poet).
To the listener who already knows the poem, the song may seem to
read it with special eloquence or it may suggest new interpretations; it may even seem wrong-headed. At the least, the listener
or scholar ought to keep a mind open to new or alternate readings; the experience of a song will almost inevitably prove
frustrating if one's only intention is to test the composer's
work against one's own reading or the composition one thinks in
advance that the composer ought to have written.

For the purpose of the present overview, the aspects of a
poem that may affect the composition of the music of a song may
be divided into three broad and necessarily interrelated areas:
diction, structure, and meaning. Each of these has applications
for all approaches to the study of the genre.

In regard to diction, the strongest control over the music
is exerted by the poetic meter. For English and German poetry
the relatively clear and regular stress patterns of the syllables
in metrical feet parallel closely the strong and weak beats of
common-practice musical style, while the grouping of feet into
poetic lines parallels the regular phrasing of the music of the
Classic and Romantic periods. The matching of textual and musical rhythms can therefore be accomplished conveniently and systematically. Indeed, it runs the risk of mechanical dullness.
The achievement of a satisfying balance between logical fitting
together of the words and music and the avoidance of unimagina-
tive predictability is an important issue in works in these
languages. In the Romance languages syllable stress patterns are
comparatively less important. As a result, the rhythm within the
phrase may be less patterned and more subtle, while the creation
of a coherent phrase-length unit is the major task. Obviously,
it is essential for the composer to understand the rhythmic
peculiarities of the spoken language. For the performer, the
style of the music can only be conveyed when this aspect of
rhythm is understood. The analyst or critic will be concerned
with the composer's skill in conveying the rhythm of language
accurately in music, as well as with the aspects of rhythm that
deviate from the linguistically directed norms and thereby serve
as vehicles for expression.

Pitch inflection is also important in language, but the
paralleling of spoken inflection in the melody of song is far
less pronounced than the treatment of rhythm. In Western European languages interrogative sentences tend to rise in pitch,
while declarative ones fall. This sort of basic pitch gesture is

commonly preserved in song. There have been some experiments
with the interrelation of vowel colors and melodic pitch, and
this is a field that may profit from further research. In general, however, melodic direction tends to be used in the art song
for the expression of meaning rather than to reinforce diction.

Where the structure of songs is concerned, the composer is
faced with potential conflicts on various levels. Within a
poetic text two types of structure may operate, a grammatical one
and a lyrical one. The former, characteristic of literary prose,
will tend toward asymmetry; the latter, more characteristic of
music, will guide the text in the direction of symmetry and
abstract design. Poetry might then be regarded as the application of music to literature. The song may emphasize either. If
the lyrical structure is stressed, the song is likely to be
dominated by regular and symmetrical phrase patterns which will
give it a strong formal unity, varied by any grammatical devia-
tions from those patterns. If the grammatical structures are
given more control, the problem will be to assure musical coherence. These are the composer's and the critic's concerns. The
performer's task is to determine how the composer intends him or
her to convey both the grammatical and the lyrical structure and
to succeed in doing so.

On a different level, there is the effect of the interaction
of textual and purely musical criteria on structure. In language, coherence may be achieved by the steady forward flow of
ideas; in music, on the other hand, which depends on the abstract
relationship of one unit to another, coherence requires restate-
ment. Crucial for the song is the success of the structure in
both poetic and musical terms. To some extent each can help to
solve the problems of the other; recurring music may help to
unify and articulate a continuous forward motion of literary
ideas, and the continuity of ideas may permit more freedom of
form in the music or compensate for the danger of seeming inco-
herence in an unfamiliar musical style. (This last point was
especially important to the composers of the Second Vienna School
during the period of experimentation with atonality.)

A classic problem in the study of the song is that of the
use of strophic or through-composed form. Given a strophic poem,
a strophic setting implies the dominance of literary form over
literary content in the composer's reading, a through-composed
setting suggests the reverse. For the scholar, analysis of a
song's form should reveal the rationale underlying the composer's
reading and the effectiveness of the specific form in communica-
ting that reading. In a strophic setting, the music must of
course suit a variety of dictions and meanings. A strophic
setting is therefore fraught with difficulty for the composer,
for the music must be written with all the stanzas equally in

mind. On another front, the performer must approach the two
forms somewhat differently. In a through-composed song the details of the composer's reading of the text are inevitably more
explicit than in a strophic one. The performer must understand
the meaning of the changing material, but need not impose a great
deal on it. With a strophic song, however, the varying content
of the stanzas must be more creatively handled by the performer--
the singer is actually called upon to interpret more than in a
through-composed song. A model case for this is Schubert's
setting of Goethe's "Heidenröslein," in which the words "Freuden"
and "leiden" must be sung to identical music.

Strophic and through-composed forms are not, of course, the
only possibilities. Another point may be illustrated by considering the fairly common symmetrical ternary form. This is generally a structure more rooted in musical than in textual principles, since the poet rarely finds it necessary to repeat the
opening stanza of a poem at the end, while this is a very satisfying plan for a piece of music. When, for example, Schumann
returns to the opening music in "Widmung" from **Myrthen,** he
recapitulates Rückert's opening lines, imposing on the text a
structure that the poet did not intend. By contrast, the application of the same form on a continuous text serves to interpret
it as having a symmetrical plan of ideas, even though the details
of the content may change in the course of the poem. Schubert,
in setting Heine's "Ihr Bild," engages in just this kind of
reading of a three-stanza text in order to highlight the connections between the outer stanzas and their contrast with the
central one.

The last few paragraphs have anticipated the discussion of
meaning in the composer's musical treatment of a poem. At its
most basic, the musical expression of textual meaning results in
"word-painting." A useful example might be the setting of the
word "drop" in Purcell's "Music for a While" (actually a song
from the music for a play, but one of those items that has become
so thoroughly absorbed into the art song repertoire that one is
forced to bend the boundaries of the definition). In this case
not only is there a sequence of illustrative downward melodic
gestures, but the detached repetitions of the word create an
onomatopoeic plopping sound. Word-painting can easily be abused,
however, and deteriorate into a mechanistic response on the
composer's part that results in sheer silliness. It is not a
very important means by which texts inspire musical ideas in most
art song.

Much more important is the ability of the composer to embody
the spirit of the poem in the music. It is not always easy to
define analytically how this is done. The most successful songs
in which this can also be explained clearly are, of course, those

of Schubert, where the accompaniments seem to express the mood so
effectively. This is achieved because the composer's reading of
the poem not only identified poetic images that might be depicted
in the music but also how that depiction could clarify the significance of the image in establishing an emotional condition;
the figures not only illustrate flowing water or a galloping
horse, but the therapeutic consolation of sitting by the brook or
the agitation of the rider. But the manner in which this vital-
ization of the mood of the poem takes place is not often so easy
to pin down, and the field for critics remains wide open. It
cannot be exaggerated that for performers--accompanists as well
as singers, as the instance of Schubert will make clear--study
and analysis of this aspect of the song is essential.

There is still room for considerable research into the means
of mood-setting employed in the theory and practice of song in
the late eighteenth and very early nineteenth centuries. The
Baroque doctrine that expressive values could be assigned to
certain conventional musical "figures" was still very much alive
through the Classic period. The most obvious example is the
theory of the affects of the different keys. Another, less often
thought of, was the potential of familiar dance styles or styles
associated with other genres for establishing the spirit of a
work. Mozart's "Lied zur Gesellenreise" (K. 468) adopts the
manner of a gavotte, and his "Als Luise die Briefe ihres unge-
treuen Liebhabers verbrannte" (K. 520) is based on the style of
the keyboard fantasy; these choices undoubtedly have expressive
significance. It has not been established how long-lived the
influence of such theories was. A music-historical study might
well investigate their traces in the Lieder of Mozart's Viennese
successors or in those of the Second Berlin School composers.
Even a century later, Mahler still employed the march and the
Ländler for expressive purposes.

Finally, there exist songs in which the content of a poem
has a direct influence on the compositional procedures or the
structure of a song. This is especially interesting in the songs
of serial composers. A simple example is Schoenberg's "Tot," op.
48, no. 2, to words by Jakob Haringer. The text suggests that
happiness and delusion are no more than two aspects of the same
thing. Schoenberg responded by creating a musical mirror-image
in the vocal line, a straightforward statement of the basic
twelve-tone row immediately followed by its retrograde, and then
a condensed version of the same procedure with only four notes.

Historical Overview

Only a very brief historical survey will be made here,

outlining the most significant factors in the development of the
art song. No attempt has been made even to list all the many
important composers. The reader is, of course, referred to the
first part of the bibliography for more comprehensive coverages.

THE SEVENTEENTH CENTURY

The enormous success of the Renaissance madrigal and related
genres during the sixteenth century contributed to the collapse
of the polyphonic style. As the century mark approached, two
different vectors combined to produce the rich new repertoire of
accompanied song. The first of these was the flexible performance practice that allowed polyphonically conceived songs to be
sung as solos with one or more instruments taking the other
parts. This produced the consort song, such as those of William
Byrd, but it was particularly accomplished by means of the lute,
which would permit a single performer to realize the entire
composition. There was an artistic as well as a practical advantage to this texture, in that it resulted in a perfectly clear
presentation of the words. The lute song was brought to its
highest artistic level in England, where its greatest master was
John Dowland. The French had a parallel tradition in the **air de
cour**, which had its own distinct national style, as did the
Italians as well.

The second reason for the rise of the solo song was the
aesthetic speculations of the late Renaissance humanist musicians
who studied the extant records of ancient Greek music. These
men, in particular the so-called Florentine Camerata, were fas-
cinated by the powerful ethical effects attributed by ancient
writers to their music and became convinced that only by ap-
proaching the style of rhetorical speaking could these effects be
achieved. This had to be accomplished by·a simplification of
texture and by a greater emphasis on the subtleties of diction
than on the portrayal of poetic images. The theory was developed
by lutenist and composer Vincenzo Galilei in his **Dialogo della
musica antica e della moderna** in 1581. The new conception of the
relative weight between diction and imagery had a profound effect
on the history of vocal style: rhythm became more flexible (leading to the recitative), melodic dissonance was emancipated for
rhetorical expression, and syllabic text-setting became the norm.

The development of the new style was given the necessary
model repertoire not by Galilei himself, but by the publication
of Giulio Caccini's **Le nuove musiche** in 1602. This source also
defined a new approach to musical texture, in its substitution of
the basso continuo for the more traditional lute tablature. The
basso continuo soon replaced the fuller-textured lute style as

the principal accompaniment type for the song.

With the abandonment of the richer polyphonic texture, composers soon found that the music required much more structural organization. In the polyphonic genres of the sixteenth century interest was maintained by the contrapuntal interplay of several voices and by the musical depiction of the moods and images of the text. As was mentioned in the preceding paragraph, the new, rhetorical style subordinated word-painting to diction. At the same time, the old, through-composed structure that was suited to leaving the composer free to respond to each new verbal image was gradually replaced by new forms. The through-composed approach survived briefly in some of the lute songs and in monodic madrigals, but the looseness of form in this repertoire was not sufficiently compensated for. Various solutions to the need for formal planning arose. In some of the lute songs the possibility of dance-like structures was explored, and the result was the use of phrase pairs. In practice, especially in France, second lines in these pairs (doubles) could be ornamented in performance.

A more sophisticated solution to the form problem was the development of the song on a ground bass or strophic bass. This arose naturally from the sixteenth-century practice of singing partially improvised melodic settings of strophic or otherwise patterned poetry over standard bass or accompaniment patterns. It did not survive the seventeenth century, though the ground-bass song had a late, brilliant flare-up in the work of Purcell.

Most durable of the musical structures of the song in the seventeenth century was the strophic form. Simple strophic songs had been used since the very beginning in the lute song and **air de cour** and among Italian basso continuo songs where they were called arias to distinguish them from the freer madrigals. The simplicity of the strophic form made these songs accessible to the widest possible public, particularly to the middle classes that were still only a relatively weak cultural force but were soon to become the dominant power in determining the direction of the evolution of the song.

The predominant structure for solo vocal pieces in the Baroque as a whole was the ternary design of the da capo aria. While this plan was more characteristic of the movements of larger, multimovement works such as opera, oratorio, and cantata than of the independent song, some examples of ternary form may be found in the art song. These are usually considerably more modest in size than the types found in the large works, and they tend to be less adventuresome in both harmonic range and the role of the accompaniment.

The growing development of abstract principles of musical design during the Baroque period is evidenced by the occasional use of instrumental ritornello sections in songs. Commonly, these would serve as interludes between strophes, providing an instrumental cadential refrain to the end of each stanza.

Particularly important in performing the songs of the seventeenth century is the matter of historical performance practice.
Imaginative realization of basso continuo and improvisation of
ornaments in melodic lines were practiced in the genre of song as
in other repertoires during this period. Whether or not indications for ornaments appear in the score, ornamentation may be
added at cadences; other standard types of passages may also call
for embellishment. When there is notated musical repetition
performers should apply their imagination to vary the music from
each statement to the next. Texts on Baroque ornamentation
practice and continuo playing should, of course, be consulted. A
couple of guiding principles may be cited, however. First of
all, musical sense and taste should be exercised; certainly the
song should not be treated as a vehicle for virtuosity but as an
opportunity for subtle expression. Second, the text must be kept
in mind; the Baroque composers believed deeply that their music
should respond to their texts, and the performer should feel
equally responsible to the poetry.

THE EIGHTEENTH CENTURY

In the earliest years of the eighteenth century there were
no important new developments in the realm of the song. In fact,
there was a drastic decline in the production of songs, which had
become divided into two styles, one too simple to bear much
interest and the other too elaborate to attract any but trained
singers whose concerns were focused elsewhere. Beginning in the
1730s, however, there was a sudden change in approach, developed
in Germany. This was the product of a broad artistic response to
a new socio-economic situation, the effect of which on the song
can hardly be overestimated. The middle class had grown by leaps
and bounds, and it provided an immense new market for styles of
poetry and music that suited its situation. The immediate need
was first filled by large collections of rather artistically
unsophisticated pieces, the **Augsburger Tafelkonfekt** and Sperontes's **Singende Muse an der Pleisse**, comprising mainly folk melodies and parodies of instrumental dance tunes. The great success
of such anthologies showed that there was a demand to be satis-
fied, and it was not long until both poets and composers were
found to leap into the breach.

The new style of poetry was introduced by Klopstock. The
German public was attracted to his works by the avoidance of
mythological imagery and courtly artificiality in favor of more
common language and a tone of elevated feeling. The music of the
Lied was given a significant impetus as well by the composers of
the so-called First Berlin School, of whom the greatest was

C.P.E. Bach, and by Gluck. Large volumes of Lieder were soon
compiled, and many songs circulated in popular periodicals addressed to the middle class. Musically, these pieces belong to
the **empfindsamer Stil**; the textures were simple, the harmonies
were occasionally colored by chromaticism for expression, and the
melodies featured expressive gestures.

The new type of Lied spread throughout the German-speaking
countries and developed rapidly. Klopstock was followed by the
poets of the Göttinger Hainbund, whose works emphasized natural
feeling and patriotic sentiment. The First Berlin School was
succeeded by a Second Berlin School among whom the most prominent
were J.A.P. Schulz, J.F. Reichardt, and K.F. Zelter. The ideal
of this group, as expressed by Schulz, was **volkstümlichkeit** (a
term impossible to translate adequately but embodying both the
ideas of "folk quality" and "national character"), manifested in
strophic form with clearly directed, symmetrical melodic and
harmonic phrasing and in simple textures and harmonies.

No other nation produced such a conscious aesthetic for
songs during the Classic era, though the rise of a new style in
general certainly influenced the song. In addition, there was no
body of song poetry of equivalent quality in other countries. In
England there were popular ballads (the broadsides) and songs for
performance in the public-garden concerts, such as those of
Thomas Arne. At the same time there grew up a vogue of national
songs, especially exploited by publishers George Thomson and
William Napier who engaged Haydn and Beethoven to arrange Scottish and Irish folk tunes.

In France the Baroque air gave way to the narrative romance.
These songs appealed to the pastoral-natural sentiment and medi-
evalist imagination of the pre-Romantic movement. By the end of
the century, they had turned in the direction of the Revolution
and patriotism.

An important factor in the development of the song during
the eighteenth century was the development of the piano. The
supersession of the lute song by the continuo-accompanied song
had meant that in general the practice of a single performer
singing and accompanying himself or herself had given way to
performance by at least two and commonly three musicians. The
piano now provided a new medium, suitable for solo performance in
the home. Indeed the simple texture of the early Classic piano
song permitted notation on only two staves, which allowed easy
reading by a single performer.

The Classic use of slower harmonic rhythm in standardized
progressions and simple accompaniment figurations also contributed to the development of the song. Clear and easily intelligi-
ble harmonic progressions and a sharply defined rhythmic grid
clarified the underlying musical direction at a subconscious
level. This, in turn, allowed the melody to become more promi-

nent on the surface, focusing attention on the singer and the
text even more sharply than in earlier songs.

THE ROMANTIC SONG

It must be stressed that there is considerable continuity
between the Classic and Romantic musical styles. By the end of
the eighteenth century the groundwork for the Romantic movement
was already well established. The literary foundation was laid
by the poetry of Goethe, which was enthusiastically taken up by
the poet's good friend the Berliner Zelter as well as by Beethoven and Schubert in Vienna.

The contribution of Schubert to the history of the Lied is
well known. It might best be summarized by observing that he
insisted that the role of the composer should be equal to that of
the poet in determining the emotional experience of the song. In
style he combined the gift of melody that the Austrian composers
learned from their Italian neighbors, the sensitivity to lyric
poetry developed by the German school, and the drama of the
ballad which dominated his own earliest work. The encounter with
Goethe's work in 1814 and 1815 led to Schubert's new insight. He
adopted the position that it was the composer's task not only to
provide the vehicle for the poem and illustrations of the meanings of the poet's words, but to interpret the poem's content at
a deeper level, determining the listener's understanding. (Of
course, it was just this imposition of the composer's reading of
the poem between the poet and the audience that met Goethe's
objection.) As was mentioned in an earlier section, Schubert
often achieved this interpretation by means of a kind of depiction of the expressive background through accompaniments that
comprise transfigured sound effects.

Solely by his music and without any explicit aesthetic
manifesto, Schubert determined the course of song composition for
the remainder of the century. From this time on, the Lied composers insisted on their role as principal interpreter of the
poem. Except in the ballad, however, which had a tremendous
vogue, his German successors generally avoided the implicit tone-
painting on which Schubert relied. In this they remained truer
to the Berlin style, especially Zelter's pupil Mendelssohn to
whom it fell to draw a Romantic final curtain on that tradition.
The songs of Schumann offer the best examples of the approach in
the generation of ca. 1810. His influence in turn branched out
to affect the work of both Brahms and Wolf.

The German poets of the first half of the nineteenth century
assisted the development of the Lied by producing a fount of
material from which Romantic and post-Romantic drew inspiration.

The publication of folk poetry by Achim and Brentano yielded folk texts directly to composers and also ideas to the poets. Among the prominent poets some are closely associated with specific contemporary composers, Müller with Schubert and Heine with Schumann, for example. Others evoked settings from more and more distant composers. Goethe continued to be popular, Eichendorff and Rückert were set from their own time to the end of the century, and Mörike had a particular late flowering in the songs of Wolf.   .

The influence of Schubert in France produced a revolution in song composition that eclipsed the romance and gave birth to the new mélodie. French composers were also fortunate in that the nineteenth century produced suitable poetry for songs. Notable are the texts of Théophile Gautier set by Berlioz. By the end of the century the symbolist movement had created a body of poetry that served French composers as well as the Romantic poets served the Germans. In addition, the symbolists' use of words more for what they evoked than for their denotative meanings was paralleled in the French composers' use of harmony for coloristic effect rather than functionally to drive the music forward. This style was perfected in the songs of Debussy.

The other Western European countries produced less in the realm of song. Vocal music in both the eighteenth and nineteenth centuries in Italy was overwhelmingly dominated by the opera, and in the Iberian countries by theater songs. In neither area did the Romantic movement produce lyric poetry that inspired composers to song, nor was there the social milieu of middle class drawing room or salon to demand such a repertoire. In England no composers of both the stature and inclination to establish a national school of song arose. The English middle and lower classes in general found their musical outlet in choral music. Ironically, the English Romantic writers' works were exported for song texts; Scott, Burns, and Byron were significant for the German Lied composers. The art song did spread, however, in response to the growth of nationalism in eastern Europe. Folk poetry and the work of native poets evoked fine song settings from Grieg, Dvorák, and Musorgsky, as well as many others.

The Romantic tendency to think in terms of expansive, organically unified works of art resulted in the development of the song cycle. Cycles of songs were not an invention of the nineteenth century; such composite works can be found as early as the late Renaissance. It was in the Romantic era that they became common, however. Beethoven's **An die ferne Geliebte** and the two Müller cycles of Schubert are the first masterpieces. Their Romantic and post-Romantic followers pursued these models. A distinction is often made between true cycles and less unified sets of songs. In practice, it would probably be more realistic to imagine all such groups of pieces as falling at specific

points along a continuum between the musically and narratively
unified cycle (Schumann's **Dichterliebe** and **Frauenliebe und -leben**
may be the most familiar examples) and collections of entirely
disparate songs.

The idea of the song cycle (Liederkreis) owes something to
the social circle (Kreis) of participating friends. The concept
of the textually and musically unified song cycle was supported
by the practice of connecting songs through some kind of dramatic
action or game (Liederspiel in either case) into a multifaceted
entertainment.

A serious, extended musical work such as a song cycle places
demands for sustained attention on its listeners that the simple,
independent, drawing-room song conceived for a private performance did not. Indeed, in the middle of the century the genre
began to move out of the home into the concert hall. This was
partly due to the need of the composers to make grander statements that were artistically suited to the public forum rather
than to the intimacy of the domestic circle. Partly it was a
reflection of changes in the socio-economic situation due to
which the middle and lower classes sought entertainment in public
rather than at home.

An obvious reflection of the artistic and social trend to a
more powerful musical expression in song was the rise of the
orchestrally accompanied song. This began in the orchestration
of songs originally intended for the piano, but by the end of the
nineteenth century the independently conceived orchestral song
cycle was well established.

THE TWENTIETH CENTURY

The art song in the twentieth century occupies a difficult
position. On the one hand it continues an honorable lineage as a
scion of a noble genre, which leaves it subject to the criticism
that it is legitimized more by its ancestry than its own accomplishments. On the other hand, an attempt to emancipate the song
from its past risks the extinction of the line. With the growing
difficulty of poetic styles and musical techniques for the listener, progress seems to have outstripped the audience's ability
to keep up. At the same time the tradition of Hausmusik is
practically defunct, domestic entertainment having been co-opted
by electronic media.

Excellent works have been composed that continue and extend
the artistic premises and style of the Classic-Romantic tradition, which is to say that they are still rooted in the tonal
musical language. This would include both post-Romantic and
Neoclassical songs.

The general trend toward more dissonant harmony, angular melody, and irregular rhythm that proceeded from the need to reach new levels of expression in the music of the period of common practice made things increasingly difficult for performers, especially singers, as well as for audiences. This difficulty is even more pronounced in atonal and serial songs. As was mentioned earlier, the composers of the Second Vienna School used song as a favored genre because of the centripetal force supplied by the text. Later serial composers have also written songs. That these range from the genuinely melodic to the nearly superhuman should only serve to prove that the ability to write idiomatically for the voice is independent of the compositional language in which a composer chooses to work.

Especially important has been the turn toward vocal works accompanied by instrumental ensembles. Perhaps the best explanation for this is that the limitation to voice and keyboard seems effete and that sheer variety of timbre compensates for the difficulty of sorting out dissonant harmonies and oddly directed lines. The problem of whether such pieces fall within the category of art song or whether they place the singer and the text in an entirely different position from the song with a single accompanist is an important one, too complex to solve here. The present guide includes some such pieces when they appear to belong to the main tradition of the art song.

The Art Song

I

GENERAL STUDIES

Historical and Systematic

1. Finck, Henry T. **Songs and Song Writers.** New York: Charles
   Scribner's Sons, 1900. xv, 254p.

   A guide to the most important (in the author's view) song
   composers of the nineteenth century and their songs. The
   discussion is quite personal and very uneven. Some individual songs are discussed at length, others are merely listed,
   and some composers' works are given only general comments.
   It is indicative that the brief chapter on French and Italian
   songs includes no mention of Duparc, Chausson, or Fauré,
   whereas the author regards Grieg and MacDowell as the greatest living song composers. Index.

2. Hall, James Husst. **The Art Song.** Norman: University of Oklahoma Press, 1953. Reprint. 1962. ix, 310p.

   Discusses the manifestations of the genre by nationality
   and in chronological order, concentrating on major composers
   and offering brief commentary on a number of mostly well-
   known songs. The opening chapter deals in a general way with
   basic issues in the aesthetics of song. The valiant attempt
   to elucidate in tabular form the differences between German
   and French song ranges from the sublime to the ridiculous
   (German Lieder are "Nourished by beer," French songs are
   "Excited by champagne"). Users of this book would be well
   advised to use the index, since the chapter headings can be
   highly misleading (the chapter entitled "Debussy," for instance, also includes Hahn, Paladhile, Ravel, and Poulenc).
   The book will probably not be of great use either to the

3

reader who seeks a continuous argument and a satisfying synthesis or to the researcher who needs a reference source. To the reader who finds a particular song treated, the specific discussion may provide some illumination. Bibliography. Index.

3. Ivey, Donald. **Song: Anatomy, Imagery, and Styles.** New York: Free Press, 1970. xii, 273p.

   Provides an excellent, detailed discussion of the relationships between poetry and music in song. The first part deals with structural matters, contrasting the problems of melodic and rhythmic settings in German and English to those in the Romance languages, and demonstrating how music can clarify poetic form or modify it for expressive intensification. The second section treats the musical expression of poetic imagery through harmony, melody, and rhythm. The third part traces the development of style in art song from the Baroque. Bibliography of books. Indexes of names and subjects, songs.

4. Meister, Barbara. **An Introduction to the Art Song.** New York: Taplinger, 1980. 224p.

   Addressed to a non-technical audience (though occasionally unable to resist such technical matters as chord functions), describes very briefly representative examples by prominent composers. Provides a cursory introduction to the genre and an outline history of vocal music to 1600, then proceeds by nationality and chronology (mostly in units devoted to single composers). A short conclusion discusses interpretation. Glossary of musical terms. Index of composers and works.

5. Northcote, Sydney. **The Ballad in Music.** London: Oxford University Press, 1942. 124p.

   Discusses a variety of genres, including the early folk ballad, the art ballad of the Romantic and post-Romantic period, the choral ballad, melodrama, instrumental works, and the drawing-room ballad. The author suggests a systematic categorization of ballads into strophic, romantic, and dramatic types. Brief bibliography including collections of ballads; list of works incorporating a discography.

6. Oehlmann, Werner. **Reclams Liedführer.** Stuttgart: Reclam, 1973. 1024p.

   Gives an excellent broad historical overview of the song repertoire in Europe from the Middle Ages to the twentieth century. Many representative songs are briefly described. Emphasis falls on the German composers; there is a brief and not very well balanced section on American composers. Indexes of songs, composers and poets.

7. Osborne, Charles. **The Concert Song Companion: A Guide to the Classical Repertoire.** London: Gollancz, 1974. 285p.

Rapidly surveys the standard repertoire. The book is divided into chapters by nationalities or languages. Some general remarks are made on composers' styles and on individual songs, but the limited size of the book precludes any depth of critical analysis. Brief bibliography. Indexes of poets and composers, songs.

8. Peake, Luise Eitel. "The Song Cycle: A Preliminary Inquiry into the Beginnings of the Romantic Song Cycle and the Nature of an Art Form." Ph.D. diss., Columbia University, 1968. 349p.

Traces the history of the song cycle back to the Baroque. Important roots of the Romantic cycle include the Baroque ballet, especially influential in England, and the social diversion with songs (Liederkreis). Also significant are the image of the circle as a poetic idea and the tendency in late eighteenth-century Germany to disguise the cycle in the work.

9. Reuter, Evelyn. **La Mélodie et le Lied.** Paris: Presses Universitaires de France, 1950. 128p.

Discusses the differences between the German and French song traditions and styles. Focuses on the aesthetic traits of each nation's songs. The influence of tonic accents, folk background, and the desire for overflowing expression contribute to the German style; the French style is traced to the semi-popular genre of the romance and to the national proclivity for the intellectual, the sensual, and restrained statement. Brief surveys are provided of the history of song through the Baroque, the Lied from 1750 to the twentieth century, and the mélodie from Berlioz (the first to use the term mélodie for art song) to Ravel and Roussel. Bibliography.

10. Sopeña Ibañez, Federico. **El nacionalismo y el 'Lied'.** Madrid: Real musical, 1979. 77p.

Considers, in addition to the movement normally referred

to as nationalism, the general differentiation of song style along national lines in the late nineteenth century. The development of the French style is studied in the mélodies of Fauré, Debussy, and Duparc. A brief discussion of the rise of the Russian style and detailed coverage of Musorgsky constitute the treatment of that nation. A single chapter mentions eastern Europe (Liszt, Dvořák, Chopin) and the northern countries (Grieg, Sibelius). The book concludes with a discussion of Wolf, whose aesthetic is held to be one of "spiritual realism." Prosy discography.

11.   Stevens, Denis. **A History of Song.** New York: Norton, 1960. 491p.

A collection of essays by various authors, treating the song generally in historical periods to ca. 1600 (Gilbert Reaney--"Middle Ages"; Denis Stevens--"Renaissance") then by nationality. The latter essays vary in approach. Several consist of very brief descriptions of many composers and works, including rather minor ones (David Cox--"Belgium," "Holland," "Switzerland"; Gilbert Chase--"Latin America," "Spain"). Others concentrate on more detailed discussions of major composers (Arthur Jacobs--"The British Isles"; David Cox--"France"; Philip Radcliffe--"Germany and Austria," "Scandinavia and Finland"; Hans Nathan--"Hungary," "United States of America"; Anthony Milner--"Italy"; Gerald Abraham--"Czechoslovakia," "Poland," "Russia"). A conclusion by Sir Michael Tippett discusses aesthetic problems. Indexes of names and titles.

12.   Taylor, David C., and Hiram Kelly Moderwell. **The Voice and Vocal Music.** Vol. 4 of **The Art of Music,** edited by Daniel Gregory Mason et al. New York: National Society of Music, 1915. xix, 388p.

Covers both singing (in an opening section by Taylor) and the history of song (Moderwell's contribution). The historical section is divided into a brief survey of song through the eighteenth century, a lengthy discussion of the nineteenth-century song, and a tentative contemporary commentary on composers from Wolf and Fauré to Schoenberg and Debussy and Ravel. Very cursory bibliography.

13.   Walker, Conway. **The Art Song and Its Composers.** Vol. 3 of **Fundamentals of Musical Art,** edited by Edward Dickinson. New York: The Caxton Institute, 1926. vi, 106p.

Addresses amateurs or beginning students. A brief survey

of song from the Greeks through the Classic period opens the
book. A chapter on characteristics of the art song introduces a series of chapters mostly on single nineteenth-
century German composers or on groups of composers. A few
major songs are described, other important ones listed.
Brief bibliographies of general books, song collections;
list of songs recorded (as of the date of the book).

Language or National Styles

ENGLISH

Great Britain

14. Banfield, Stephen. **Sensibility and English Song: Critical
      Studies of the Early 20th Century.** 2 vols. Cambridge:
      Cambridge University Press, 1985.

      (Developed from Banfield's 1979 Oxford University disserta-
      tion.) Focusing on the development of art song in England
      in the twentieth century, inquires why and how composers set
      certain texts in songs. Discusses the relationship of works
      to their biographical and historical contexts, and engages
      in extensive critical discussion of individual songs. Ap-
      pendices. Song lists; bibliography. Index.

15. Brett, Philip. "The English Consort Song, 1570-1625." **Pro-
      ceedings of the Royal Musical Association** 88 (1961-62):
      73-88.

      Surveys the history of the genre. Indicates the variety
      of material covered by the term "consort song," which in-
      cludes not only solo songs accompanied by viols, but also
      those with choruses and a variety of possible performance
      media, including lutes and harpsichords or ensembles of
      singers. Songs for dramatic presentation are also men-
      tioned. The quality of the repertoire is uneven, reaching
      its culmination in the compositions of William Byrd.

16. Duckles, Vincent. "The English Musical Elegy of the Late
      Renaissance." In **Aspects of Medieval and Renaissance Mu-
      sic: A Birthday Offering to Gustave Reese,** edited by Jan
      LaRue et al., 134-53. New York: Pendragon, 1966.

Discusses the repertoire of commemorative expressions of grief in English music around 1600, a fruitful source for study because it embodies a unified group of pieces all involving deep emotion. The repertoire includes partsongs, consort songs, and lute ayres. The general aesthetic of the genre and style traits are covered. Striking is the general restraint of musical expression, which suggests that the approach to lamenting is more solemn than impassioned.

17. Gibbon, John Murray. **Melody and the Lyric: From Chaucer to the Cavaliers.** London: Dent, 1930. xii, 240p.

Argues that the English lyricists wrote their poetry with existing dance tunes in mind. Popular songs and songs from plays are included, as well as lute songs in the second half of the book, which deals with songs from the period covered by the present bibliography. Many texts and tunes are cited. Index of songs.

18. Johnstone, H. Diack. "English Solo Song, c. 1710-1760." **Proceedings of the Royal Musical Association** 95 (1968-69): 67-80.

Provides an overview of the subject. The repertoire may be divided into two categories, ballad and art song. The former, strophic and popular in style, were promulgated by their inclusion among the attractions at the pleasure gardens in London. The art song, generally in binary form and more sophisticated in style, shows Continental influences. Characteristic of all this repertoire is typical English tunefulness.

19. Jorgens, Elise Bickford. **The Well-Tun'd Word: Musical Interpretations of English Poetry, 1597-1651.** Minneapolis: University of Minnesota Press, 1982. xx, 298p.

Developed from the author's dissertation (New York University, 1975), discusses the setting of the Elizabethan and Stuart lyric in solo song. There is a thorough discussion of general problems in musical setting of poetic accentuation and of structure and meaning. The repertoire is treated according to contrasting approaches to text setting--those of the French measured air, the dance tune, and the Italian monody--and the synthesis of these approaches. Bibliography. Index.

20. Kidson, Frank. "A Study of Old English Song and Popular Melody Prior to the 19th Century." **The Musical Quarterly**

1 (1915): 569-82.

Surveys the history of song in England to 1800. Particularly helpful are the general remarks on the rise of solo
English song in the seventeenth century and the depiction of
the pleasure gardens in the eighteenth. Many composers,
songs, and singers are listed.

21. Mellers, Wilfred. **Harmonious Meeting: A Study of the Rela-
    tionship between English Music, Poetry and Theatre, c.
    1600-1900.** London: Dobson, 1965. 317p.

    Within the context of a study of the development of En-
    glish vocal music, follows the development of song from the
    lute ayres of Campion and Dowland to the dramatic style of
    Purcell (Chapters 7-12). The approach is through analysis
    of representative individual works. Reference to scores is
    required; a few rare examples are included in the appen-
    dices. Plates. Discography. Index.

22. Monson, Craig. **Voices and Viols in England, 1600-1650: The
    Sources and the Music.** Studies in Musicology 55. Ann
    Arbor, Mich.: UMI Research Press, 1982. xvi, 360p.

    From Monson's dissertation (University of California,
    Berkeley, 1974), describes in detail the twenty-four extant
    sources for the consort song and verse anthem in the first
    half of the sixteenth century. The complete contents of
    each source are tabulated. There appears to have been an
    abrupt change of taste after 1600, in which the madrigal was
    succeeded by the voice-and-viols repertoire and a more se-
    rious type of expression associated with it. This combined
    some of the technical advances developed in the madrigals of
    the 1590s with an older, native tradition. Illustrations.
    Bibliography. Indexes.

23. Northcote, Sydney. **Byrd to Britten: A Survey of English
    Song.** London: John Baker, 1966. 152p.

    Provides a cursory overview of the material, generally
    with one chapter to each century and one paragraph to each
    composer. The author does not hesitate to express personal
    opinions or to digress from the topic. Appendices list
    publications of twentieth-century English songs and Handel
    opera arias. Index.

24. Pattison, Bruce. **Music and Poetry of the English Renais-
    sance.** 2nd ed. London: Methuen, 1948. ix, 222p.

Devotes a single chapter to the ayre, of which a good portion is spent on the sixteenth-century lute song in Italy
and France and on Italian monody. The focus of the chapter
is on Campion's principles, but illustrations are also taken
from Rosseter, Danyel, and Dowland. Substantial bibliography. Index.

25. Ruff, Lillian M., and D. Arnold Wilson. "The Madrigal, the
     Lute Song, and Elizabethan Politics." **Past and Present** 44
     (August 1969): 3-51.

Traces the reflection of political atmosphere in the texts
of both genres during a period of controversy. The lute-
song texts are broadly characterized by pessimism and metaphysical ideas. A table lists the total published output of
each genre from 1588 to 1632.

26. Spink, Ian. "English Cavalier Songs, 1620-1660." **Proceedings
     of the Royal Musical Association** 86 (1959-60): 61-78.

Discusses the history and style of the songs of mid-
seventeenth-century England. The development of an English
recitative style is attributed less to Italian influence
than to native roots. Its beginnings were to be found in
the masque songs, and its development took place most notably in dialogues and laments. Henry Lawes's song "O I Am
Sick" is included in its entirety.

27. ———. **English Song: Dowland to Purcell.** London: Batsford,
     1974. 312p.

Surveys the development of English song in the seventeenth
century. While the author considers the aesthetic goal in
this repertoire to be the achievement of expression by the
synthesis of text and music, he clearly outlines the style
change from contrapuntally conceived lute song to continuo-
accompanied monody. Purcell's mastery of large-scale
structures is placed at the apex of the development. Lists
of sources; bibliography; index.

28. Warlock, Peter [Philip Heseltine]. **The English Ayre.** London:
     Oxford University Press, 1926. Reprint. Westport, Conn.:
     Greenwood, 1970. 142p.

Discusses the major composers of ayres. The text concentrates on the biographies of the composers and includes
details of publication of their songs, often citing complete
texts of prefaces and dedicatory letters. There is little

discussion of the music itself; some of the best pieces are identified, but only a few are treated in detail. Facsimiles. Chronological table of publications and contemporary events; list of editions.

29. Weiss, Wolfgang. "Die Airs im Stilwandel." **Anglia: Zeitschrift für englische Philologie** 87 (1969): 201-16.

Deals with poetry of the seventeenth-century English song. Because of the constraints of musical structure, song composers chose texts in the older style of the **ordo naturalis,** which relied on logical form, rather than the increasingly popular **ordo artificialis,** which featured expressive disorder.

United States of America

30. Adkins, Aldrich Wendell. "The Development of the Black Art Song." D.M.A. thesis, University of Texas, 1971. 161p.

Not examined. In the abstract for **Dissertation Abstracts** (32A/11 [1972]: 6471-A) Adkins states that the study identifies characteristics of black American music derived from African musical culture and the influences of white American musical style. The post-Civil War period led to black art poetry and the training of black musicians in conservatories. These composers developed folk idioms into black art song. Stages in the use of African inherited idioms are identified: from 1900 to 1934 these appeared cautiously; between 1935 and 1950 they were employed more confidently; and after 1950 they are used along with avant-garde techniques.

31. Friedberg, Ruth C. **American Art Song and American Poetry.** Vol. 1, **America Comes of Age.** Metuchen, N.J.: Scarecrow, 1981. viii, 167p.

The first volume of a projected three-volume work, takes up specific songs in turn, describing the relationships between words and music in each. Composers covered are Edward MacDowell, Charles Martin Loeffler, Charles Griffes, Charles Ives (who merits a complete chapter), Douglas Moore, William Grant Still, Ernst Bacon, Roy Harris, and Aaron Copland. Bibliography. Indexes.

32. Thorpe, Harry Colin. "Interpretative Studies in American

Song." The Musical Quarterly 15 (1929): 88-116.

Aims to increase interest in American art song, which the
author believes to be unjustly neglected. Thorpe discusses
six of his favorite songs, generally characterizing the
poems and tracing the course of the music. The songs are:
"The Sea" by Edward MacDowell, "Into a Ship Dreaming" by
Bainbridge Crist, "In the Yellow Dusk" by Edward I.
Horsman, "A Clear Midnight" by H. Reginald Spier, "Serenade" by John
Alden Carpenter, and "To Helen" by Oscar G. Sonneck.

33. Upton, William Treat. Art Song in America: A Study in the
    Development of American Music. Boston: Oliver Ditson,
    1930; supplement 1938. Reprint. New York: Johnson Reprint
    Co., 1969. xi, 279, 41p.

    Discusses the various generations of song composers in the
    United States, with brief descriptions of the song style of
    each composer. Upton maintains that the initial impulses of
    American song writers were rooted in folk song and guided by
    the German tradition until the twentieth century, when im-
    pressionism and nationalism began to have considerable in-
    fluence. He concludes that by the 1930s a certain impasse
    had been reached, partly due to the influence of Wagner, and
    argues that the experimentation and diversity of style he
    observed in that decade could be expected to clear a path
    for a rebirth of the song. Index.

34. ————. "Some Recent Representative American Song-Compos-
    ers." The Musical Quarterly 11 (1925): 383-417.

    Gives a long list of composer and songs. Special atten-
    tion is paid to Alice Barnett, John Alden Carpenter, Bain-
    bridge Crist, Charles T. Griffes, A. Walter Kramer, and
    Wintter Watts. Watts is judged the most "American," Carpen-
    ter least.

35. Yerbury, Grace D. Song in America from Early Times to about
    1850. Metuchen, N.J.: Scarecrow, 1971. 305p.

    Derived from Yerbury's dissertation research ("Styles and
    Schools of Art-Song in America, 1720-1850," Ph.D. diss.,
    Indiana University, 1953), divides the early American song
    repertoire into schools of style centered around particular
    cities (mostly in the eighteenth century) or leading compos-
    ers (in the nineteenth century). Yerbury argues that these
    composers were more interested in preserving a European
    heritage, especially the English, than in developing an

original American style. A substantial portion of the book
is given over to bibliographies of songs. Appendix of two
songs by Herrmann Saroni. Index.

Miscellaneous

36. Flothuis, Marius. "Vocal Compositions by Dutch Composers
     based on English Texts." **Musical Opinion** 88 (1964-65):
     471-72.

Lists a number of compositions by Dutch composers in the
English language. There were very few such works prior to
1940, the greatest influence in music of the Netherlands
coming from Germany at that time, but the importance of
English radio and the presence of British and American
troops in World War II gave a sudden impetus to settings of
English texts. The works listed include songs and works in
larger genres; some descriptive comments on the music are
made.

FRENCH

37. Bellaigue, Camille. "Les 'Mélodies' françaises." **Revue des
     deux mondes** 53 (1919): 448-68.

Enthusiastically describes the repertoire from the change
of style after the period of the romance and the establish-
ment of the mélodie, attributed here to Gounod. Works of
Gounod, Paladhile, Massenet, Widor, Hahn, Bizet, Saint-
Saëns, Fauré, Chausson, and Duparc are discussed. Bellaigue
feels that in the mélodie France found a legitimate counterpart to the German Lied. The article calls for a new optimism in the French genre in the twentieth century.

38. Cammaert, Gustave. "Les Brunettes." **Revue belge de musicolo-
     gie** 11 (1957): 35-51.

Describes the repertoire of brunettes, especially those of
the three volumes published by Ballard in 1703, 1704, and
1711. The texts are generally amorous, in a variety of
veins, and/or pastoral. The poetic structures are most
often quatrains and sixains, with some huitains as well.
Musically, the pieces may be characterized by tempo, either
slow with ornamented repetitions (**simples et passionés**) or
fast. The forms employed are generally binary, but a vari-

ety of types may be found. The historical context of the
brunettes, which followed the seventeenth-century airs and
led to the romances of the later eighteenth century, is also
clarified.

39. Duméril, Edmond. **Le Lied allemand et ses traductions poé-
     tiques en France.** Bibliothèque de la revue littéraire
     comparée 98. Paris, 1933. Reprint. Geneva: Slatkine, 1975.
     xii, 402p.

     Seeks to demonstrate the influence of German Lied poetry
     on the Romantic movement in French literature and on the
     rise of symbolism. Considered are the linguistic problems;
     the contributions of such leading figures as Mme de Staël,
     Gérard de Nerval, Henri Blaze, and others; the effects of
     Edouard Schuré's history of the Lied; Verlaine and Mallarmé.
     Bibliography. Index of names.

40. Gérold, Théodore. **L'Art du chant en France au XVIIe siècle.**
     Publications de la Faculté des Lettres de l'Université de
     Strasbourg 1. Strasbourg: Université de Strasbourg, 1921.
     xv, 279p.

     Traces the history of French song in the seventeenth
     century, beginning with the heritage of the sixteenth cen-
     tury and evolving by the influence of virtuoso technique and
     dramatic innovations to the style used in the period of
     Lully. The teaching of the style is outlined, including
     technique, ornamentation, and diction. Appendix of repre-
     sentative pieces. Bibliography.

41. Gougelot, Henri. **La Romance française sous la Révolution** et
     l'Empire. 2 vols. Melun: Librairie d'Argences, 1938, 1943.
     371, 208p.

     In the first first volume, **Etude historique et critique,**
     discusses the literary content and style, the composers, and
     the music of the romance from 1789 to 1813. The author
     grants that much of the repertoire is of little artistic
     value, but finds texts that do have a sincerity of poetic
     sentiment and music that laid the groundwork for the Roman-
     tic movement. Plates. Bibliography. Index of names. The
     supplementary volume, entitled **Choix de textes musicaux,**
     contains excerpts from Baron Thiébault's 1813 **Du Chant et
     particulièrement de la romance,** and facsimile reproductions
     of seventy-two songs that the author believes to be the best
     of the repertoire. Notes on the sources are provided.
     Plates.

42. Lockspeiser, Edward. "The French Song in the 19th Century."
     The Musical Quarterly 26 (1940): 192-99.

     Distinguishes between the earlier romance and the mélodie.
     Representatives of the romance, Masini, Monpou, and Berlioz,
     are discussed. The mélodie is said to have originated with
     Duparc's "Invitation au voyage," but the poetry of Verlaine
     is credited with establishing its style.

43. Masson, Paul-Marie. "Les 'Brunettes'." **Sammelbände der In-
     ternationalen Musikgesellschaft** 12 (1910-11): 347-68.

     Discusses the history and style of the brunette. These
     songs originated in the seventeenth century and were pub-
     lished by Ballard from 1703 on. Their topics are pastoral.
     In style, they are simple and clear, elegant and natural.
     Often they adopt dance rhythms, and almost always they
     employ binary form.

44. Meister, Barbara. **Nineteenth-Century French Song: Fauré,
     Chausson, Duparc, and Debussy.** Bloomington, Ind.: Indiana
     University Press, 1980. xiii, 402p.

     Provides a reference source of analytical comments on all
     the songs with piano accompaniment of these four composers,
     including translations of the texts. A brief historical and
     biographical introduction is included. Index of songs by
     first lines.

45. Noske, Frits. **French Song from Berlioz to Duparc: The Origin
     and Development of the Mélodie.** 2nd ed., rev. Translated
     by Rita Benton. New York: Dover, 1970. xiv, 454p.

     Originally published in French as **La Mélodie française de
     Berlioz à Duparc: Essai** de **critique historique** (Amsterdam:
     North-Holland; Paris: Presses Universitaires de France,
     1954), this book is the standard text on its subject. It
     traces the roots of the Romantic mélodie in the decline of
     the earlier romance in the 1830s and the development of the
     genre to roughly 1880. There is an introductory excursion
     into French prosody and into music in French Romantic poet-
     ry. The body of the text consists of critical discussion of
     a great many pieces. Among the several appendices are
     unknown songs by Liszt and Fauré, and an extensive catalogue
     of songs. Bibliography. Index.

46. Packer, Dorothy S. "Horatian Moral Philosophy in French
     Song, 1649-1749." **The Musical Quarterly** 61 (1975): 240-71.

16

Draws attention to an aspect of the texts of French vaude-
villes. The poets of these songs used them to purvey a
Horatian manner of life based on good sense, simplicity, and
moderation.

47. Verchaly, André. "Poésie et air de cour en France jusqu'à
1620." In **Musique et poésie au XVIe siècle**, 211-24. Paris:
Centre national de la recherche scientifique, 1954.

Treats the history and style of the **air de cour** in the
first two decades of the seventeeth century. Attention is
focused on the structure and subjects of the poetry and the
technical musical means used. The author feels that in this
period the union of poetry and music was very close and that
it gave way increasingly during the remainder of the century. Pierre Guédron's setting of Malherbe's "Que n'estes
vous lassées" is included as a score example.

48. ————. "La Poésie française baroque et sa musique (1580-
1645)." In **Actes des Journées internationales d'étude du
baroque, Montauban 1968**, 127-36. Montauban: Association de
la faculté des lettres et sciences humaines, 1969.

Not examined. The abstract by the author for **RILM**
(70/432) indicates that the **air de cour** is the focus of the
study. Its style was sometimes governed more by literary
influences, sometimes by musical trends. The music might
better be referred to as mannerist than Baroque.

49. Walker, D.P. "The Influence of **musique mesurée à l'antique**,
Particularly on the **Airs de cour** of the Early Seventeenth
Century." **Musica disciplina** 2 (1948): 141-63.

Suggests that certain characteristics of the **air de cour**
may be attributed to the sixteenth-century **musique mesurée**,
particularly the homophonic texture and unmetered rhythms
made up of only two note values. The treatment of the
texts, however, which is often not good in the **airs de cour**,
leaves the question of a direct influence unresolved

GERMAN (including Austria and Switzerland)

50. Abert, Hermann. "Entstehung und Wurzeln der begleiteten
deutschen Sololiedes." In **Gesammelte Schriften und Vor-
trägen**, edited by Friedrich Blume, 156-72. Halle: Max
Niemeyer, 1929. Reprint. Tutzing: Hans Schneider, 1968.

Argues that the German seventeenth-century solo song represented by Heinrich Albert was not modeled on the Italian
monody but evolved directly from the German chorale and
folksong tradition of the sixteenth century.

51. Alberti-Radanowicz, Editha. "Das Wiener Lied von 1789-1815."
In **Studien zur Musikwissenschaft: Beihefte der Denkmäler
der Tonkunst in Oesterreich**, Vol. 10, edited by Guido
Adler, 37-78. Vienna: Universal Edition, 1923.

Surveys the repertoire that links Mozart's and Schubert's
Lieder. Historical material includes a list of the publications in Vienna during the period in question; discussion of
the poetry (mostly sentimental love poems and some evocative
lyrics); and brief discussions of individual composers. The
bulk of the study consists of a detailed description of the
stylistic features of the music. The author's list of Lied
types includes folk-style songs, Singspiellieder, ariettas,
mood-painting songs, romances, and ballads.

52. Baron, John H. "Dutch Influences on the German Secular Solo-
Continuo Lied in the Mid-Seventeenth Century." **Acta musicologica** 43 (1971): 43-55.

Demonstrates that the repertoire of monophonic household
songs that developed in Puritan Holland in the sixteenth
century provided source material for German composers of
secular continuo Lieder. The influence is illustrated by
examples from the Lieder of Philip von Zesen. The author
shows how the German songs developed a more sophisticated
style than their Dutch models in form and in text-music
relationships.

53. ————. "Foreign Influences on the German Secular Solo Continuo Lied of the Mid-Seventeeth Century." Ph.D. diss.,
Brandeis University, 1967. 439p.

Not examined. According to the abstract (**Dissertation
Abstracts** 28A [1968]: 4197-A) attempts, to identify the
influence of various national styles on the continuo Lied.
The Italian monody provided the basso continuo technique but
had unexpectedly little effect on German vocal style.
French and Dutch influences were stronger on both the poetry
and the musical treatment of its rhythm.

54. Beaufils, Marcel. **Le Lied romantique allemand.** Paris: Gal-
limard, 1956. Reprint. 1982.   347p.

Reflects on the history of the Lied from Mozart to Schoenberg. While not contributing sophisticated analysis or
original findings, the text is engagingly written and manages to capture the essential aesthetic developments effectively. This book does not fall into the usual trap of
stringing together innumerable descriptions of individual
songs. Annotated discography (by Gilles Cantagrel) to 1981.

55. Bie, Oscar. **Das deutsche Lied.** Berlin: S. Fischer, 1926.
     227p.

Comments in a personal but insightful style on the nineteenth- and early twentieth-century Lied. The study focuses
on four major composers, Schubert, Schumann, Brahms, and
Wolf, with brief discussions of their contemporaries. In
addition to discussing the composers' styles and specific
songs, the study incorporates aesthetic and historical observations on the nature and development of the genre.

56. Bischoff, Hermann. **Das deutsche Lied.** Berlin: Marquardt,
     n.d. 117p.

Reviews the history of the Lied from the seventeenth
century to the end of the nineteenth. The book discusses
individual composers briefly, making comments on the style
and contributions of each. Portraits, complete songs. Bibliography.

57. Bortolotto, Mario. **Introduzione al Lied romantico.** Milan:
     Ricordi, 1962. 204p.

Discusses the stylistic development of the German Lied in
the nineteenth century, concentrating on major composers.
There is a brief historical and aesthetic introductory section; substantial discussion of Beethoven, Schubert, and
Schumann; an overview of the mid-century composers from
Mendelssohn to Brahms; and a fairly extensive treatment of
Wolf, Mahler, and Strauss. The text itself is interesting
and readable, but the reader is handicapped by the absence
of clear chapter divisions. Index of names.

58. Brody, Elaine, and Robert A. Fowkes. **The German Lied and Its
     Poetry.** New York: New York University Press, 1971. viii,
     316p.

Presents discussions of a number of major Lieder, pursuing
a historical outline. The authors have contributed quite
independently to the treatment of each piece, Fowkes discus-

sing the poetry and Brody the music. The critical level is
not especially deep--a result of the origin of the text in a
university course. Bibliography. Indexes.

59. Bücken, Ernst. **Das deutsche Lied: Probleme und Gestaltung.**
     Hamburg: Hanseatische Verlagsanstalt, 1939. 196p.

     Surveys the history of the Lied from the Baroque to the
     early twentieth century, concentrating on characterizations
     of style. The Classic period is treated geographically
     (Prussian and southern styles), while the nineteenth century
     is discussed according to a variety of headings (Romantic
     song, folk-type songs, the Biedermeier, the Wagner-Liszt
     circle, Brahms, and Wolf). The treatment of the twentieth-
     century Lied is, of course, dated. List of editions; no
     other scholarly apparatus.

60. Danuser, Hermann. "Der Orchestergesang des Fin de siècle:
     Eine historische und ästhetische Skizze." **Die Musikfor-
     schung** 30 (1977): 425-52.

     Views the prominence of the orchestral Lied as a charac-
     teristic product of the period from about 1890 to the First
     World War. The argument is developed from a sociological
     viewpoint, based on the rise of the song recital, the de-
     cline of chamber music in the context of orchestral con-
     certs, and the obsolescence of the concert performance of
     arias. The orchestral song is contrasted to the concert
     aria and the keyboard-accompanied song.

61. Diez, Werner. "Sehnsucht nach der Vergangenheit: Bemerkungen
     zum deutschen Kunstlied am Ende der Romantik." **Neue Zeit-
     schrift für Musik** 130 (1969): 239-44.

     Investigates the relationship between the approaches to
     Lied composition of the post-Romantic composers and of their
     Romantic and late Romantic predecessors. Characteristic is
     a historical consciousness of the tradition leading to Wolf,
     which commonly resulted in an attempt at simplification.
     Pfitzner and Schoeck are given most thorough consideration.

62. Dürr, Walther. **Das deutsche Sololied im 19. Jahrhundert:
     Untersuchungen zu Sprache und Musik.** Taschenbücher zur
     Musikwissenschaft 97. Wilhelmshaven: Heinrichshofen, 1984.
     351p.

     Investigates ways in which text and music may interact in
     songs, illustrating the possibilities by analyses of a num-

ber of specific works. Concludes that the mark of Romantic
Lieder is a "polyrhythm" among text, singing voice, and
instrumental part. Indexes.

63.   Earl, Don Lee. "The Solo Song Cycle in Germany (1800-1850)."
      Ph.D. diss., Indiana University, 1952. 260p.

      Not examined. According to the abstract in **Dissertation
      Abstracts** (12 [1952]: 799-800), the study distinguishes true
      song cycles from song collections and investigates the man-
      ner in which unity is established in the cycles. Aside from
      the unifying force of the texts of sets based on poetic
      cycles, the song cycles tend to be held together by limited
      use of melodic recurrence and by a logically conceived
      sequence of keys. A recurrence of meter in the concluding
      song was also discovered in some instances.

64.   Friedlaender, Max. **Das deutsche Lied im 18. Jahrhundert:
      Quellen und Studien.** Stuttgart and Berlin: Cotta, 1902. 2
      vols. Reprint. Hildesheim: Olms, 1970. 3 vols.   lviii,
      384; vii, 360; 632p.

      Despite its early date, constitutes the standard reference
      source on the eighteenth-century Lied. After a brief his-
      torical overview of the Lied from the sixteenth century
      through the nineteenth, Volume 1 provides a bibliography of
      eighteenth-century song collections in chronological order
      and, in a separate section, descriptive commentary on each.
      A second fascicle of the first volume prints 236 songs.
      Volume 2 lists, with brief commentary, the most significant
      of the repertoire, organized by poets and texts. Appendices
      include a tabulation of the appearances of each individual
      poet in the entire repertoire, a supplement to the main body
      of Volume 2, and indexes.

65.   Frotscher, Gotthold. "Die Aesthetik des Berliner Liedes in
      ihren Hauptproblemen." **Zeitschrift für Musikwissenschaft** 6
      (1923-24): 431-48.

      Outlines some of the artistic principles underlying the
      song composition of the eighteenth-century Berlin composers,
      quoting from writings of the time. The relationships of
      text and music in terms of diction, structure, and expres-
      sion are mentioned.

66.   Grasberger, Franz. **Das Lied.** Vol. 1 of **Kostbarkeiten der
      Musik.** Tutzing: Hans Schneider, 1968.   211p.

Focuses on seven masterpieces: Mozart, "Das Veilchen":
Beethoven, "Zärtliche Liebe"; Schubert, "Gretchen am Spinnrade"; Schumann, "Mondnacht"; Brahms, "Wiegenlied"; Wolf,
"Verborgenheit"; Strauss, "Traum durch die Dämmerung." Biographical information takes precedence over actual discussion of the music. Facsimiles.

67. Hazay, Oe. von. **Entwicklung und Poesie des Gesanges, und die**
     wertvollen Lieder der Gesamt-Musikliteratur. 2nd ed. 2
     vols. Leipzig: Max Hesse, 1915. xi, 760p.

     Includes both sacred and secular song through the entire
     history of music. The discussion of art song occupies the
     latter part of the first volume and the first part of the
     second. The repertoire is divided into historical sections,
     separating nineteenth-century composers into Romantic, post-
     Romantic (free dissonance), nationalist, and "modern" (for
     1915) groups. The discussion is by individual composers,
     and general information is included to the detriment of any
     detailed treatment of the songs. An appendix lists the most
     important repertoire by composers. Index.

68. Hering, Hans. "Das Klavierpart im Lied des 19. Jahr-
     hunderts." **Melos/Neue Zeitschrift für Musik** 4 (1978): 95-
     101.

     Reflects on the role of the piano part in the Lieder of
     Schubert, Schumann, Brahms, and Wolf. Concludes that the
     process of emancipation of the piano took place in a variety
     of ways: Schubert allowed the piano to reflect the psychic
     state of the song; Schumann expanded its participation in
     the musical structure; Brahms limited the piano's role some-
     what; while Wolf expanded it to the point that it led to the
     orchestrally accompanied song.

69. Jöde, Ulf. **Die Entwicklung des Liedsatzes in der deutschen**
     Musikbewegung. Wolfenbüttel: Möseler, 1969. 332p.

     Not examined. Constitutes Jöde's Ph.D. dissertation (Uni-
     versity of Hamburg, 1969). The author's abstract in **RILM**
     (69/2032) indicates broad coverage of the songs of the
     German youth-music movement. The approach is historical and
     the coverage includes a large number of composers. Note-
     worthy are the rediscovery of old songs and the effect of
     Hindemith on the movement.

70. Jolizza, W.K. von. **Das Lied und seine Geschichte.** Vienna:
     Hartleben, 1910. xii, 691p.

Surveys the history of the song from antiquity to the
first decade of the twentieth century. In the early chapters complete pieces are interspersed with the prose text.
At the nineteenth century the discussion tends to decline
into mere listings of songs in the context of the composers'
lives and very general statements about style. An appendix
collects aphorisms about song. Bibliography. General index
and index of songs.

71. Kravitt, Edward F. "The Ballad as Conceived by Germanic
    Composers of the Late Romantic Period." **Studies in Roman-
    ticism** 12 (1973): 499-515.

    Emphasizes the distinction between the ballad and the Lied,
    and the fact that the ballad demands freedom of narrative
    structure and vivid, dramatic portrayals. Argues that Mah-
    ler, Wolf, and Strauss failed to suit their music to these
    requirements in their settings of ballad texts. Cites the
    writings and compositions of Martin Plüddemann as the most
    faithful to the ballad tradition.

72. ————. "The Lied in 19th-Century Concert Life." **Journal of
    the American Musicological Society** 18 (1965): 207-18.

    Traces the history of the rise of the Liederabend out of
    the drawing room and salon, via the pot-pourri concert.
    Comments of contemporary critics are quoted.

73. ————. "The Orchestral **Lied**: An Inquiry into Its Style and
    Unexpected Flowering around 1900." **The Music Review** 37
    (1976): 209-26.

    Observes that the orchestral scorings of songs of Wolf,
    Mahler, Reger, Pfitzner, and Strauss were inspired by a
    variety of factors. Among these were the need to reach the
    new concert audience, the composers' activity as conductors,
    and a desire to achieve greater expressive effect. Equally
    varied were the approaches of these composers to the compo-
    sition or transcription of Lieder for orchestral accompani-
    ment.

74. ————. "Tempo as an Expressive Element in the Late Romantic
    Lied." **The Musical Quarterly** 59 (1973): 497-518.

    Establishes the historical tradition of rubato and exam-
    ines rhythmic fluctuations in the songs of the late Romantic
    composers. Freedom of tempo is traced to the need to re-
    flect the inner, emotional time experienced by the speaker

of the poetic text. Various means of indicating rhythm changes are illustrated, including proportional notation, measured tempo indications, and changing or flexible meter signatures.

75. Kretzschmar, Hermann. "Das deutsche Lied seit dem Tode Richard Wagners." In **Gesammelte Aufsätze über Musik und Anderes**. Vol. 1, **Gesammelte Aufsätze über Musik aus den Grenzboten**, 284-300. Leipzig: Breitkopf & Härtel, 1910. Also in Vol. 2, **Gesammelte Aufsätze aus den Jahrbüchern der Musikbibliothek Peters**, 23-29. Leipzig: C.F. Peters, 1911.

Scans the field of song composition in the period 1883-97 through the eyes of a contemporary. Wagner's influence on the Lied is seen in the elevation of the sentiments expressed, the expansion of form, and the increase in relationship between vocal part and accompaniment. Many of the composers mentioned are now minor or even insignificant figures. Hugo Wolf, who forms the climax of the discussion, is regarded as "a genius from whose brilliance various rays will some day fall on the whole of song composition."

76. ———. "Das deutsche Lied seit Robert Schumann." In **Gesammelte Aufsätze über Musik und Anderes**. Vol. 1, **Gesammelte Aufsätze über Musik aus den Grenzboten**, 1-35. Leipzig: Breitkopf & Härtel, 1910.

Summarizes the work of the most significant Lied composers of the 1850s, 1860s, and 1870s. (The essay was written in 1881.) A large number of composers is discussed. Kretzschmar stresses that since Schumann the tendency has been to allow the spirit or the expression of the text to dominate over musical form, so that as compared to the first half of the century melody has lost some symmetry but gained in poetic force.

77. ———. **Geschichte des neuen deutschen Liedes, I. Teil: Von Albert bis Zelter**. Leipzig: Breitkopf & Härtel, 1911. Reprint. Hildesheim: Olms, 1966. viii, 356p.

Presents a detailed survey of the history of the Lied in the seventeeth and eighteenth centuries. The book is divided into two large chapters. The first begins with the appearance of monodic style at the beginning of the seventeenth century in Italy and concludes at the end of the century (the "liederloser Zeit"). The second chapter covers the eighteenth century from the reawakening of the Lied

through the First and Second Berlin Schools and their contemporaries.   Index of names.

78.   Landau, Anneliese. **The Lied: The Unfolding of Its Style.**
      Lanham, Md.: University Press of America, 1980. vi, 138p.

      Attempts to trace an increasing sensitivity of Lied com-
      posers to their poets, from Haydn to Hindemith. Coverage is
      uneven, and discussions occasionally include unmotivated
      detail.   In addition to German composers, Musorgsky, Cop-
      land, and Britten are mentioned. Discography; bibliography.

79.   Lindner, Ernst Otto. **Geschichte des deutschen Liedes im**
      XVIII. Jahrhundert. Edited by Ludwig Erk. Leipzig: Breit-
      kopf und Härtel, 1871. Reprint. Wiesbaden: Sändig, 1968.
      xvi, 144, 167p.

      Provides a thorough history of the German (not including
      Austrian) Lied from Reinhard Keiser to the composers of the
      1780s.   Includes a substantial and valuable appendix of 122
      pieces of music. Indexes of songs, names.

80.   Moser, Hans-Joachim. **Das deutsche Lied seit Mozart.** 2nd ed.
      Berlin and Zürich, 1937. Reprint. Tutzing: Hans Schneider,
      1968. 440p.

      Consists of two discrete sections: a brief but thorough
      historical survey of the Lied from the Classical period to
      the early twentieth century; and analytical discussions of
      major works grouped into ten programs, each consisting of a
      cycle or set of Lieder by a single major composer. Indexes
      of names, songs.

81.   Müller, Günther. **Geschichte des deutschen Liedes vom Zeit-**
      alter des Barock bis zur Gegenwart. Munich: Drei Masken,
      1925. Reprint. Bad Homburg: Hermann Gentner, 1959. [iv],
      336, 48p.

      Traces the history of the Lied from the point of view of
      the poetry. The discussion is oriented toward literary
      criticism of the texts, with occasional brief remarks about
      relevant musical settings. The book is divided into two
      main sections at the year 1750, each section subdivided
      according to poetic types. Index. Appendix of music for
      selected songs from Schein to Zelter.

82.   Nef, Albert. **Das Lied in der deutschen Schweiz Ende des 18.**
      und Anfang des 19. Jahrhunderts. Zurich: Hug, 1909. vii,

167p.

Discusses the first years of the solo song in Switzerland. Characteristic of the history of songs in Switzerland in this period in contrast to that of Germany is a close relation to polyphonic song and spiritual songs, an enthusiasm for patriotic songs, and a tendency not to export the songs to other countries. Appendices include biographies of composers Johannes Schmidlin (1722-1772), Johann Heinrich Egli (1742-1810), and Johann Jakob Walder (1750-1817); an extensive list of repertoire; and a musical supplement of thirty-one songs.

83. Nettl, Paul. "The Austrian Baroque Lied." **Journal of Renaissance and Baroque Music (=Musica disciplina)** 1 (1946): 101-110.

Makes a brief, general survey. The sources for these songs were not primarily printed but rather the Jesuit plays and manuscripts prepared for religious and court use. The main influences on the style are the Austrian folk dance and folksong, peasant songs, and some Italian arias and French tunes. The Lied in Bohemia and the songs of Count Sporck are also mentioned.

84. ―――. **Das Wiener Lied im Zeitalter des Barock.** Vienna, Leipzig: Passer, 1934. 50, 31p.

Discusses the style of Viennese Lieder in the seventeenth century. An introduction considers the German and Italian influences on Austrian style. Composers given substantial treatment include Schnüffis, Prinner, the Emperor Leopold I, and Schmelzer. Appendix containing thirteen complete songs.

85. Ossenkop, David Charles. "The Earliest Settings of German Ballads for Voice and Clavier." Ph.D. diss., Columbia University, 1968. 749p.

Investigates the treatment of ballad texts in song settings between 1756 and 1815. Principal is the question of whether strophic narrative poems were to be set to music in strophic form, strophic variations, or sectional, cantata-like structures. Most of the earliest settings are strophic, although more complex poems may be cantata-like. In the later part of the period in question Reichardt employed elaborate strophic variations, while Zumsteeg tended to a cantata form with more operatic style. A dramatic approach was also characteristic of the Austrian and Bohemian compos-

ers. Elements of this genre became important roots of the
Romantic Lied.

86.   Pollak-Schlaffenberg, Irene. "Die Wiener Liedmusik von 1778-
      1789." **Studien zur Musikwissenschaft: Beihefte der Denk-
      mäler der Tonkunst in Österreich** 5 (1918): 97-151.

      Reviews the history and describes the style of songs
      published in Vienna between the first song publication there
      and Mozart's first published songs.   The Viennese song grew
      from the Singspiellied rather than the German dance tune.
      Characteristic of the Austrian as opposed to the German
      style were the influence of the Italian opera aria and the
      independence of the keyboard part.   Music examples are ap-
      pended.

87.   Porter, Cecelia Hopkins. "The **Rheinlieder** Critics: A Case of
      Musical Nationalism." **The Musical Quarterly** 63 (1977): 74-
      98.

      Describes the spate of nationalistic German songs that
      arose after 1840 as a response to the French threat to take
      the Rhein.   The movement was spawned by Nikolaus Becker's
      poem "Der deutsche Rhein."   The large number of folk-style
      and patriotic songs that ensued were critiqued partly as
      expressions of patriotic emotion and partly for musical
      value.   In addition, bourgeois commercial spirit and jour-
      nalistic interest are reflected in the history of these
      songs.

88.   ————. "The Rhenish Manifesto: 'The Free German Rhine' as
      an Expression of German National Consciousness in the
      Romantic Lied." Ph.D. diss., University of Maryland, 1975.
      xiii, 629p.

      Considers the enormous output of Lieder evoked by the
      French threat to the Rhine in 1840.   The social history of
      these pieces gives a picture of the political and cultural
      situation of the era.   In style, these Lieder, whose compos-
      ers included Schumann, Mendelssohn, Loewe, and Franz, mani-
      fest the quality of **Volkstümlichkeit** that symbolized patri-
      otic feeling. Appendices. Bibliography. Index of names.
      Glossary of German terms.

89.   Reissmann, August. **Das deutsche Lied in seiner historischer
      Entwicklung.** Kassel: Bertram, 1861.   290, 41p.

      An early, classic study but now somewhat dated, gives a

perceptive outline history of the Lied from the Middle Ages
to the mid-nineteenth century. The crucial division is
placed at the rise of the **volkstümliches Lied** in the eighteenth century. A concluding section of the study discusses
the ballad and the influence of the Lied on other genres. A
supplement comprises representative pieces up to the eighteenth century.

90. ———. **Geschichte des deutschen Liedes.** Berlin: Guttentag,
     1874. vii, 284, 48p.

The successor to Reissmann's earlier book (item 89 above),
offers an overview of the history of the Lied from its
origins to the middle of the nineteenth century. The author
attempts to identify the important items of the repertoire,
discussing some songs individually and listing many others.
The emphasis is on the development and realization of aesthetic principles. Appendix of exemplary pieces.

91. Rentzow, Hans. **Die mecklenburgischen Liederkomponisten des
     18. Jahrhunderts.** Niederdeutsche Musik 2. Hanover: Nagel,
     1938. 178, 8p.

Rentzow's dissertation (University of Rostock, 1936),
outlines the history of the Lieder of the Mecklenburg composers from 1757 to 1807. The style began under the influence of Hamburg and by the end of the century resembled the
simple, strophic Berlin type. At the turn of the century
the composers began to elaborate the style in texture, vocal
melody, and form. Especially noteworthy is their reliance
on particular poets. Music examples are relegated to the
end of the book. List of songs and song collections.

92. Schäfke, Rudolf. "Vom Liedschaffen der Gegenwart" **Melos** 4
     (1925): 534-40.

Stresses that twentieth-century composers have turned away
from the orchestrally conceived song style of the late Romantic period and instead concentrate on transparency in
scoring, which allows the voice to sound clearly, and on
linear texture. Representative composers are discussed--
Hans Pfitzner, the representative of the conservative tradition; Carl Prohaska; Lothar Windsperger; Erwin Lendvai;
Anton Webern; and Paul Hindemith, whose **Marienleben** is noteworthy for its application to the genre of song forms bor-
rowed from absolute music.

93. Schneider, K.E. **Das musikalische Lied in geschichtlicher**

Entwickelung. 3 vols. Leipzig: Breitkopf & Härtel, 1863, 1864, 1865. xxiv, 323; xvi, 514; viii, 370p.

The third section, entitled "Dritte Periode: Das stro-phische Stimmungslied," traces the history of the Lied from the early seventeenth to the early nineteenth century. The author emphasizes the seemingly unprepossessing beginnings of the genre and that only in the German-speaking nations was fruitful development of song achievable in this period.

94. Schollum, Robert. "Anmerkungen zur Geschichte des öster-reichischen Kunstliedes." In **Musik und Dichtung: Anton Dermota zum 70. Geburtstag (4. Juni 1980)**, edited by Herbert Zeman, 7-19. Vienna: Oesterreichische Nationalbib-liothek, 1980.

Not examined. According to the abstract in **RILM** (80/3966), traces the history of the Lied in Austria from the eighteenth to the twentieth century. Focuses on the varying emphases placed on textual and musical considerations.

95. ————. **Das österreichische Lied des 20. Jahrhunderts.** Pub-likationen des Instituts für Oesterreichische Musikdoku-mentation 3. Tutzing: Hans Schneider, 1977. 169p.

Not examined. The author's **RILM** abstract (77/883) states that the history of Austrian song from Schubert is briefly outlined, and the discussion concentrates on composers born between 1857 and 1930. Included are the Second Vienna School composers and many others. Relationships of text and music are studied. Bibliography. Index.

96. Schumann, Elisabeth. **German Song.** New York: Chanticleer, 1948. 72p.

An excellent brief and informal history of the Lied from the Middle Ages to the early twentieth century. The book concentrates on the great Romantic song composers and has a single chapter to survey lesser masters. Besides brief characterizations of a number of masterpieces, the author gives occasional personal evaluations. A final chapter discusses the singing of Lieder, illustrating general prin-ciples by Schubert's "Die Forelle" and Brahms's "Vergeb-liches Ständchen." Illustrations and color plates. Index.

97. Schuré, Edouard. **Geschichte des deutschen Liedes.** Berlin: Sacco, 1870. 408p.

Discusses the Lied as a poetic form, with emphasis on the folk tradition. The first chapters are devoted to various topical sub-genres, taken up in the order in which they arose, to the seventeenth century. The final three chapters deal with the revival of the Lied as an artistic genre and its history from the seventeenth to the nineteenth century. The Lied is said to draw its strength and its cultural force from its broad appeal to all levels of German social life. A few translations of Lieder into French are appended.

98. Schwab, Heinrich W. "Kunstlied: Krise einer Gattung." **Musica** 35 (1981): 229-34.

Reviews the social and aesthetic history of the Lied through the nineteenth century. Points out that the artistic sophistication of the genre led it from the home to the concert hall in the middle of the century, and that the continuation of this artistic development into the twentieth century has led to its decline as a concert genre and its appeal to intimate, informed audiences in more chamber-music-like settings. Illustrations.

99. ———. **Sangbarkeit, Popularität und Kunstlied: Studien zu Lied und Liedästhetik der mittleren Goethezeit 1770-1814.** Studien zur Musikgeschichte des 19. Jahrhunderts 3. Regensburg: Bosse, 1965. 205p.

Examines two of the major concepts in the history of the Lied before Schubert's first masterpieces, making extensive reference to contemporary writings. The principle of **Sangbarkeit** brought about a poetic approach that operated in conscious relation to singing, a close relationship between poets and composers, and new styles in both music and poetry. The idea of **Popularität** produced a simpler melodic style, a tendency to melodic conventions, and a German style independent of Italian and French models. The style of "Kunstlied" as opposed to the "volkstümliches Lied" can be defined on the basis of these aesthetic principles, considering the choice of high quality texts, the increasingly declamatory melodic style, and the obbligato role of the accompaniment. Bibliographies of primary and secondary literature. Index.

100. Seyfert, Bernhard. "Das musikalische-volkstümliche Lied von 1770-1800." **Vierteljahrsschrift für Musikwissenschaft** 10 (1894): 33-102.

Supplements the great nineteenth-century histories of the
Lied. Among the many composers mentioned, Hiller is credited with raising public interest in the genre with his
Singspiele; Schulz with identifying the Hainbund's poems as
the best texts and with establishing the simple folk style;
Reichardt with achieving a more expressive melodic and
harmonic language. Attention is also given to the important role of the Lied in various areas of eighteenth-
century society. Supplement of complete songs. (An extensive set of comments by Max Friedlaender on this article
appears on pages 234-38 of the same volume.)

101.   Spitta, Philipp. "Ballade." In **Musikgeschichtliche Auf-
       sätze**, 403-61. Berlin: Paetel, 1894. Reprint. Hildesheim:
       Olms, 1976.

       Outlines the history of the German ballad from Bürger's
       "Lenore" in 1773 through the works of Loewe.

102.   Stein, Jack M. **Poem and Music in the German Lied from Gluck
       to Hugo Wolf.** Cambridge, Mass.: Harvard University Press,
       1971. 238p.

       Attempts to investigate, by means of specific analyses,
       the nature of the synthesis of poetry and music in the
       Lied. Stein seems to be searching for the perfect treat-
       ment of poetry by the composer, defining that by whether
       the composer's reading accurately reflects Stein's own.
       Musical values are not securely established, and the book
       becomes a series of notes on a large number of songs,
       employing superficial analysis and assertions about their
       effectiveness. Bibliography. Index of poems and songs;
       general index.

103.   Stoljar, Margaret Mahoney. **Poetry and Song in Late Eigh-
       teenth-Century Germany: A Study in the Musical Sturm und
       Drang.** London: Croom Helm, 1985. xii, 217p.

       Examines the development of the Lied in the period 1770-
       90. Stoljar gives an illuminating outline of the social
       and literary context of the genre, then discusses with
       great insight (though sometimes questionable assumptions
       about certain aspects of eighteenth-century music history)
       the contributions of several central figures, both poets
       and composers. Classified bibliography. Index.

104.   Stuber, Robert. **Die Klavierbegleitung im Liede von Haydn,
       Mozart und Beethoven: Eine Stilstudie.** Biel: Schüler,

1958. 132p.

From the author's dissertation (University of Berne, 1952), considers various aspects of the accompaniment in the songs of the Viennese Classic composers. The first chapters establish the nature of basso continuo style and contrast to it the variety of keyboard textures in the Classic songs. The relationship of the voice to the keyboard part is examined, particularly with regard to the doubling of the melody and various ways of expanding on that principle, and to the use of the keyboard to complete the rhythmic movement. The accompaniment grows more independent over the course of the period. Finally, attention is given to a variety of ways in which the accompaniment responds to the content of the text; here the groundwork was laid for Schubert's and the Romantic Lied style. Bibliography.

105. Thomas, R. Hinton. **Poetry and Song in the German Baroque.** London: Oxford University Press, 1963. xii, 219p.

Traces Baroque song from its roots in the polyphonic Lied through the continuo Lied to the arias of the generation of Handel and Telemann. Both poets and composers are discussed. The approach is the treatment of the development of poetry and the illustration by representative examples of the manner in which it was set. Appendices include complete music examples and a note on recordings. Bibliography.

106. Ursprung, Otto. "Vier Studien zur Geschichte des deutschen Liedes: IV. Der Weg von den Gelegenheitsgesängen und dem Chorlied über die Frühmonodie zum neueren deutschen Lied." **Archiv für Musikwissenschaft** 6 (1924): 262-323.

Discusses the polyphonic Lied and the earliest German continuo songs, ending with Heinrich Albert. Emphasis is placed on the political situation in Germany in the late sixteenth and early seventeenth centuries. Extensive lists of published music are provided.

107. Vetter, Walther. **Das frühdeutsche Lied: Ausgewählte Kapitel aus der Entwicklungsgeschichte und Aesthetik des ein- und mehrstimmiges deutschen Kunstliedes im 17. Jahrhundert.** 2 vols. Universitas-Archiv 8. Münster: Helios, 1928. xv, 350; xii, 159p.

Reflects a detailed and ground-breaking study of the

aesthetic and the musical development from polyphonic to
monodic Lied in the seventeenth century. The approach is
through close consideration of specific works. Vetter
stresses the aspects of the German tradition that are
independent of Italian and French developments. The second
volume prints 311 Lieder. Indexes to each volume.

108. ———. "Wort und Weise im deutschen Kunstlied des 17.
      Jahrhunderts." **Zeitschrift für Musikwissenschaft** 10
      (1927-28): 624-31.

      Shows how a German style of declamation in monodic song
      was based in the German polyphonic Lied rather than in
      Italian solo song models. Especially important is the
      adoption of the rhythmic traits of dance music by German
      Lied composers.

109. ———. "Zur volklichen und landschaftlichen Bestimmung des
      deutschen begleiteten Sololiedes." **Jahrbuch der Musikbib-
      liothek Peters** 44 (1937): 58-76. Reprinted in **Mythos-
      Melos-Musica: Ausgewählte Aufsätze zur Musikgeschichte** 1.
      Leipzig: Deutsche Verlag für Musik, 1957.

      Attempts to identify national German traits in the solo
      Lied of the Baroque. Argues that the true roots of an
      independent national style are to be found in the Pomera-
      nian repertoire.

110. Whitton, Kenneth. **Lieder: An Introduction to German Song.**
      London: Julia McRae; New York: Franklin Watts, 1984.
      xii, 203p.

      An enthusiastic introduction to the Lied, addressed to
      music-lovers rather than scholars. The opening historical
      review is well grounded in a good perspective on the reper-
      toire. There is an interesting consideration of practical
      problems of performance, a set of brief commmentaries on
      twenty-five prominent songs, and a cursory discussion of
      important recordings. Appendices; brief bibliography.
      General and title indexes.

111. Wiora, Walter. **Das deutsche Lied: Zur Geschichte und Aes-
      thetik einer musikalischen Gattung.** Wolfenbüttel and
      Zurich: Möseler, 1971. 195p.

      A two-part study. The first section of the book dis-
      cusses the nature of the Lied as a genre. The term is
      taken in a somewhat general sense, not restricted to but

centered on the simple, strophic type. The various aesthetic and stylistic manifestations of the genre are surveyed. The second part of the book takes a historical
approach. The history of the Lied is outlined in six
stages from the Carolingian era to the twentieth century,
then, in more detail, several crucial stages in the eighteenth and nineteenth centuries are treated in depth. Substantial bibliography.

112.   ———. "Die Gattung 'Lied'." In **Festschrift für Ernst
Hermann Meyer zum sechszigsten Geburtstag,** edited by
Georg Knepler, 141-50. Leipzig: Deutsche Verlag für
Musik, 1973.

Not examined. The author's abstract in **RILM** (76/290)
indicates that the essay pursues the idea that the Lied is
centered on the strophic form and traces some of the types
of development that it has undergone in relation to that
constant.

113.   ———. "Die Romantisierung alter Mollmelodik im Liede von
Schubert bis Wolf." **Deutsches Jahrbuch der Musikwissenschaft** 11 (1966): 61-71.

Shows how the German nineteenth-century composers adapted
the repertoire of folk-melody models in their songs. Examples from older sources are matched with phrases from
Beethoven, Reichardt, Schubert, Schumann, Loewe, and Wolf.
Wiora reasons that this indicates how strong a force the
folk Lied remained in the art Lied, even while the genre
continued to develop.

114.   Worbs, Hans Christoph. "Die Schichtung des deutschen Lied-
gutes in der zweiten Hälfte des 17. Jahrhunderts." **Archiv
für Musikwissenschaft** 17 (1960): 61-70.

Stresses the multiplicity of subgenres of the Lied in the
late seventeenth century. Among these were folksongs,
student songs, songs with spiritual and didactic intent for
domestic use, social songs, and sophisticated songs for an
audience of connoisseurs.

115.   Zeman, Herbert. "Dichtung und Musik: Zur Entwicklung des
österreichischen Kunstliedes vom 18. zum 19. Jahrhundert." In **Musik und Dichtung: Anton Dermota zum 70.
Geburtstag (4. Juni 1980),** edited by Herbert Zeman, 20-
34. Vienna: Oesterreichische Nationalbibliothek, 1980.

Not examined. According to the **RILM** abstract (80/3970),
points out the connection of the songs of the Viennese
Classical composer to the German-language poetry of the
period. Indicates the varying moods of the song texts.

ITALIAN

116. Aldrich, Putnam. **Rhythm in Seventeenth-Century Italian
     Monody.** New York: Norton, 1966. 188p.

     Investigates the practical problems of transcription and
     performance of the Italian monody repertoire to the 1630s.
     The method employed is to read the theoretical treatises of
     the time, especially Antonio Brunelli's **Regole utilissime,**
     then to apply them to a selected repertoire. Major empha-
     sis is given to the relation of musical rhythm to dance and
     verse rhythms. The last quarter of the text consists of an
     anthology of transcriptions in an idiosyncratic layout that
     the author hopes will clarify the musico-poetic structure.
     Tables. Index.

117. Baron, John H. "Monody: A Study in Terminology." **The Musi-
     cal Quarterly** 54 (1968): 462-74.

     Traces the development of the term "monody" from its
     first use--by Giovanni Battista Doni in 1635--to the pres-
     ent. Baron argues for a narrow application of the term
     for only the Florentine rhetorical recitative style.

118. Einstein, Alfred. "Die Aria di Ruggiero." **Sammelbände der
     Internationalen Musikgesellschaft** 13 (1911-12): 444-54.

     Investigates the use of formulaic settings for the sing-
     ing of poetry in sixteenth- and seventeenth-century Italy.
     The name of the so-called "Aria di Ruggiero," used for
     singing texts in **ottava rima,** can be traced to a passage in
     Ariosto's **Orlando furioso** that was set to this formula by
     Antonio Cifra.

119. Fortune, Nigel. "Italian Secular Monody from 1600 to 1635:
     An Introductory Survey." **The Musical Quarterly** 39 (1953):
     171-95.

     Suggests that the genre of monody, overshadowed by opera
     in scholarly perspective, should be better known and under-
     stood. Outlines the background of the genre and discusses

the situation of the composers and the circulation of the repertoire. The three important centers of its development are identified and compared: Florence, important early but less so after 1620; Rome, slower in adopting the new type; and Venice, which took the lead in publication and in developing the style. The texts at first were comparable to those of the serious polyphonic madrigal but later tended toward the popular.

120. Leitgeb, Walburga. "Studien zum italienischen Lied in Wien zur Zeit der Klassik (1750-1820)." Ph.D. diss., University of Vienna, 1980. 723p.

Not examined. The **RILM** abstract (80/575) indicates that the study describes the situation around 1800, focusing on two collections by Antoni. The singer Angelica Catalani is also discussed. Work-list; bibliography.

121. Lupo, Bettina. "Romanze, notturni, ariette nel primo ottocento." **La rassegna musicale** 14 (1941): 81-95.

Begins with a discussion of the French romance. Identifies as major factors in the history of Italian song in the early nineteenth century the growth of a popular nationalism and the focus of musical life on the opera. The social situation of the song is described, and names of some important singers, poets, and composers are listed. By comparison with the Lied, the Italian song suffers from its weaker poetic material, emphasis on vocalism rather than poetic interpretation in the melody, and relegation of the accompaniment to a subordinate role.

122. Racek, Jan. **Stilprobleme der italienische Monodie: Ein Beitrag zur Geschichte des einstimmigen Barockliedes.** Prague: Státní Pedagogické Nakladatelství, 1965. 310p.

Expands a 1938 study published in Czech. Covers the history of monody from about 1600 to 1670. Begins with the theoretical and aesthetic background, followed by a consideration of the texts, then extensive examination of melody and harmony. A treatment of form constitutes the core of the book, showing the development from madrigal and aria to cantata and oratorio. The last chapter deals with expression and various specific styles. The period 1620-40 is regarded as the crucial phase in the history of monodic song. List of sources. Appendix of music.

123. ———. "Zum Wort-Ton-Problem in der Vokalmusik am Ende des

16. und am Anfang des 17. Jahrhunderts." In **Colloquium Music and Word, Brno 1969,** edited by Rudolf Pečman, 27-34. Brno: International Musical Festival, 1973.

Argues that the monodic repertoire of the Florentine camerata took its compositional structure from both rhythmic and expressive characteristics of its texts. This repertoire is seen as representing a landmark in the history of the relationship between text and music.

124.   Schmitz, Eugen. "Zur Frühgeschichte der lyrischen Monodie Italiens im 17. Jahrhundert." **Jahrbuch der Musikbibliothek Peters** 18 (1911): 35-48.

Compiles a brief introduction to the monody as a preface to a later study of the cantata. Of particular concern are the differentiation of madrigal from aria style and stylistic distinctions among sections; the accompaniment, especially with regard to the ostinato or strophic bass, the ritornello, dance styles, and imitation of the vocal line in the bass; and dramatic monodies and dialogues.

125.   —————. "Zur Geschichte des italienischen Continuo-Madrigals im 17. Jahrhundert." **Sammelbände der Internationalen Musikgesellschaft** 11 (1909-10): 509-28.

Connects the continuo madrigal to the rise of the cantata in the first half of the seventeenth century. Particularly important is the appearance of passages of recitative style in the monodic madrigals.

126.   Torchi, L. "Canzoni ed arie italiane ad una voce nel secolo XVII." **Rivista musicale italiana** 1 (1894): 581-656.

Pleads for a revival of interest in Italy's musical heritage of the seventeenth century in the face of the expanding influence of German music and Wagnerism. The stylistic characteristics of seicento solo vocal music are illustrated by analysis of numerous works.

POLISH

127.   Simon, Alicia. **The Polish Songwriters.** Warsaw: Tosspo, 1936. 50p.

Makes a brief historical survey of the development of the

art song in Poland and by Polish composers. The study is organized in four sections: pre-Romantic (Elsner, Kurpiński, and others), Romantic (Chopin, Moniuszko, and others), late Romantic, and modern (Szymanowski and others). Composers and songs are listed and some characteristics of style identified.

RUSSIAN

128. Oliphant, E.H.C. "A Survey of Russian Song." **The Musical Quarterly** 12 (1926): 196-230.

Comments on a large number of songs from a survey of nearly six hundred pieces. The problem of translation is demonstrated. Composers from Glinka to Prokofiev and Stravinsky are grouped into four periods. The bulk of the article is made up of descriptive and evaluative remarks on the composers' song oeuvres in general and on representative songs.

SCANDINAVIAN

Norway

129. Olson, Robert Wallace. "A Comparative Study of Selected Norwegian Romances by Halfdan Kjerulf, Edvard Grieg, and Eyvind Alnaes." D.M.A. diss., University of Illinois, 1973. 328 p.

Not examined. According to the author's abstract in **RILM** (74/571), the study traces Norwegian art song from 1840 to 1930, with attention to the influence of Norwegian folksong and the German Lied. Bibliography; work-lists.

Sweden

130. Larson, Carl Robert. "A History of Swedish Solo Song." Ph.D. diss., University of Iowa, 1968. 408p.

Not examined. The abstract by the author in **RILM** (69/3407) indicates that the history includes relationships

of Swedish song to song in other countries.   An appendix
contains 750 songs.   Bibliography; work-list.

SPANISH AND PORTUGUESE (including Latin America)

131.   Araújo, Mozart de. **A modinha e o lundu no século XVIII.**
       São Paulo: Ricordi Brasileira, 1963.   159p.

       Consists of a historical discussion of Brazil's national
       song genres, together with complete music and texts for
       thirty-two songs.

132.   ————. "The **Lundu** and **Modinha** of Brazil in the Nineteenth
       Century." **College Music Symposium** 7 (1967): 103-7.

       A synopsis of a conference paper. Explains briefly how
       the **lundu** migrated from a popular form to the salon and art
       music while, by contrast, the **modinha** developed from an
       art-song genre through the salon and ultimately attained
       the character and function of popular music.

133.   Mariz, Vasco. **A cancão brasileira: Erudita, folclórica,
       popular.** 4th ed. Rio de Janiero: Cátedra, 1980.   419p.

       (Supersedes an earlier version with the title **A cancão de
       camara no Brasil.** Porto: Progredior, 1948.) The first part
       of the book traces the history of the art song in Brazil
       since the mid-nineteenth century.   There is a brief discus-
       sion of general problems of song composition.   The histori-
       cal survey groups the composers into generations, and each
       composer is given a sub-chapter.   The development of na-
       tionalism is outlined, reactions against nationalist ten-
       dencies are discussed, and an independent, post-nationalist
       movement is identified.   Appendices include an essay on
       important performers, a list of songs, and a guide to
       pronunciation in singing Brazilian art songs.   Bibliogra-
       phy.   Index of names.

II

STUDIES OF INDIVIDUAL COMPOSERS AND WORKS

Isaac Albéniz
(1860-1909)

134. Llorens, José María. "El 'Lied' en la obra musical de Isaac Albéniz." **Anuario musical** 15 (1960): 123-40.

Describes Albéniz's songs in chronological order. Remarkable is the variety of languages in which he composed-- Italian, English, and French, as well as Spanish. The influences on his style are noted, especially those of Schumann and the nineteenth-century French composers.

Heinrich Albert
(1604-1651)

135. Müller-Blattau, Joseph. "Eine Liedkantate von Simon Dach und Heinrich Albert: Studie zur Geschichte des früh-deutschen Liedes." In **Musa-Mens-Musici, im Gedenken an Walther Vetter,** edited by Heinz Wegener, 99-107. Leipzig: VEB Deutscher Verlag für Musik, 1969.

Demonstrates Albert's care in setting Dach's text, an unusual song-cantata in honor of the poet Martin Opitz.

Dominick Argento
(b. 1927)

136. Sabatino, Trucilla Marie. "A Performer's Commentary on **To be Sung upon the Water** by Dominick Argento." D.M.A. diss., Ohio State University, 1980. 108p.

Not examined. According to the abstract in **RILM** (80/5833), discusses structure and text-music relations. The 1974 cycle for high voice, clarinet and bass clarinet, and piano, is a tribute to Schubert. Appendix of letters from Argento to the author.

Michael Arne
(ca. 1740-1786)

137. Parkinson, John A. **An Index to the Vocal Works of Thomas Augustine Arne and Michael Arne.** Detroit Studies in Music Bibliography 21. Detroit: Information Coordinators, 1972. 82p.

Lists all the songs alphabetically, with keys to the collections or larger works from which they come. The lost works of each composer are listed in the appendices.

Thomas Augustine Arne
(1710-1778)

138. Farish, Stephen Thomas, Jr. "The Vauxhall Songs of Thomas Augustine Arne." D.M.A. thesis, University of Illinois, 1962. 170p.

Not examined. The abstract (**Dissertation Abstracts** 23 [1963]: 4375-76) indicates that the study identifies the stereotypical style of the composer, but emphasizes his willingness to adapt it to the demands of particular texts. Influences on Arne's style were the popular ballad, especially in the earlier songs; the florid Italian **opera seria** aria, the strongest influence; and the **opera buffa** style, which he employed in the later part of his career.

*   Parkinson, John A. **An Index to the Vocal Works of Thomas Augustine Arne and Michael Arne.**

Cited above as item 137.

Carl Philipp Emanuel Bach
(1714-1788)

139. Busch, Gudrun. **C.Ph.E. Bach und seine Lieder.** Kölner Beiträge zur Musikforschung 12. Regensburg: Bosse, 1957. 407, 110p.

Places the songs of C.P.E. Bach in context, concluding
that in his Gellert settings of 1758 he broke free from the
stylistic constraints of the First Berlin School and indicated the progress of the Lied's compositional style in the
Second Berlin School and after. Bach's song oeuvre, including sacred songs, is put into historical and biographical perspective and subjected to thorough analysis.
Appendices include a chronological list of songs, index,
and musical examples. Bibliography.

Ernst Bacon
(b. 1898)

140. St. Edmunds, John. "The Songs of Ernst Bacon." **Sewanee
Review** 49 (1941): 499-501.

Praises Bacon's style for such qualities as forthright-
ness, toughness, virility, and grandeur of imagination.
The music is characterized by its use of counterpoint that
justifies syncopation and dissonance.

Béla Bartók
(1881-1945)

141. Collins, Adrian. "Bartók, Schoenberg, and Some Songs."
Music and Letters 10 (1929): 177-81.

Discusses the Five Songs, op. 16, by Bartók. Bartók's
music is found to have an underlying sense of consonance
that provides coherence despite the dissonance that expresses the sentiments of the texts.

142. Dille, Denijs. "Ein unbekanntes Bartók-Manuskript." **Oester-
reichisches Musikzeitschrift** 22 (1967): 283-84.

Provides information about the date of the manuscript of
Bartók's orchestral setting of Reinhold Becker's completion
of Beethoven's "Erlkönig" sketch and suggests that Bartók
might have attempted to derive some income from it during
the period of 1905 when he had no regular position.

143. Gervers, Hilda. "Béla Bartók's **Ot dal** (Five Songs) Opus
15." **The Music Review** 30 (1969): 291-99.

Examines the history and style of the set. The authorship of the texts is suppressed according to Bartók's own

wish. The songs represent the characteristic elements of
Bartók's mature style, including melody and rhythm related
to Hungarian folk music and a harmonic system based on
polar axes within the circle of fifths.

Gabriel Bataille
(ca. 1575-1630)

144. Verchaly, André. "Gabriel Bataille et son oeuvre person-
nelle pour chant et luth." **Revue de musicologie** 29
(1947): 1-24.

Reports on the life of Bataille and the style of his
songs. Little is known of his biography. In addition to
numerous transcriptions for voice and lute, forty-six airs
he actually composed are extant, and they constitute models
of the genre both in text and music. In general, his style
is simple, though in dramatic situations it can be more
ambitious. Work-list.

Sir Arnold Bax
(1883-1953)

145. Banfield, Stephen. "Bax as a Song Composer." **The Musical
Times** 124 (1983): 666-69.

Explains why Bax is little regarded as a song composer,
principally judging that Bax's idiom was unsuited to the
intimate and simple genre of song. (This article is a pre-
publication extract from Banfield's **Sensibility and English
Song**; see item 14 above.)

Ludwig van Beethoven
(1770-1827)

146. Boettcher, Hans. **Beethoven als Liederkomponist.** Augsburg:
Filser, 1928. Reprint. Walluf: Sändig, 1974. xii, 180p.

Examines Beethoven's Lieder in considerable detail. The
variety of texts is emphasized and subjected to systematic
discussion. A complete survey of Beethoven's song forms
leads to the conclusion that for Beethoven the dramatic
shape of the content became more important than literary

structure. Study of the composer's choices of keys reveals
that the expressive meanings associated with specific to-
nalities evolved from more conventional to more personal
usage. Historical evaluation produces the argument that
Beethoven freed the Lied from its earlier social position
as drawing-room or salon music to a more significant status
as personal expression of the composer as individual. Form
diagrams. Index of names. Table compiling information on
all songs and song fragments.

147. Bücken, Ernst. "Die Lieder Beethovens: Eine stilkritische
      Studie." **Beethoven Jahrbuch** 2 (1925): 33-42.

      Illustrates Beethoven's attention to several important
      issues in the composition of songs as it developed in the
      nineteenth century. Among these are the use of lyrical or
      declamatory vocal writing, the evocation of Romantic feel-
      ings, the depiction of phenomena of nature. Beethoven's
      most important contribution is seen in his subjection of
      poetic form to the force of musical structure.

148. Curzon, Henri de. **Les Lieder et airs détachés de Beethoven.**
      Paris: Fischbacher, 1905.   54p.

      Makes a general survey of the songs and independent arias
      in chronological order. Offers brief descriptive comments
      on the music. Work-list.

149. Friedlaender, Max. "Nachwort." In Beethoven, **An die ferne
      Geliebte: Ein Liederkreis**, 45-72. Leipzig: Insel Verlag,
      1924. Extracted in **Inselalmanach**, 1925: 63-76.

      A substantial historical and critical discussion. The
      author places the work between the eighteenth-century can-
      tata and the nineteenth-century song cycle. The informa-
      tion regarding the identity of the "Immortal Beloved" is
      out of date. The comments on the music make considerable
      reference to Nottebohm's publication of the sketches.

150. Hopkinson, Cecil, and C.B. Oldman. "Thomson's Collections
      of National Song with Special Reference to the Contribu-
      tions of Haydn and Beethoven." **Edinburgh Bibliographical
      Society Transactions** 2 (1938-45): 1-64. Corrections and
      additions in 3 (1948-55):121-24.

      Begins with history and general description of George
      Thomson's collections. List of editions; bibliography;
      descriptions of editions; facsimiles of title pages. The-

matic catalogues for both Haydn's and Beethoven's settings.

151. Kerman, Joseph. **"An die ferne Geliebte."** In **Beethoven Studies,** edited by Alan Tyson, 123-57. New York: Norton, 1973.

Makes a broad-based and detailed study of the cycle, including literary and musical analysis, biographical and historical context, and criticism. The author concludes that **An die ferne Geliebte** introduced aspects of Beethoven's late style, notably the folk-like melodic construction and an expanded approach to tonal planning. Sketch facsimile.

152. Lissa, Zofia. "Beethovens Bearbeitungen zweier polnischer Volkslieder." In **Bericht über den internationalen Beethoven-Kongress 10.-12. Dezember 1970 in Berlin,** edited by Heinz Alfred Brockhaus and Konrad Niemann, 447-52. Berlin: Neue Musik, 1971.

Discusses Beethoven's two arrangements of Polish songs in the set of **Chants des divers** [sic] **nations** of 1816-18 (WoO 158a). Hypothesizes that Beethoven must have heard the songs first-hand, probably from someone serving in the household of a member of the Polish aristocracy in Vienna. Emphasizes Beethoven's grasp of the stylistic details of Polish folk music.

153. Lockwood, Lewis. "Beethoven's Sketches for **Sehnsucht** (WoO 146)." In **Beethoven Studies,** edited by Alan Tyson, 97-122. New York: Norton, 1973.

Thoroughly investigates the large number of sketches for the song. Demonstrates that Beethoven's compositional procedure was not simply a progression in one direction from unformed early ideas to a perfected composition, but in this case a variety of approaches to musical ideas based on the structure of the poem. Facsimiles and transcriptions of sketches.

154. Massenkeil, Günther. "Religiöse Aspekte der Gellert-Lieder Beethovens." In **Religiöse Musik in nicht-liturgische Werken von Beethoven bis Reger,** edited by Walter Wiora with Günther Massenkeil and Klaus Wolfgang Niemöller, 83-96. Studien zur Musikgeschichte des 19. Jahrhunderts 51. Regensburg: Bosse, 1978.

Deals with both textual content and musical style. The

composer's use of Gellert's texts reflects his own religious opinions. The music itself embodies some characteristics associated with the style of sacred music.

155. Müller-Blattau, Joseph. "Beethoven vertont Goethe: Er-
reichtes und Geplantes." In **Goethe und die Meister der
Musik,** 46-61. Stuttgart: Klett, 1969.

Using Beethoven's settings of Goethe poems, shows the
development of the composer's style, both as regards the
composition of songs and in relation to the complete oeuvre. Special attention is given to the four settings of
"Sehnsucht."

156. Poser, Martin. "Beethoven und das Volksliedgut der
Britischen Inseln." In **Bericht über den internationalen
Beethoven-Kongress 20. bis 23. März 1977 in Berlin,**
edited by Harry Goldschmidt, Karl-Heinz Köhler, and
Konrad Niemann, 405-9. Leipzig: VEB Deutscher Verlag für
Musik, 1978.

Considers Beethoven's arrangements of Scottish, Irish,
Welsh, and English folk songs for George Thomson. Emphasis
is placed on the fact that although the idiom of the melodies was very foreign to Beethoven, he nevertheless absorbed them into art works with the stamp of his own style.

157. Ringer, Alexander L. "The Art of the Third Guess: Beethoven
to Becker to Bartók." **The Musical Quarterly** 52 (1966):
304-12.

Traces the history of Beethoven's projected setting of
"Erlkönig." He made two sketches for a song on Goethe's
text before abandoning it. In 1897 Reinhard Becker published a completed version, which Bartók later orches-
trated. Facsimiles of the Beethoven sketches and of the
manuscript of the opening of Bartók's version.

158. Schmidt-Görg, Joseph. "Zur Entstehungszeit von Beethovens
Gellert-Liedern." **Beethoven-Jahrbuch** 5 (1961-64): 87-91.

Revises the previous dating for the origin of the set of
songs, placing them in the context of Beethoven's wrestling
with his growing deafness between the summer of 1801 and
the writing of the Heiligenstadt Testament in October 1802.
A copyist's manuscript allows them to be dated not later
than 8 March 1802.

159. Schneider, Anneliese. "Bemerkungen zur Konzeption des
      Liederkreises Op. 98, **An die ferne Geliebte.**" In **Bericht
      über den internationalen Beethoven-Kongress 10.-12.
      Dezember 1970 in Berlin,** edited by Heinz Alfred Brockhaus
      and Konrad Niemann, 327-32. Berlin: Neue Musik, 1971.

      Seeks to demonstrate how Beethoven united the principles
      of musical coherence with attention to details of the text.
      Points out a variety of traits, including the treatment of
      strophic and overall form, the textures of the piano part,
      and figurational or motivic reflections of mood and mean-
      ing.

160. Schollum, Robert. "Zu Form und Wiedergabe von Liedern Beet-
      hovens." In **Bericht über den internationalen Beethoven-
      Kongress 10.-12. Dezember 1970 in Berlin,** edited by Heinz
      Alfred Brockhaus and Konrad Niemann, 575-79. Berlin: Neue
      Musik, 1971.

      Re-evaluates Beethoven's songs. Emphasized are the vari-
      ety of influences on his style, his sociological position
      as contrasted to that of his successors, the importance of
      musical-rhetorical figures in the songs, and the importance
      of the sonata form.

161. Thürmer, Helmut. "Zum Deklamationsproblem in den Liedern
      Beethovens." In **Gesellschaft für Musikforschung Kongress-
      bericht, Bonn 1970:** 598-99.

      Reflects on contradictions between metrical and specific
      accents in Beethoven's Lieder. Emphasizes that Beethoven's
      responses to problems of poetic declamation should not be
      used indiscriminately to classify his songs as Classic or
      Romantic.

162. Tyson, Alan. "Beethoven's English Canzonetta." **The Musical
      Times** 112 (1971): 122-25.

      Authenticates the song "La Tiranna," on an English text
      by William Wennington, as a work of Beethoven, by means of
      sketches in "Grasnick 1." The composition may be dated
      about December 1798. The complete song, as edited by
      Tyson, is included.

Georg Benda
(1722-1795)

163.   Drake, John D. "The Songs of Georg Benda." **The Musical Times** 113 (1972): 964-65.

Establishes Benda's position as a song composer--he was not a very prolific one or especially devoted to the genre--and describes the style of the works. Generally the composer's song oeuvre is characterized by diversity of approach, with styles ranging from the declamatory (even recitative-like) to the aria-like, according to his interpretation of the individual texts.

William Sterndale Bennett
(1816-1875)

164.   Temperley, Nicholas. "Sterndale Bennett and the Lied." **The Musical Times** 116 (1975): 958-61, 1060-63.

Offers a re-evaluation of Bennett's work in the field of song. Temperley provides biographical background and the history of Bennett's songs. Analyses of some representative songs show Bennett to have been influenced by the German Lied, but not as exclusively by Mendelssohn as is commonly assumed. Work-list.

Alban Berg
(1885-1935)

165.   Chadwick, Nicholas. "Berg's Unpublished Songs in the Oesterreichische Nationalbibliothek." **Music and Letters** 52 (1971): 123-40.

Groups the ninety songs of the Helene Berg collection into four stylistic periods. The first-period songs show the influences of Schubert, Wagner, and Mahler. The second-period songs are more progressive and suggest the influence in addition of Schumann, Wolf, and others. In the third group Berg seems to have turned toward Brahms as a model, due to the guidance of Schoenberg. The final songs show the emergence of Berg's personal style, still under the influence of Schoenberg. The author specifically takes issue with Redlich's dating of some of the songs.

166.   ————. "A Survey of the Early Songs of Alban Berg." 2

vols. Ph.D. diss., Oxford University, 1972. 163; 142p.

Not examined. The **RILM** abstract by the author (72/1907) indicates that Berg's early style (1900-10) is traced to the "conservative" school of Brahms and Schoenberg. Bibliography; work-list.

167. ————. "Thematic Integration in Berg's Altenberg Songs." **The Music Review** 29 (1968): 300-304.

Traces some occurrences of key motives in Berg's orchestral Lieder op. 4 from the introduction of the first song to the final song.

168. DeVoto, Mark. "Alban Berg's Picture Postcard Songs." Ph.D. diss., Princeton University, 1966. iv, 139p.

Not examined. According to the author's abstract (**Dissertation Abstracts** 28A [1967]: 1836-A), performs an analysis of motivic content on the five Altenberg orchestral songs, revealing symmetrical (**Bogenform**) structure in individual songs and over the set as a whole. The history of the Altenberg songs is also treated. Appendices include accounts of the disastrous premiere performance and a study of the pencil score of the two concluding songs.

169. Leibowitz, René. "Alban Berg's Five Orchestral Songs after Postcard Texts by Peter Altenberg, Op. 4." **The Musical Quarterly** 34 (1948): 487-511.

Gives an analytical description of each of the songs. The characteristics of Berg's style that are emphasized are its free chromaticism, the application of counterpoint and variation technique to a small amount of motivic material to create structural unity, compactness and economy, and the rich and imaginative use of the very large orchestra. Portraits of Berg; complete piano-vocal score of the fifth song.

170. Stroh, Wolfgang Martin. "Alban Bergs Orchesterlieder." **Neue Zeitschrift für Musik** 130 (1969): 89-94.

Analyzes the Altenberg songs, op. 4, demonstrating that Berg's development of serial techniques in them is intimately connected with the poetic texts. By contrast, in the later aria "Der Wein" the twelve-tone method is taken for granted, and the compositional technique is more independent of the text.

171. Wilkey, Jay Weldon. "Certain Aspects of Form in the Vocal
     Music of Alban Berg." Ph.D. diss., Indiana University,
     1965. 281p.

     Not examined. The author's abstract (**Dissertation
     Abstracts** 26 [1966]: 4720-21) indicates that the disserta-
     tion illustrates by analyses of all the vocal works (not
     only songs) the development of Berg's style from its roots
     in Romanticism to serialism. Also considered are his uses
     and developments of standard musical forms.

                         Ludwig Berger
                         (1777-1839)

172. Siebenkäs, Dieter. **Ludwig Berger: Sein Leben und seine
     Werke unter besonderer Berücksichtigung seines Liedschaf-
     fens.** Berliner Studien zur Musikwissenschaft 4. Berlin:
     Merseburger, 1963. 316p.

     Recounts the composer's biography. Siebenkäs regards
     Berger as having achieved the transition from the style of
     the Second Berlin School to the genuinely Romantic Lied.
     Though his songs were rooted in the tradition of domestic,
     amateur performance and folk-like style, he provided the
     bridge to Romanticism for the North German composers in the
     genre. Appendices include Berger's extant letters, lists
     of his students, catalogue of his works. Bibliography.
     Index.

                         Hector Berlioz
                         (1803-1869)

173. Dickinson, A.E.F. "Berlioz's Songs." **The Musical Quarterly**
     55 (1969): 329-43.

     Describes and critiques the songs, focusing on those
     arranged for orchestra. The songs are admitted to be weak
     by comparison to those of Schubert, but they were important
     in establishing Berlioz's mastery of lyrical writing ful-
     filled in the operas.

174. Warrack, John. "Berlioz's 'Mélodies'." **The Musical Times**
     110 (1969): 252-54.

     Emphasizes Berlioz's tendency to use uneven phrasings,
     which are one of his most original characteristics but

perhaps account for the public's resistance to his songs.
Warrack finds the piano parts not as organically related to
the text and melody as in the Lieder of his German contemporaries, but the harmonies are often fascinating.

Julius Bittner
(1874-1939)

175. Brantl, Renate. "Das Klavierlied von Julius Bittner (1874-
      1939)." Ph.D. diss., University of Vienna, 1979. 228p.

      Analyzes the Lieder of the Viennese jurist and poet-
      composer. A brief biographical sketch is given. The texts
      are analyzed in detail. The traits of Bittner's musical
      style are outlined (with copious musical illustrations) in
      the areas of declamation, the role of the piano parts,
      harmony, and formal and tonal structures. Special consid-
      eration is given to the **Sechs Lieder von der unglücklichen
      Liebe der edlen Dame Pang Tschi Yü** because of the effects
      of the exotic subject matter on the musical style. Biblio-
      graphy; detailed thematic catalogue.

Antoine Boësset
(1586-1643)

176. Cohen, Albert. "A Study of Notational and Performance Prob-
      lems of an Early **Air de cour: Je voudrois bien, o Cloris**
      (1629) by Antoine Boësset (c.1586-1643)." In **Notations
      and Editions: A Book in Honor of Louise Cuyler,** edited by
      Edith Borroff, 55-68. Dubuque, Iowa: Wm.C. Brown, 1974.

      Illustrates problems and principles in making an edition
      of a seventeenth-century vocal work intended for partially
      improvised performance. Boësset's song, which is selected
      as exemplary here, presents the problem of sources that
      indicate solo voice and lute, an embellished version of the
      voice line, and vocal ensemble setting. A facsimile of one
      source and a transcription that includes a composite ren-
      dering of the various possibilities are included. Biblio-
      graphy.

Alexander Porfir'yevich Borodin
(1833-1887)

177. Abraham, Gerald Ernest Heal. "Borodin's Songs." In **On**

Russian Music, 169-78. London: W. Reeves, 1929. Reprint.
New York: Books for Libraries Press, 1970.

Presents the historical background of Borodin's twelve
songs, and critical remarks on their style. Abraham judges
the pieces to be diverse in expression and of uniform high
quality, representing a stance midway between the roughness
of Musorgsky's and the shallowness of Tchaikovsky's works
in this genre.

Cosimo Bottegari
(1554-1620)

178. MacClintock, Carol. "A Court Musician's Songbook: Modena MS
C 311." Journal of the American Musicological Society 9
(1956): 177-85.

Discusses Cosimo Bottegari's book of songs. Contents
include transcriptions of polyphonic madrigals by leading
sixteenth-century composers, lute songs and arie senza
parole, short popular-style songs; sacred songs; lute
pieces. General commentary is given on the music.

Johannes Brahms
(1833-1897)

179. Barlmeyer, Werner. "'Von ewiger Liebe': Noch einmal zur
Textvorlage von Brahms' op. 43,1." Melos/Neue Zeitschrift
für Musik 4 (1978): 101-2.

Traces the origin of the text back through August Heinrich Hoffmann von Fallersleben (identified by Eric Sams,
see item 207 below) to a transcription of a Sorbic song by
the folklorist Leopold Haupt of Görlitz.

180. Bell, A. Craig. The Lieder of Brahms. Darley: Grian-Aig,
1979. vi, 137, xxp.

Surveys Brahms's song oeuvre. An introductory chapter
discusses the composer's style in general, after which the
songs are dealt with by opus number with descriptive comments and indications of the character of each. Appendices
include a chronological list of songs, sources of texts,
cursory bibliography, indexes.

181. Bernet Kempers, Karel Philippus. "Die 'Emanzipation des

Fleisches' in den Liedern von Johannes Brahms." **Studien für Musikwissenschaft** 25 (1962): 28-30.

Points out that among Brahms's song texts are a number that reflect the new, realist view of love as sensual, a characteristic of the "junges Deutschland" movement.

182. Boros, R. "Petöfi--in der Vertonung von Brahms." **Studia musicologica Academiae scientiarum hungaricae** 8 (1966): 391-99.

Brahms set as Lieder and part-songs several Petöfi texts thoroughly reworked by the German philosopher and poet G.F. Daumer. The author presents critical analyses of Brahms's settings of "Sah dem edlen Bildnis" (op. 46, no. 2) and "Wir wandelten" (op. 96, no. 2).

183. Boyer, Margaret Gene. "A Study of Brahms' Setting of the Poems from Tieck's **Liebesgeschichte der schönen Magelone und des Grafen Peter von Provence.**" Ph.D. diss., Washington University, 1980. 113p.

Not examined. According to the **RILM** entry (80/646), pursues the relationship of the work to biographies of the poet and the composer, analyzes four of the songs, and considers the degree to which the songs can be regarded as constituting a cycle.

184. Boyer, Thomas. "Brahms as Count Peter of Provence: A Psychosexual Interpretation of the **Magelone** Poetry." **The Musical Quarterly** 66 (1980): 262-86.

Accounts for Brahms's interest in Tieck's poetic cycle through a parallel between the composer's and Count Peter's experiences of a dichotomy between sex and pure love. Several of Brahms's musical treatments of the texts are explained as reflections of his critical responses to them.

185. Bozarth, George S. "Brahms's 'Liederjahr of 1868'." **The Music Review** 44 (1983): 208-22.

Argues from examination of the original sources for songs attributed by Max Kalbeck to the year 1868 that many of these pieces must be re-dated. Bozarth demonstrates that Brahms commonly composed groups of songs on texts by individual poets, only gathering them together later for publication.

186. ———. "The Lieder of Johannes Brahms--1868-1871: Studies in Chronology and Compositional Process." Ph.D. diss., Princeton University, 1978. vi, 245p.

Focuses on the **Lieder und Gesänge** opp. 57 and 58, but covers several other sets of songs (opp. 33, 43, 46-49) and other works. The first part of the study reviews and corrects the understanding of the chronology of Brahms's song oeuvre, using the surviving source material. The songs of opp. 57 and 58 are placed in the years 1867-71. The process of composition in these works is then examined in detail, from the choice of texts, through the sketch and draft stages, to the autograph manuscript and printed editions. Brahms worked out ideas in two-line (melody and bass) texture, then filled in the accompaniment. He continued to work out details through the last stages of the compositional process. Facsimiles, transcriptions, tables, diagrams. Appendices list Brahms's extant sketches and criteria for diplomatic descriptions of manuscript sources. A catalogue of sources for opp. 33, 43, 46-49, 57, and 58 is included. Bibliography.

187. ———. "Johannes Brahms und die Liedersammlungen von David Gregor Corner, Karl Severin Meister und Friedrich Wilhelm Arnold." **Die Musikforschung** 36 (1983): 177-99.

Explores the sources Brahms used for folk-song arrangements and some sacred pieces. The collections of Catholic pieces by Corner and Meister, and Arnold's collections of folk songs and the **Lochheimer Liederbuch** are discussed. The article provides insight into the compositional conception of a variety of Brahms's works.

188. Evans, Edwin. **Handbook to the Vocal Works of Brahms.** Vol. 1 of **Historical, Descriptive, and Analytical Account of the Entire Works of Johannes Brahms.** London: Wm. Reeves, 1912. Reprint. New York: Burt Franklin, 1970. xviii, 599p.

Provides notes on individual pieces in order by opus number. A brief introductory chapter discusses "Brahms as a Song Composer." For each song such data as key, tempo, and range are given, with observations on the form and content of the text (with translations, which are not always complete) and occasional cursory descriptions of the music. Appendices include a chronology, list of Brahms's vocal works by genre, index of titles and first lines, index of poets and other sources of texts, list of edi-

tions, index of names (other than poets), and a list of
Evans's translations of Lied texts into English.

189. Federhofer, Hellmut. "Zur Einheit von Wort und Ton im Lied
     von Johannes Brahms." **Gesellschaft für Musikforschung
     Kongressbericht, Hamburg** 1956: 97-99.

     Discusses the text-setting of "Das Mädchen spricht," op.
     107, no. 3. Federhofer defends Brahms's barring of two
     lines that Riemann (see item 205 below) had suggested could
     more appropriately be rebarred.

190. Fellinger, Imogen. "Zur Entstehung der 'Regenlieder' von
     Brahms." In **Festschrift Walter Gerstenberg zum 60. Ge-
     burtstag,** edited by Georg von Dadelsen and Andreas
     Holschneider, 55-58. Wolfenbüttel: Möseler, 1964.

     Investigates the history of the two songs op. 59, nos. 3
     and 4. Brahms's compositional process went through several
     stages, which can be reconstructed principally through
     letters.

191. Fiske, Roger. "Brahms and Scotland." **The Musical Times** 109
     (1968): 1106-11.

     Actually discusses the influence of Scottish poetry--
     Ossian, Percy, Burns, and Scott--on German Romantic music
     in general as well as Brahms in particular. Although
     Brahms set only one Scottish text as a Lied, "Murrays
     Ermordung" (op. 14, no. 3), he set others in other vocal
     media. Fiske hypothesizes that some of the melodies of
     Brahms's piano pieces can be associated with Scottish poems
     that the composer at one time thought of setting as songs.

192. Fox Strangways, A.H. "Brahms and Tieck's 'Magelone'." **Music
     and Letters** 21 (1940): 211-29.

     Recounts the narrative of the cycle and draws attention
     to some of Brahms's expressive musical effects in each
     song. There is a digression on the characters of Romanti-
     cism in the major nineteenth-century composers' works.
     Singing translations of all Tieck's texts into English are
     provided.

193. Friedlaender, Max. **Brahms's Lieder: An Introduction to the
     Songs for One and Two Voices,** translated by C. Leonard
     Leese. London: Oxford University Press, 1928. xiii,
     263p. (Originally published in Berlin in 1922 as **Brahms**

Lieder: Einführung in seine Gesänge für eine und zwei
Stimmen.)

Supplies brief notes on the individual songs, organized
according to opus numbers. The discussion of each song
includes compositional history, Brahms's literary source
and his alterations in the text, information on Brahms's
manuscript versions and the publication of the song, and
descriptive characterization of the setting. Indexes of
poets, titles and first lines.

194. Gennrich, Friedrich. "Glossen zu Johannes Brahms' 'Sonnet'
op. 14 Nr. 4 'Ach könnt' ich, könnte vergessen sie'."
Zeitschrift für Musikwissenschaft 10 (1927-28): 129-39.

Traces back the history of the text Brahms used for this
song. It was originally a song attributed to the thir-
teenth-century trouvère Thibaut IV, which was published in
the rise of the Romantic movement in eighteenth-century
France and translated into German by Herder. Brahms, quite
independent of any knowledge of its earlier musical settings, managed to achieve an interpretation that has some
features in common with them and captured the spirit of the
medieval lyric.

195. Gerber, Rudolf. "Formprobleme im Brahmsschen Lied." **Jahrbuch der Musikbibliothek Peters** 29 (1932): 23-42.

Seeks to demonstrate how musical forms in Brahms's Lieder
are governed by the composer's readings of the texts.
Brahms achieved unity by using the strophic model and
variety by applying the variation principle. A number of
individual songs are discussed, ranging in order of complexity from the strict strophic type to free forms.

196. Guck, Marion A. "Analysis Symposium: Brahms, 'Der Tod, das
ist die kühle Nacht,' op. 96, no. 1." **In Theory Only** 2/6
(September 1976): 27-34.

Not examined. According to the author's RILM abstract
(76/7172), the song is analyzed using an adaptation of
Schenkerian methods. Ambiguity in the song's structure is
discussed.

197. Harrison, Max. **The Lieder of Brahms.** New York: Praeger,
1972. 152p.

A wide-ranging critical study of Brahms's songs, consid-

erably hampered by the obscurity of its organization--there
are no chapter divisions. List of songs by opus number;
bibliography. Index.

198. Helms, Siegmund. **Die Melodiebildung in den Liedern von
     Johannes Brahms und ihr Verhältnis zu Volksliedern und
     volkstümlichen Weisen.** Bamberg: Rudolf Rodenbusch, 1968.
     270p.

     The author's dissertation at the Freie Universität in
     Berlin, traces the influence of other melodies in about one
     third of all of Brahms's songs. The first half of the
     study catalogues all the citations and influences of these
     melodies in Brahms's Lieder. The second part presents
     analytical observations on specific aspects of the melodic
     style. Facsimiles, table, diagrams. Appendices list
     source materials and include musical quotations of folk
     melody material.

199. Kross, Siegfried. "Zur Frage der Brahmsschen Volkslied-
     bearbeitungen." **Die Musikforschung** 11 (1958): 15-21.

     Lists Brahms's folksong arrangements, indicating their
     sources and the collections in which they are found.

200. Mies, Paul. **Stilmomente und Ausdrucksstilformen in
     Brahms'schen Lied.** Leipzig: Breitkopf & Härtel, 1923.
     Reprint. Walluf: Sändig, 1975. 147p.

     Studies the structural and expressive components of
     Brahms's Lied style. Characteristic for Brahms's form is
     the emphasis on unification, both at the level of motivic
     working-out and in large form, and this increased as the
     composer matured. A large number of specific expressive
     gestures are listed, with identifications of the signifi-
     cance of each. Tables. Index of songs.

201. Misch, Ludwig. "Kontrapunkt und Imitation im Brahmsschen
     Lied." **Die Musikforschung** 11 (1958): 155-60.

     Identifies the use of contrapuntal technique in Brahms's
     songs. Although such instances are relatively rare in the
     Lieder compared to other genres, Misch is able to point out
     instances of combinations of melodic lines, canonic imita-
     tion, and augmentation and diminution.

202. Pisk, Paul A. "Dreams of Death and Life: A Study of Two
     Songs by Johannes Brahms." In **Festival Essays for Pauline**

Alderman: A Musicological Tribute, edited by Burton L.
Karson, 227-34. Provo, Utah: Brigham Young University
Press, 1976.

Indicates aspects of the technical construction of
Brahms's "Der Tod, das ist die kühle Nacht" (op. 96, no. 1)
and "Immer leiser wird mein Schlummer" (op. 105, no. 2)
that the author believes to have emotional force. He
concludes that the intellectual in Brahms's songs is balanced by the expressive. Form diagram.

203. Rieger, Erwin. "Die Tonartencharakteristik im einstimmigen
Klavierlied von Johannes Brahms." Studien für Musikwissenschaft 22 (1955): 142-216.

Investigates the use of tonality for expressive purposes
in Brahms's Lieder. After an introductory survey of the
affective uses of keys, Rieger identifies the songs in each
of the thirty-one keys Brahms uses and their common emotional content. Also considered are the expressive effects
of key contrasts and relationships within songs. Brahms
used keys for expression in nearly sixty per cent of his
songs, but he followed a plan of his own and did not adopt
any standard, conventional system.

204. Riemann, Hugo. "Brahms' Taktfreiheiten im Lied." Die Musik
25/2 (1933): 595-96.

Defends Brahms against the suggestion that he committed
errors in rhythmic declamation in his songs. The argument
is based on the historical observation that regular pat-
terning of beats is a consequence of the influence of the
dance on musical rhythm and that freer approaches have been
characteristic of vocal music.

205. ———. "Die Taktfreiheiten in Brahms' Liedern." Die Musik
12/1 (October-December 1912): 10-21.

Argues that the rhythms in the songs of Brahms reflect a
sensitivity to text declamation that is distorted by the
uniformly regular strong and weak beats of the standard
notation. Brahms is regarded as taking an approach similar
to that of the seventeenth-century composers. Riemann
proposes rebarrings of "Immer leiser wird mein Schlummer"
(op. 105, no. 2) and "Schwalbe, sag mir an" (op. 107, no.
3) that he believes reflect the composer's intentions.

206. Sams, Eric. Brahms Songs. BBC Music Guides 23. Seattle:

University of Washington Press, 1972.   68p.

Makes a critical survey of Brahms's Lieder, following a
generally chronological plan, but concentrating on matters
of style and content rather than a simple song-by-song
treatment. The figure of Clara Schumann assumes special
importance. No index or bibliography.

207.   ———. "Von ewiger Liebe." **Neue Zeitschrift für Musik** 133
       (1972): 257.

Corrects the earlier attribution to Josef Wenzig of the
translation of the text of Brahms's song. The actual poet
was Heinrich Hoffmann von Fallersleben, and Brahms apparently found the text in a book belonging to Schumann.

208.   Sannemüller, Gerd. "Die Lieder von Johannes Brahms auf
       Gedichte von Klaus Groth." **Jahresgabe der Klaus-Groth-
       Gesellschaft** 16 (1972): 23-35.

Not examined. The **RILM** abstract (75/1308) emphasizes
that the eleven songs on Groth texts represent Brahms's
general style in the subordination of detail to mood in the
melody and in the adoption of varied strophic form.

209.   Stohrer, Sister Mary Baptist. "The Selection and Setting of
       Poetry in the Solo Songs of Johannes Brahms." Ph.D.
       diss., University of Wisconsin, 1974.   v, 241p.

Considers the composer's use of relatively undistin-
guished poetry. Suggests that the quality of a song is not
necessarily dependent on the quality of its text as a
literary work. Concludes that Brahms's songs do not permit
generalized judgments. Appendices list poets with brief
biographies, and song texts set by Brahms. Bibliography.

210.   Walker, Ernest. "The Songs of Schumann and Brahms: Some
       Contacts and Contrasts." **Music and Letters** 3 (1922): 9-
       19.

Stresses that the two composers share a general aesthetic. Within that context, Schumann is more sensitive
and responsive to his texts, while Brahms displays more
rigorous musical technique.

Pierre de Bréville
(1861-1949)

211.   Daitz, Mimi Segal. "Grieg and Bréville: 'Nous parlons alors
       de la jeune école française ...'." **19th-Century Music** 1/3
       (March 1978): 233-45.

       Discusses the diary entry made by Bréville regarding a
       meeting with Grieg in July 1887. The Norwegian composer
       expressed his interest in the use of modal inflection in
       Bréville's "Chanson triste."

212.   ————. "The Songs of Pierre de Bréville (1861-1949)."
       Ph.D. diss., New York University, 1973. ix, 351p.

       Provides historical and biographical background and anal-
       yses of the composer's eighty-two published songs.   Notes
       on and translations of all the texts are provided.   Each
       song is analyzed in chart form, and nine pieces are dis-
       cussed in detail. Although in many respects the composer's
       style was quite consistent, the songs are grouped into six
       periods, based on biographical and stylistic criteria.
       Analytical timelines. Appendices, including a complete
       list of Bréville's compositions and writings. Bibliogra-
       phy.

Frank Bridge
(1879-1941)

213.   Keating, Roderic Maurice. "The Songs of Frank Bridge."
       D.M.A. diss., University of Texas, 1970. 115p.

       Not examined. The author indicates in the abstract in
       RILM (70/2090) that there are 54 songs, 23 unpublished.
       They are placed in historical and stylistic context, espe-
       cially vis à vis the "English musical renaissance" and the
       pervading trends in English style after 1920.   Bibliogra-
       phy; work-list.

Benjamin Britten
(1913-1976)

214.   Brewster, Robert Gene. "The Relationship between Poetry and
       Music in the Original Solo-Vocal Works of Benjamin
       Britten through 1965." Ph.D. diss., Washington Univer-
       sity, 1967. vi, 255p.

Surveys Britten's songs. A chapter of historical background on song in England and a discussion of Britten's
song cycles introduce the dissertation. The poetry and the
music are discussed independently, then related in a separate chapter. The relationships examined have to do with
mood, form, rhythm, rhyme, enjambment and caesura, cyclic
devices, and word-painting. Bibliography; list of poets
and poems.

215.   Noble, Jeremy. "Britten's 'Songs from the Chinese'." **Tempo**
       52 (Autumn 1959): 25-29.

Discusses the cycle of six songs for voice and guitar.
Attention is drawn to the appropriateness of this scoring
for these texts and to the framing and shaping of the whole
cycle. Each song is described in a few paragraphs.

216.   Whittall, Arnold. "Tonality in Britten's Song Cycles with
       Piano." **Tempo** 96 (Spring 1971): 2-11.

Categorizes the eight mature cycles into those that cen-
ter on a single tonality and those that progress from one
tonality to another. Whittall analyzes the means by which
Britten expands tonal areas for expressive purposes by
means of chromaticism and modulation.

Henry T. Burleigh
(1866-1949)

217.   Allison, Roland Lewis. "Classification of the Vocal Works
       of Harry T. Burleigh (1866-1949) and Some Suggestions for
       Their Use in Teaching Diction in Singing." Ph.D. diss.,
       Indiana University, 1966.   394p.

Not examined. According to the author's abstract in
Dissertation Abstracts (27A [1967]: 3889-A), gives biography and a survey of the composer's vocal works, including
157 songs and three cycles. The difficulty of the songs is
evaluated, and their use to develop vocal skills recom-
mended and demonstrated by recorded examples. The dissertation also discusses dialect and the singing of Negro folk
music.

William Byrd
(1543-1623)

218. Brett, Philip, and Thurston Dart. "Songs by William Byrd in
      Manuscripts at Harvard." **Harvard Library Bulletin** 14
      (1960): 343-65.

      Beginning from a discussion of an incomplete set of part-
      books for consort songs (Harvard College Library MS Mus
      30), deals with a number of such sources compiled in London
      ca. 1590-1615. These sets were apparently written by a
      group of professional copyists in close touch with William
      Byrd and intended for customers with sympathies toward the
      Roman church. The music tends to be rather conservative
      for the time. Plates showing copyists' handwritings, texts
      of some unpublished song texts, and a list of the collec-
      tions discussed are included.

219. Brett, Philip. "Word-Setting in the Songs of Byrd." **Pro-
      ceedings of the Royal Musical Association** 98 (1971-72):
      47-64.

      Treats Byrd's style in handling his texts. Places empha-
      sis on the composer's careful setting of poetic form and on
      his expressive restraint, which is traceable to the in-
      fluence of the ideal of decorum.

Giulio Caccini
(ca. 1545-1618)

220. Chan, Mary Elizabeth Joiner. "Caccini's 'Amarilli mia bel-
      la': Its Influence on 'Miserere my maker'." **Lute Society
      Journal** 10 (1968): 6-14.

      Not examined. In **RILM** (76/9345) the author states that
      two song settings that begin "Miserere my maker," in
      British Library MS Add. 15117 and in Cambridge, King's
      College, Rowe MS 2, represent adaptations of Caccini's
      familiar song.

221. Feller, Marilyn. "The New Style of Giulio Caccini, Member
      of the Florentine Camerata." In **International Musicologi-
      cal Society Kongressbericht, Köln** 1958, 102-104. Kassel:
      Bärenreiter, 1959.

      Points out the importance and value of tracing the his-
      tory of Caccini's monodies from his first song in 1589

through his 1614 collection. The development of the style
is clearer in his works than in those of his compatriots.
It is possible to identify his attempts to clarify the
writing of the music and the progress of his compositional
experimentation.

222. Hitchcock, H. Wiley. "Caccini's 'Other' **Nuove musiche**."
      Journal of the American Musicological Society 27 (1974):
      438-60.

      Discusses Caccini's **Nuove musiche e nuova maniera di
      scriverle** of 1614. The collection follows the pattern and
      style of the more familiar 1602 **Le nuove musiche,** but is
      larger and different in some musical aspects. The so-
      called "new manner of writing them" refers to the explicit
      indication of **passaggi,** tremolos, and trills. The book and
      its preface represent Caccini's continuing struggle for
      recognition in the musical rivalries of Florence. Facs-
      imile of title page.

223. ————. "Vocal Ornamentation in Caccini's **Nuove musiche**."
      The Musical Quarterly 56 (1970): 389-404.

      Reasons that most of the necessary ornamentation is ac-
      tually written out in **Le nuove musiche** (1602), and that
      only cadential and expressive ornaments need to be applied.
      Hitchcock believes that the "new" element in this collec-
      tion is the specification of ornamentation, an attempt on
      Caccini's part to preserve the "balance between declamation
      and decoration" that he intended.

                        Thomas Campion
                        (1567-1620)

224. Campion, Thomas. **Songs and Masques, with Observations on
      the Art of English Poesy.** Edited by A.H. Bullen. London:
      A.H. Bullen, 1903. xxxix, 288p.

      Includes Campion's English poetry--without music--as well
      as his important essay "Observations on the Art of English
      Poesie." An introduction by the editor is supplemented by
      a brief discussion of Campion's music by Janet Dodge.

225. Davis, Walter R. "Melodic and Poetic Structure: The
      Examples of Campion and Dowland." **Criticism** 4 (1962): 89-
      107.

Contrasts the styles of Campion's and Dowland's lute
songs. Campion's style is identified with the epigram in
its emphasis on clarity, sectionalism, and contrast. Dowland's, on the other hand, stresses repetition, development, and progressive amplification of a central idea.

226. Doughtie, Edward. "Sibling Rivalry: Music vs. Poetry in
     Campion and Others." **Criticism** 20 (1978): 1-16.

Evaluates Campion's settings of several of his texts and
compares them to those of other lute-song composers. Concludes that Campion intended to write music that did not
compete with the poems and that he therefore did not con-
sistently succeed in achieving music that interpreted and
thereby elevated the words.

227. Eldridge, Muriel T. **Thomas Campion: His Poetry and Music
     (1567-1620).** New York: Vantage, 1971. 165p.

Evaluates the work of Campion. Introductory sections
give background to the music and poetry of the time and the
lute song. Campion's biography is outlined. Eldridge
describes twelve individual songs, taking up first poem
then music in a relatively simple manner and appending
personal comments. She concludes that Campion succeeded in
matching poetry and music. Addendum of materials on the
Campion Society. Bibliography.

228. Greer, David. "'What If a Day': An Examination of the Words
     and Music." **Music and Letters** 43 (1962): 304-19.

Lists the numerous sources of this popular song and
examines its influence on other pieces in the seventeenth
century. Both music and texts appear to have been modeled
on "What If a Day," which has been attributed to Campion.

229. Harper, John. "A New Way of Making Ayres? Thomas Campion:
     Towards a Revaluation." **The Musical Times** 110 (1969):
     262-63.

Illustrates that Campion's songs achieve a unity and
balance between his texts and the various elements of
musical structure in each individual piece. Comparing
Campion to Donne and Dowland, Harper argues that he should
not be judged by Donne's poetry or Dowland's music but by
criteria specific to Campion himself.

230. Joiner, Mary. "Another Campion Song?" **Music and Letters** 48

(1967): 138-39.

Proposes that the song "Tarry sweete love," preserved in
a manuscript at Christ Church, Oxford (Mus. 439), may be by
Campion. The second line of the text is used as an example
by Campion in "Observations in the Art of English Poesie."
Neither the approximate date of the manuscript nor the
musical style would call the attribution to Campion into
question. The complete music is included.

231. Sternfeld, Frederick W. "A Song from Campion's **Lord's
     Masque." Journal of the Warburg and Courtauld Institutes**
     20 (1957): 373-75.

     Discusses and gives facsimile and transcription of the
     song "Woo her and win her," from 1613. Judges the song to
     be a "model of simplicity" whose "eloquence has not faded
     with age."

232. Swaen, A.E.H. "The Authorship of 'What If a Day,' and Its
     Various Versions." **Modern Philology** 4 (1907): 397-422.

     Surveys the sources of the song, of which Campion claimed
     to be the author. Campion's authorship is denied, though
     no other author can be proposed. Swaen regards the two-
     stanza version by Richard Alison from 1606 as providing the
     best text.

                      Giovanni Francesco Capello
                          (fl. 1610-19)

233. Kurtzmann, Jeffrey. "Giovanni Francesco Capello, an Avant-
     Gardist of the Early Seventeenth Century." **Musica disci-
     plina** 31 (1977): 155-82.

     Covers the works of the Venetian early Baroque composer.
     His only secular collection was the **Madrigali et Arie**
     (1617).

                        Giacomo Carissimi
                          (1605-1674)

234. Rose, Gloria. "The Cantatas of Giacomo Carissimi." **The
     Musical Quarterly** 48 (1962): 204-15.

     Emphasizes the wide variety of styles and forms in the

cantatas of Carissimi. In addition to composite, multimovement structures, there are a number of single-movement
songs in the older strophic and strophic-variation forms,
as well as binary and ternary forms. The composer's style
is characterized by moderation and by exceptional skill in
text setting.

Benjamin Carr
(1768-1831)

235. Lehmann, Carroll J. "Benjamin Carr: His Contribution to
Early American Solo Vocal Literature." D.M.A. thesis,
University of Iowa, 1975. vii, 172p.

Outlines Carr's activities in general before proceeding
to detailed treatment of the songs. The composer influenced his successors by his use of three-staff rather than
two-staff scoring, his increasing of the independence of
the accompaniment, his relatively advanced harmonic style,
and his choice of fine poetry. Bibliography. Appendices
include a selection of complete songs, a list of the songs,
and correspondence of the composer.

Mario Castelnuovo-Tedesco
(1895-1968)

236. Lyle, Watson. "The Shakespeare Songs of Mario Castelnuovo-
Tedesco." **The Chesterian** 17 (1935-36): 140-43.

Characterizes in extremely cursory fashion each of the
thirty-six songs. The author's judgement is that the songs
are varied in compositional approach and in quality.

Antonio Cesti
(1623-1669)

237. Burrows, David, comp. **Antonio Cesti (1623-1669).** Wellesley
Edition Cantata Index Series 1. Wellesley College, 1964.

Gives titles, musical incipits, sources, and structure
diagrams. While many of the cantatas are sectional, employing contrasting passages of recitative and lyrical
style, a few are simple strophic arias that may be classi-
fied as art songs.

238. ⸺. "The Cantatas of Antonio Cesti." Ph.D. diss.,
     Brandeis University, 1961. 254p.

     Describes the cantatas and their style, and places them
     in historical perspective. The work of Cesti corresponds
     to the period in which the cantata changed from a unified
     song to a multi-movement cycle. Appendices include a dis-
     cussion of the sources for the repertoire, thematic index,
     and a selection of pieces. Bibliography.

                        Theodore Chanler
                         (1902-1961)

239. Cox, Donald R. "Theodore Ward Chanler: A Biographical and
     Analytical Study of the Man and Three Song Cycles."
     D.M.A. thesis, University of Southern Mississippi, 1976.
     98p.

     Includes a biographical sketch of the composer and re-
     views his ideas on music and song from his articles in
     Modern Music. The songs of three cycles, **The Children** on
     texts of Leonard Feeney and **Eight Epitaphs** and **Four Rhymes
     from "Peacock Pie"** on poems by Walter de la Mare, receive
     brief descriptive and interpretive commentary. List of
     Chanler's songs; bibliography.

240. Kolb, Bruce Lanier. "The Published Songs of Theodore
     Chanler." D.M.A. diss., Louisiana State University, 1976.

     Not examined. According to the author's abstract in **RILM**
     (76/10010), covers Chanler's biography and song aesthetics,
     as well as analyzing the thirty-two published songs.   In-
     fluences of Fauré and Stravinsky are noted. Appendices.

241. Nordgren, Elliott Alfred. "An Analytical Study of the Songs
     of Theodore Chanler (1902-1961)." Ph.D. diss., New York
     Univerisity, 1980. 392p.

     Not examined. The **RILM** abstract indicates that the study
     treats Chanler's song aesthetic, which focuses on pre-
     serving the musical qualities of the texts, and describes
     the composer's style as relatively conservative.

242. Tangeman, Robert. "The Songs of Theodore Chanler." **Modern
     Music** 22 (May-June 1945): 227-32.

     Briefly describes the songs. The oeuvre is characterized

as mature and thoughtful in style.   List of Chanler's
songs.

Ernest Chausson
(1855-1899)

243. Crankshaw, Geoffrey. "The Songs of Chausson." **The Monthly
     Musical Record** 83 (1953): 148-51.

     Praises Chausson's subtlety of expression and achievement
     of balance between text and music.   Opp. 2 and 8 are given
     brief, favorable comment, while the Maeterlinck **Serres
     Chaudes** (op. 24) are judged to be less successful.   Three
     individual settings--of Mauclair's "Les Heures," Verlaine's
     "La Chanson bien douce," and Moréas's "Dans la forȩt"--are
     identified as especially successful.

Frédéric Chopin
(1810-1849)

244. Brown, Maurice J.E. "The Posthumous Publication of Chopin's
     Songs." **The Musical Quarterly** 42 (1956): 51-65.

     Recounts the complex history of the publication of
     Chopin's nineteen Polish songs.   The music was only gath-
     ered with some difficulty.   The first substantial collec-
     tion, consisting of sixteen songs, was issued in Berlin in
     1857 (by Schlesinger) and in Warsaw in 1858 (by Gebethner).
     A seventeenth song was added in an 1872 edition.   The
     remaining two pieces finally appeared in the twentieth
     century.

245. Prilisauer, Richard. "Frédéric Chopins 'Polnische Lieder'."
     Chopin-Jahrbuch 2 (1963): 117-32.

     Complains that Chopin's songs have been the objects of
     prejudice.   Prilisauer feels that they ought not to be
     judged by the principles generally applied to German Roman-
     tic Lieder, but that they can only be understood when their
     expression is regarded as belonging more to the music than
     to the text.   Especially important is the recognition of
     their roots in the mazurka and waltz.   A list of editions
     is given, and these are compared, principally on the basis
     of the success of the German translations of the Polish
     texts.

246. Stookes, Sacha. "Chopin: The Song-Writer." **The Monthly Musical Record** 80 (1950): 96-99.

Describes the songs as belonging to the general manner of the mazurkas, rather than to the virtuosic world of the études or the Bellinian cantabile style of the nocturnes. The later songs, composed after Chopin went to Paris, are seen to show some awareness of Schubert.

Aaron Copland
(b. 1900)

247. Daugherty, Robert Michael. "An Analysis of Aaron Copland's **Twelve Poems of Emily Dickinson.**" D.M.A. diss., Ohio State University, 1980.   224p.

Not examined.   According to the **RILM** abstract (80/5827), discusses Copland's response to the images in the texts. Suggests that stronger verbal imagery evokes symbolic motives in the settings.   Bibliography.

248. Young, Douglas. "Copland's Dickinson Songs." **Tempo** 103 (1972): 33-37.

Notes that the genre of song cycles is unusual among Copland's songs and the output of American composers in general.   In this cycle Copland matches the precision but not the mystical character of the poetry.   His style here recalls that of Fauré.

Peter Cornelius
(1824-1874)

249. Konold, Wulf. "Peter Cornelius und die Liedästhetik der Neudeutschen Schule." **The International Review of Music Aesthetics and Sociology** 1 (1970): 187-94.

Places Cornelius in the context of the school of Liszt and Wagner, opposed to the formalistic ideas of Hanslick. Although Cornelius did not formulate a systematic aesthetic of song, his writings allow Konold to place him in that group that regarded text and music as a unity, reflecting respectively the specific content and the expression of feeling in the total work of art.

250. Marx-Weber, Magda. "Cornelius' Kritik des Liedes." In **Peter**

Cornelius als Komponist, Dichter, Kritiker und Essayist,
edited by Hellmut Federhofer and Kurt Oehl, 169-77.
Studien zur Musikgeschichte des 19. Jahrhunderts 48.
Regensburg: Bosse, 1977.

Quotes extensively from Cornelius's writings and those of
his contemporaries. The main issues of the day were concerned with finding a style for the Lied that would go
beyond the models of Schubert and Schumann. New types of
texts and a more spontaneous and natural overall impression
were among the criteria Cornelius espoused.

251. Massenkeil, Günther. "Cornelius als Liederkomponist." In
Peter Cornelius als Komponist, Dichter, Kritiker und
Essayist, edited by Hellmut Federhofer and Kurt Oehl,
159-67. Studien zur Musikgeschichte des 19. Jahrhunderts
48. Regensburg: Bosse, 1977.

Discusses the position of Cornelius's songs in his oeuvre
and in their historical context. Especially emphasizes the
connection of his Lieder to the Hausmusik of the nineteenth
century.

252. Porter, E.G. "The Songs of Peter Cornelius." The Music
Review 27 (1966): 202-6.

Expresses regret at the general absence of Cornelius's
settings from the standard song repertoire. The influence
of the New German School and the composer's exploration of
more declamatory language than the lyricism of Schubert,
Schumann, and Franz is emphasized. A few strikingly effec-
tive or characteristic examples are adduced.

Luigi Dallapiccola
(1904-1975)

253. Eckert, Michael. "Text and Form in Dallapiccola's Goethe-
Lieder." Perspectives of New Music 17 (Spring-Summer
1979): 98-111.

Shows how images in the content of the texts are reflected in the composer's treatments of the row in this set
for mezzo-soprano and three clarinets.

John Danyel
(1564-ca. 1626)

254. Judd, Percy. "The Songs of John Danyel." **Music and Letters**
      17 (1936): 118-23.

      Judges Danyel's twenty known works to be uniformly of
      high quality. His personal style is characterized by con-
      trapuntal treatment of the lute parts, sweeping and well-
      planned vocal lines, freedom of structure, and sensitivity
      to his texts. There are two cyclical sets of three songs
      each.

255. Scott, David. "John Danyel: His Life and Songs." **Lute
      Society Journal** 13 (1971): 7-17.

      Outlines the career of the composer, including a good
      deal of thoughtful speculation to fill the gaps between the
      sketchy known details. Each of Danyel's songs is described
      in a paragraph.

Claude Debussy
(1862-1918)

256. Bathori, Jane [Jeanne Marie Berthier]. **Sur l'interprétation
      des mélodies de Claude Debussy.** Paris: Editions
      Ouvrières, 1953. 40p.

      Offers practical instructions to the performer on such
      matters as dynamics, articulation, phrasing, and elision.
      The author was one of the most important interpreters of
      Debussy's songs.

257. Böhmer, Helga. "Alchimie der Töne: Die Mallarmé-Vertonungen
      von Debussy und Ravel." **Musica** 22 (1968): 83-85.

      Compares briefly the approaches of Debussy and Ravel to
      the poetry of Mallarmé. Each composer made four song
      settings, in two cases independently selecting the same
      texts.

258. Briscoe, James Robert. "The Compositions of Claude
      Debussy's Formative Years." Ph.D. diss., University of
      North Carolina, 1979. xvi, 448p.

      Relates the style of Debussy's early works to the styles
      of his predecessors, tracing it especially to the late

nineteenth-century French composers but also the Russians
and Wagner, and demonstrates how traits of Debussy's late
writing are anticipated in the early works. The mélodies
are the most numerous and significant genre among the
pieces discussed. Tables. Thematic catalogue of works
included; list of unavailable works from the period in
question; bibliography.

259.   ———. "Debussy's Earliest Songs." College Music Symposium
        24/2 (Fall 1984): 81-95.

Outlines the biographical background to the composition
of Debussy's mélodies of the 1880s and draws attention to
early appearances of central traits of the composer's
style, using quotations from these works.

260.   Cobb, Margaret C., compiler and annotator. The Poetic
        Debussy: A Collection of His Songs Texts and Selected
        Letters. Translated by Richard Miller. Boston: North-
        eastern University Press, 1982. xxii, 318p.

Gives all the texts of Debussy's songs, in order of
composition, with excellent translations and notes. Also
included are selected letters that indicate the composer's
literary awareness and sensitivity, also with translations
and notes. A small third section gives notes on compositions other than songs that are based on literary texts.
Appendices; bibliography. Indexes.

261.   Fischer, Kurt von. "Bemerkungen zu den zwei Ausgaben von
        Debussys Ariettes oubliées." In Symbolae historiae
        musicae: Hellmut Federhofer zum 60. Geburtstag, edited by
        Friedrich Wilhelm Riedel and Hubert Unverricht, 283-89.
        Mainz: Schott, 1971.

Not examined. According to the author's abstract in RILM
(73/582), the article examines the differing details in the
1888 and 1903 editions and argues that Debussy attempted to
clarify form, improve declamation, and coordinate the music
with the sense of Verlaine's texts.

262.   Hardeck, Erwin. Untersuchungen zu den Klavierliedern Claude
        Debussys. Kölner Beiträge zur Musikforschung 44. Regens-
        burg: Bosse, 1967. v, 264p.

Traces the development of stylistic/aesthetic trends in
Debussy's songs. In Hardeck's view, the earliest songs
were influenced less by Debussy's French predecessors than

by the Russian composers and Wagner, and they are remarkable for their independence of style. The symbolist movement became the basis for Debussy's songs in the late
1880s, though in an altogether personal manifestation.
From 1904 (after **Pelléas et Mélisande**) a strain of classi-
cism may be identified. Bibliography.

263. Hirsbrunner, Theo. "Musik und Dichtung im französischen Fin
de Siècle am Beispiel der **Proses lyriques** von Debussy."
In **Musik und Dichtung: Kaleidoskop ihrer Beziehungen**,
edited by Günter Schnitzler, 152-74. Stuttgart: Klett-
Cotta, 1979.

Concludes that Debussy in the **Proses lyriques** achieved
the fusion of poetry and music that the symbolists sought.
"His **Proses lyriques** are unrealisable, invisible lyrical
dramas subordinated under a poetic-musical language."

264. ———. "Musik und Sprache bei Gabriel Fauré und Claude
Debussy." **Melos/Neue Zeitschrift für Musik** 1 (1975): 365-
72.

Compares Fauré's and Debussy's settings of Verlaine's
"C'est l'extase." Fauré employs a more traditional musical
idiom in a more complex fashion, while Debussy's setting
uses a more modern style and achieves greater simplicity.

265. ———. "Zu Debussys und Ravels Mallarmé-Vertonungen."
Archiv für Musikwissenschaft 35 (1978): 81-103.

Contrasts the approaches of the two composers, each of
whom set a handful of Mallarmé texts. Characteristic of
the difference between them is that Ravel's songs emphasize
tightness of form while Debussy's give themselves up to the
poems' expansive and obscure aspects.

266. Hsu, Samuel. "Imagery and Diction in the Songs of Claude
Debussy." Ph.D. diss., University of California, Santa
Barbara, 1972. 218p.

Not examined. The author's abstract in **RILM** (73/3786)
reports that Debussy's songs are approached through criteria established in the aesthetics of symbolist poetry.
Bibliography; work-list.

267. Moe, Orin, and William B. Chappell. "Debussy and
Baudelaire: **Harmonie du Soir**." **Bonnes Feuilles** 4/1-2
(Spring 1975): 122-48.

Not examined. The authors' abstract for **RILM** (76/7481) reports that the relationships of the text and the music are discussed with reference to both structure and imagery. The music articulates a dialectic in the poem that had not been observed by literary critics.

268. Nichols, Roger. "Debussy's Two Settings of 'Clair de lune'." **Music and Letters** 48 (1967): 229-35.

Compares the settings of Verlaine's poem made by Debussy in 1882-84 and in 1892. The period that separates the two settings was a crucial one in Debussy's maturation as a composer, and the comparison of the songs illustrates the increase in his sensitivity to both details and atmosphere, his skill in text-setting, his development of sensuous and static harmonic style, and especially his mastery of form and textural balance.

269. Porter, Laurence M. "Text versus Music in the French Art Song: Debussy, Fauré, and Verlaine's **Mandoline**." **Nineteenth-Century French Studies** 12 (1983-84): 138-44.

Contrasts the two composers' approaches to Verlaine's text. Debussy's setting is parodistic and rich in detail but choppy in structure, while Fauré's sets a mood of assurance and effects a coherent structure.

270. Ruschenberg, Peter. "Stilkritische Untersuchungen zu den Liedern Claude Debussys." Ph.D. diss., University of Hamburg, 1966.

Not examined. The dissertation is abstracted in **Die Musikforschung** 20 (1967): 316-17. Several common assumptions about Debussy's songs are challenged. Rather than symbolist poetry, texts oriented toward nature unify his work. His forms are not free but closely bound to the texts and defined by recurring motives. The declamation of the vocal lines reflects French prosody. A personal rhythmic figure pervades all the songs. Finally, the use of whole-tone language is traceable more to the expansion of the Western tonal system than to exoticism. Influences on Debussy's style are listed. An appendix includes the previously unpublished songs "Caprice" and "Jane."

271. Trevitt, John. "Debussy **inconnu**: An Inquiry." **The Musical Times** 114 (1973): 881-86; 1001-05.

Discusses the problems of the lack of knowledge of

Debussy's song oeuvre. The history of the songs is summarized, with emphasis on their importance for the understanding of the development of Debussy's style. List of
songs.

272.   Wenk, Arthur. **Claude Debussy and the Poets.** Berkeley: University of California Press, 1976. x, 345p.

Analyzes the texts and music of the most important of
Debussy's settings. The poets discussed are Banville,
Baudelaire, Verlaine, Mallarmé, and Louÿs, as well as
Debussy himself. The emphasis is placed on the nature of
the inspiration Debussy derived from his text in each case
and on the compositional techniques with which he responded
to that inspiration. Appendices include work-list, variant
readings of texts, meters used by the composer, translations. Bibliography. Index.

273.   Youens, Susan. "From the Fifteenth Century to the Twentieth: Considerations of Musical Prosody in Debussy's
Trois Ballades de François Villon." **The Journal of Musicology** 2 (1983): 418-33.

By means of several examples, defines the special problems of declamation in the setting of French; explains
Debussy's apparently somewhat ambiguous attitude toward
these problems; and analyzes perceptively representative
lines from the Villon ballade settings.

Frederick Delius
(1862-1934)

274.   Gooch, Bryan N.S. "Ernest Dowson and Frederick Delius: On
Songs of Sunset as Mentioned in Arthur Hutchings'
Delius." **The Music Review** 36 (1975): 140-41.

Reproaches Hutchings for the misattribution of Dowson's
texts for Delius's song cycle as well as for other fail-
ings, and generally laments the failure of studies of
either poet or composer to give significant attention to
the relationships between the two.

275.   Holland, A.K. **The Songs of Delius.** London: Oxford University Press, 1951. 56p.

Gives an overview of Delius's songs. The composer is
regarded as not particularly bound by the details of his

texts, which he used as bases for personal expressions that are made through musical means. He wrote songs on texts from Scandinavia, France (Verlaine), Germany (Nietzsche), and Great Britain and adapted his style somewhat to each nationality or language. The songs are discussed and critiqued individually. Work-list.

Norman Dello Joio
(b. 1913)

276. Bumgardner, Thomas Arthur. "The Solo Vocal Works of Norman Dello Joio." D.M.A. diss., University of Texas, 1973. 217p.

Not examined. According to the author's abstract in **RILM** (74/641), the study focuses on the influence of the texts on the music. Bibliography; work-list.

Brian Dennis
(b. 1941)

277. Hill, Peter. "The Chinese Song-Cycles of Brian Dennis." **Tempo** 137 (June 1981): 23-29.

Surveys Dennis's nine cycles of songs on T'ang dynasty poems. The composer's attraction for the poems reflects the affinity of his musical style in the early 1970s for their apparent simplicity, strict structure, and use of symmetrical oppositions. Over the period of these compositions, he gradually turned toward more flexible creative processes.

Richard Dering
(ca. 1580-1630)

278. Platt, Peter. "Perspectives of Richard Dering's Vocal Music: Together with a Performer's Guide." **Studies in Music** (Australia) 1 (1967): 56-66.

Not examined. The author's **RILM** abstract (67/712) indicates that Dering wrote Italian continuo madrigals in the Italian style of the time. The English songs include cries for solo voice and viols.

Paul Dessau
(1894-1979)

279. Rienäcker, Gerd. "Gesänge der Hoffnung und Zuversicht: Paul Dessaus Liederzyklen nach Texten von Heine und Neruda." **Musik und Gesellschaft** 36 (1976): 71-76.

Not examined. The abstract in RILM (76/11132) by the author indicates that the cycles represent a "synopsis of ideals." The contrasting spirit of the two groups of songs is emphasized.

Bernard van Dieren
(1887-1936)

280. Grouse, Gordon. "Bernard van Dieren: Three Early Songs in Relation to His Subsequent Development." **The Music Review** 29 (1968): 116-22.

Describes the style and character of the **Drei Lieder** of 1907. Although they are quite conservative, they contain moments which prefigure the composer's later style. During his second period van Dieren moved in the direction of atonality, while in his maturity he emphasized polyphonic textures.

281. Pirie, Peter J. "The Songs of van Dieren." **Monthly Musical Record** 88 (1958): 144-46.

Surveys the songs. Emphasizes the variety that results from van Dieren's adaptation of his technique to very diverse poetry in several languages. The constant features of his style are identified as polyphonic texture, serenity, and delicacy of harmonic color and melodic inflection.

Gaetano Donizetti
(1797-1848)

282. Sorce Keller, Marcello. "Gaetano Donizetti: un bergamasco compositore di canzoni napoletane." **Studi donizettiani** 3 (1978): 100-107.

Not examined. The author's RILM abstract (79/2848) indicates that analysis of three songs shows how Donizetti avoided the clichés of Neapolitan song.

John Dowland
(1563-1626)

283. Brown, Patricia A. "Influences on the Early Lute Songs of
      John Dowland." **Miscellanea musicologica** (Australia) 3
      (1968-69): 21-33.

      Not examined. The author's **RILM** abstract (69/3498) indi-
      cates that the article considers the relationships of
      Dowland's 1597 ayres for four parts with lute tablature to
      both English and Continental styles.

284. Dowling, Margaret. "The Printing of John Dowland's **Second
      Book of Songs or Ayres."** **The Library,** 4th series, 12
      (1932): 365-80.

      Traces the litigious publication history of Dowland's
      1600 collection.

285. Fellowes, Edmund H. "The Songs of Dowland." **Proceedings of
      the Musical Association** 56 (1929-30): 1-26.

      Gives an introduction to Dowland's lute songs, including
      historical background and descriptive commentary on a num-
      ber of pieces to illustrate the principles of Dowland's
      style.

286. Poulton, Diana. **John Dowland.** London: Faber & Faber;
      Berkeley: University of California Press, 1972. 520p.

      An extensive study of the composer's life and music. The
      large chapter on the songs discusses the sources, the
      pieces themselves, and some aspects of performance. The
      treatment of texts and music tends to be descriptive and
      sometimes critical but not analytical. Bibliography of
      printed music and books; table of manuscript sources. In-
      dexes.

287. Toft, Robert. "Musicke a Sister to Poetrie: Rhetorical
      Artifice in the Passionate Airs of John Dowland." **Early
      Music** 12 (1984): 190-99.

      Applies the standard repertoire of rhetorical devices to
      a discussion of both texts and music of Dowland's songs.
      Toft illustrates a number of figures by examples particu-
      larly from "Sorrow sorrow stay" and "In darknesse let mee
      dwell." The techniques are clearly identified and convinc-
      ingly demonstrated.

288.   Wells, Robin Headlam. "John Dowland and Elizabethan Melan-
       choly." **Early Music** 13 (1985): 514-28.

       Explores the literary conventions of expression on which
       Dowland's melancholy songs are based. Wells cautions
       against regarding these songs as personal statements re-
       flecting the composer's own experience, and instead views
       them as products of exceptional vision and skill in a
       standard genre.

                        John Duke
                        (1899-1984)

289.   Compton, Earl Wilson. "A Singer's Guide to the Songs of
       John Duke." D.M.A. thesis, Eastman School of Music, 1974.
       xv, 212p.

       Discusses the songs by types--atmospheric, cantabile,
       spirited and dramatic, declamatory and humorous. Perhaps
       the most helpful parts of the thesis are the appendices,
       which include notes on each song giving range, voice type,
       rhythmic character, and brief comments; a chronological
       list of the songs identifying poets, dates of composition,
       and publishers; and a list of songs grouped by voice type.

                        Henri Duparc
                        (1848-1933)

290.   Northcote, Sydney. **The Songs of Henri Duparc.** London:
       Dobson, 1949. 122p.

       Gives a fine introduction to the composer and his works.
       Introductory chapters cover the music-historical context,
       the composer's biography, and the poets whose texts in-
       spired him. Each of the songs is taken up, with an English
       translation, analytical comments, and remarks on problems
       of performance. A final chapter briefly surveys Duparc's
       other works. Portraits, facsimile. Bibliography; disco-
       graphy.

                        Antonín Dvořák
                        (1841-1904)

291.   Cerný, Miroslav. "Zum Wort-Ton-Problem im Vokalwerk Antonín
       Dvořáks." In **Colloquium Music and Word, Brno 1969,** edited

by Rudolf Pečman, 139-57. Brno: International Musical
Festival, 1973.

Discusses the problem of diction in Dvořák's text setting
in general, including songs, duets, choral pieces, and
larger vocal genres. Dvořák is given a significant position in the history of thé development of Czech vocal
music.

292. Robertson, Alec. "Dvořák's Songs." **Music and Letters** 24
(1943): 82-89.

(Duplicates a chapter from Robertson's biography of the
composer.) Surveys the songs chronologically, covering
them in a very dispassionate way. Although the quality of
the songs is not uniform, Robertson judges the best to be
very successful.

Gottfried von Einem
(b. 1918)

293. Schollum, Robert. "Die Klavierlieder Gottfried von Einems."
Oesterreichische Musikzeitung 28 (1973): 80-86.

Describes the general style of Einem's forty-two songs
and comments specifically on a few individual ones. The
composer takes a somewhat operatic approach, making each
song a miniature scene. Characteristically the vocal lines
are declamatory, and the piano's role is kept concise.

Hanns Eisler
(1898-1962)

294. Elsner, Jürgen. "Die Majakowski-Vertonungen Hanns Eislers."
Musik und Gesellschaft 18 (1968): 434-44.

Not examined. According to the abstract in **RILM**
(68/3589), demonstrates by analysis of four songs the composer's sympathy with the aesthetic principles of the October Revolution.

295. Grabs, Manfred. "'Wir, so gut es gelang, haben das Unsre
getan': Zur Aussage der Hölderlin-Vertonungen Hanns
Eislers." **Beiträge zur Musikwissenschaft** 15 (1973): 49-
59.

Not examined. The RILM abstract (73/766) reports that the article demonstrates that Eisler's montage technique affects the meanings of and classical models in Hölderlin's poetry.

296. Hennenberg, Fritz. "Zur Dialektik des Schliessens in Liedern von Hanns Eisler." Sammelbände zur Musikgeschichte der Deutschen Demokratischen Republik, Vol. 2, 181-227. Berlin: Neue Musik, 1971.

Not examined. According to the RILM abstract (71/2569), investigates means by which Eisler avoids conventional cadence formulas.

297. Mainka, Jürgen. "Musikalische Betroffenheit: Zum Begriff des Gestischen." Beiträge zur Musikwissenschaft 15 (1973): 61-80.

Not examined. The RILM abstract (73/805) by the author states that Eisler's settings of Anacreon are analyzed with regard to sudden contrast in the areas of tonality, intervals, rhythm, dynamics.

298. ———. "Der Mächtigen Krieg ist euer Tod." Zeitschrift für Kunst und Gesellschaft 8 (1976): 77-97.

Not examined. The RILM abstract (76/6152) indicates that the discussion treats Eisler's setting of Tucholsky, Brecht, and Weinert from 1925 to 1934, with special references to the use of the Classic-Romantic idiom.

299. Rösler, Walter. "Zu einigen Tucholsky-Liedern Hanns Eislers." Beiträge zur Musikwissenschaft 15 (1973): 81-92.

Not examined. The abstract in RILM (73/838) indicates that the article deals with evidence of the chanson tradition in the songs, and that in them musical quotation is employed as a parodistic or satirical element.

300. Trexler, Roswitha, with Fritz Hennenberg. "Wie ich Eislers Hölderlin-Fragmente singe." Melos/Neue Zeitschrift für Musik 4 (1978): 107-10.

Proposes a special interpretive approach to the performance of Eisler's songs. A degree of detachment from the material is needed in order to convey the questioning and even contradictory responses to the content of the texts.

Gabriel Fauré
(1845-1924)

301. Bland, Stephen F. "Form in the Songs of Gabriel Fauré."
     Ph.D. diss., Florida State University, 1976. 108p.

     Consists of formal analysis of Fauré's songs. Bland
     demonstrates the broad trend over Fauré's career as a song
     composer away from strophic toward through-composed struc-
     tures. In all of the songs it is characteristic of Fauré
     to blur sectional divisions within each piece.

302. Bowman, Robin. "Eight Late Songs of Fauré: An Approach to
     Analysis." **Musical Analysis** 1/1 (Winter 1972): 3-5.

     Tabulates data on melodic intervals in the vocal lines of
     Fauré's **Mirages,** op. 113, and **L'Horizon chimérique,** op.
     118. Bowman thereby observes that there is a tendency
     toward rising scalar lines concluded by a large falling
     interval. Similar approaches to other musical elements are
     suggested. The author believes that such an approach would
     best reveal composers' musical thinking.

303. Chalupt, René. "Gabriel Fauré et les pòetes." **La Revue
     musicale** 3/4 (October 1922): 220-25.

     Draws attention to Fauré's constant contact with the
     leading literary styles throughout his career. His choice
     of song texts was marked by eclecticism.

*   Hirsbrunner, Theo. "Musik und Sprache bei Gabriel Fauré und
     Claude Debussy."

     Cited above as item 265.

304. Jankelevitch, Vladimir. **Fauré et l'inexprimable.** Paris:
     Plon, 1974. 383p.

     Treats the work of Fauré from an aesthetic/critical point
     of view. The composer's creative career is viewed as a
     self-contained, uniformly directed progression toward sim-
     plicity and austerity. Jankelevitch identifies three sty-
     listic periods: 1870-1890, 1890-1907, and 1907-1922. (The
     first part of the study was originally published in 1938 as
     Fauré et ses mélodies [Paris: Plon]. The present edition
     incorporates two further sections, one of notes on Fauré's
     piano and chamber works, and the other dealing with ambi-
     guity, equanimity, and charm in Fauré's style.) Appendices.

305. Kurtz, James Lawrence. "Problems of Tonal Structure in
      Songs of Gabriel Fauré." Ph.D. diss., Brandeis Univer-
      sity, 1970. 124p.

      Not examined. According to the abstract (**Dissertation
      Abstracts** 31A [1971]: 3583-84A), applies voice-leading
      analysis to four songs: "Les Présents," op. 46, no. 1;
      "Puisque l'aube grandit," op. 61, no. 2; "Soir," op. 83,
      no. 2; and "Inscription sur le sable," op. 106, no. 8. The
      manner of establishing a tonal structure is discovered to
      be based not on functional harmony but on linear and modal
      means.

306. Orrey, Leslie. "The Songs of Gabriel Fauré." **The Music
      Review** 6 (1945): 72-84.

      Surveys the songs. Emphasis is placed on the composer's
      musical language and its development, with no concern for
      the works as settings of poetry. Orrey's purpose is to
      call for wider knowledge of Fauré's works.

*   Porter, Laurence M. "Text versus Music in the French Art
      Song: Debussy, Fauré, and Verlaine's **Mandoline**."

      Cited above as item 270.

307. Ravel, Maurice. "Les Mélodies de Gabriel Fauré." **La Revue
      musicale** 3/4 (October 1922): 214-19.

      Reports one composer's view of another, from an inter-
      view. Ravel regards Fauré as having shown his greatest
      genius in the mélodie. His achievement was to raise the
      French song above the level of the salon romance and cast
      off the dominance of the German Lied.

308. Sommers, Paul Bartholin. "Fauré and His Songs: The Rela-
      tionship of Text, Melody and Accompaniment." Ph.D. diss.,
      University of Illinois, 1969. 175p.

      Not examined. The abstract in **RILM** (69/4261) states that
      the study identifies fundamental problems in song compos-
      ing, especially those related to the French language, and
      traces the composer's style development in representative
      songs of three periods: to 1890, 1890-1905, and 1906-1924.

Alfonso Ferrabosco
(ca. 1578-1628)

309. Doughtie, Edward. "Ferrabosco and Jonson's 'The Houre-glasse'." **Renaissance Quarterly** 22 (1969): 148-50.

Draws attention to a set of part-books at Carlisle Cathe-dral in which music by Alfonso Ferrabosco previously known with the text "All you forsaken lovers come" is paired with Ben Jonson's poem "The Houre-glasse." Suggests that the Jonson text may be the original one.

310. Duffy, John Charles. "The Vocal Works of Alfonso Ferrabosco the Younger, c. 1578-1628." Ph.D. diss., Boston Univer-sity, 1979. 656p.

Not examined. The abstract in **RILM** (79/2515) states that Ferrabosco's works are analyzed. The composer's awareness of major-minor pairing is examined. His more advanced songs anticipate the style of the basso continuo song.

Thomas Ford
(d. 1648)

311. Siemens, Reynold. "If Music and Sweet Poetry Agree: Thomas Ford's 'Since First I Saw Your Face'." **Renaissance Quar-terly** 21 (1968): 153-61.

Analyzes the song from the perspectives of the matching of verbal and musical rhythm and of the reflection of text meanings in the music. Shows how Ford suited the music not only to the first but as well to the second and third stanzas of the poem.

Robert Franz
(1815-1892)

312. Aldrich, Richard. "Robert Franz on Schubert and Others." **The Musical Quarterly** 14 (1928): 486-94.

Quotes at some length from Franz's letter to the Dresden-ite Twietmeyer, dating from 1868 to 1875. Despite the article's title, the material reveals much more about Franz than about Schubert or other musicians, especially his resentment of what he perceived to be a lack of apprecia-tion of his work.

313. Boonin, Joseph M. **An Index to the Solo Songs of Robert Franz.** Music Indexes and Bibliographies 4. Hackensack, New Jersey: Joseph Boonin, 1970. v, 19p.

Lists Franz's songs by opus number, with indication of available commercial editions. Included are a list of the contents of the editions of selected songs, an index of the songs by titles and first lines, and an index by poets.

314. Porter, Ernest G. "Robert Franz on Song." **The Music Review** 26 (1965): 15-18.

Relates statements made by Franz in letters to the style of his Lieder. He believed that the genre had reached a critical point that required a retrospective approach. He described his own approach to composition as one of seeking a balance between spontaneous inspiration and conscious work. Technical refinement is most evident in the composition of the piano parts.

315. ————. "The Songs of Robert Franz." **The Musical Times** 104 (1963): 477-79.

Calls for greater knowledge and appreciation of Franz. In describing his style, Porter acknowledges that the composer was no innovator but stresses his lyrical melody and expressive accompaniments. Franz songs are compared to settings of the same texts by Schubert, Schumann, and Wolf, indicating how differently two composers can interpret a single poem.

Vincenzo Galilei
(late 1520s-1591)

316. Palisca, Claude V. "Vincenzo Galilei and Some Links between 'Pseudo-Monody' and Monody." **The Musical Quarterly** 47 (1960): 344-60.

Argues that Galilei's ideal for the texture of songs was the simple, homorhythmic style employed in frottole and other popular Italian songs. Further, the "arias" such as Ruggiero and Romanesca were not basses but vocal discant formulas, and their orientation to the soprano part, which distinguished them from contrapuntal music, made them attractive models to Galilei. He is thus seen not as a progressive but as a traditionalist who sought to maintain existing, popular styles.

Charles Gounod
(1818-1893)

317. Langevin, Kenneth W. **"Au Silence des belles nuits:** The
      Earlier Songs of Charles Gounod." Ph.D. diss., Cornell
      University, 1978.   212p.

      Not examined. According to the **RILM** abstract (78/721),
      relates the composer's background to his song oeuvre, es-
      tablishes style criteria by analysis of his first published
      song, and discusses the remainder of the works in chrono-
      logical order.

Percy Grainger
(1882-1961)

318. Dreyfus, Kay. **Percy Grainger's Kipling Settings: A Study of
      the Manuscript Sources.**   Music Monograph 3. Western
      Australia: University of Western Australia, 1980.   viii,
      131p.

      Not examined. According to the abstract in **RILM**
      (80/880), discusses the compositional history of the works
      and the composer's view of the material. The settings,
      including songs and choral works, range over Grainger's
      entire career.

Alexandr Tikhonovich Grechaninov
(1864-1956)

319. Pastukhov, V.L. "The Songs and Romances of A.T. Gretchani-
      noff." **Tempo** 25/11 (Autumn 1952): 11-18.

      Introduces Grechaninov's song oeuvre in general, over two
      hundred fifty pieces in a wide variety of styles. The
      works are grouped into categories: songs on folk themes
      (both Russian and other nationalities); epic ballads; chil-
      dren's songs; lyrical songs, including several cycles;
      songs in operatic style; character and humorous songs; and
      neo-Classic songs.

Edvard Grieg
(1843-1907)

320. Desmond, Astra. "Grieg's Songs." **Music and Letters** 22

(1941): 333-57. Reprinted in revised form as "The Songs" in **Grieg: A Symposium,** edited by Gerald Abraham, 71-92. Norman, Oklahoma: University of Oklahoma Press, 1950.

Provides an overview of Grieg's song output, with descriptions and criticisms of some of the most important songs. The importance of the language of the texts is emphasized, as is Grieg's success in emancipating himself from German style. Chronological list of songs.

321. Orr, C.W. "A Word for Grieg's Songs." **Monthly Musical Record** 113 (1933): 37.

Commends Grieg's songs for their simplicity and vocal grace. Several of the best songs are named.

322. Weismann, Wilhelm. "Edvard Grieg als Liederkomponist." **Zeitschrift für Musik** 99 (1932): 765-67.

Introduces Grieg's song style in general. Emphasizes the composer's reliance on strophic form, which in turn focuses attention on his inclination to express the crucial impression of the poetry in simple, direct, and naive terms.

Charles Tomlinson Griffes
(1884-1920)

323. Johnson, Richard Oscar. "The Songs of Charles Tomlinson Griffes." D.M.A. diss., University of Iowa, 1977. 192p.

Not examined. The **RILM** abstract (78/862) indicates that the songs are analyzed in regard to form, harmony, melody, poetry, meter, and rhythm. The development of Griffes's style is traced.

324. Upton, William Treat. "The Songs of Charles T. Griffes." **The Musical Quarterly** 9 (1923): 314-29.

Explores Griffes's songs in chronological order, describing the character of many of them and showing the development of his style. He began with German texts under the influence of Brahms and Strauss, later manifesting a more French style. The songs are praised for their sincerity, skillful construction, and unity of form.

Ivor Gurney
(1890-1937)

325. Hold, Trevor. "Two Aspects of 'Sleep': A Study in English
      Song-Writing." **The Music Review** 41 (1980): 26-35.

      Offers a comparative analysis of the settings of Thomas
      Nashe's poem by Ivor Gurney and by Peter Warlock. De-
      scribes Gurney's setting as highly impassioned and roman-
      tic, while Warlock's is calm and classicistic. Emphasizes
      that both songs are masterful compositions and that the
      contrast between them shows how varied musical readings of
      a single text can be.

326. Moore, Charles Willard. **Maker and Lover of Beauty: Ivor
      Gurney, Poet and Songwriter.** Rickmansworth, Herts.:
      Triad, 1976. 28p.

      Recounts the life and career of the composer. Employs
      unpublished materials by Marion Scott, personal correspon-
      dence, interview. Does not shrink from a frank discussion
      of Gurney's personality and mental collapse. Illustra-
      tions.

327. ————. "The Solo Vocal Works of Ivor Gurney (1890-1937)."
      D.M. diss., Indiana University, 1967. 183p.

      Not examined. According to the abstract in **RILM**
      (67/949), gives biographical and style-analytical informa-
      tion. Both published and unpublished material was con-
      sidered.

Reynaldo Hahn
(1875-1947)

328. Schuh, Willi. "Zum Liedwerk Reynaldo Hahns." **Schweizer
      Beiträge zur Musikwissenschaft** 2 (1974): 103-26.

      Not examined. According to the **RILM** abstract (74/2937),
      provides biographical material as well as analyses of some
      songs.

George Handford
(ca. 1585-1647)

329. Doughtie, Edward O. "Two Songs from Renaissance England."

Forum (University of Houston) 9/1 (Spring 1971): 74-81.

Presents two lute songs by George Handford from his manuscript book of **Ayres** (Trinity College, Cambridge, MS R.16.29). The songs, "Say ye gods" and "Now each creature," are published here for the first time. Doughtie describes Handford as a competent minor composer.

Josef Matthias Hauer
(1883-1959)

330. Krejcí, Karel Jan. "Vollkommene Einheit von Wort und Musik: Josef Matthias Hauers Hölderlinliedern." **Neue Zeitschrift für Musik** 131 (1970): 241-45.

Argues that Hauer's development of a rigorously intellectual twelve-tone technique of composition can be traced in relation to his setting of Hölderlin's texts. Krejči believes that once one hears these songs it is no longer possible to conceive the texts and the music separately. Portrait of Hauer.

Joseph Haydn
(1732-1809)

331. Angermüller, Rudolph. "Neukomm's schottische Liedbearbeitungen für Joseph Haydn." **Haydn-Studien** 3 (1974): 151-53.

Demonstrates that Haydn's pupil Sigismund Neukomm made the arrangements of Haydn's settings of Scottish songs for voice, piano, violin, and cello.

332. Brown, A. Peter. "Joseph Haydn and Leopold Hofmann's 'Street Songs'." **Journal of the American Musicological Society** 33 (1980): 356-83.

Compares settings of three texts by Hofmann and Haydn. Haydn wrote his settings in deliberate competition with those of Hofmann, whom he regarded as a rival, and appears to have picked on Hofmann's weakest songs. While Hofmann adopted a simple, conservative style in the North German tradition, Haydn exploited the more flexible melody and richer harmony of the Viennese Lied. Complete musical and poetic texts of all three songs are included. Tables.

333. Feder, Georg. "Zu Haydns schottischen Liedern." **Haydn-**

Studien 1 (1965): 43.

Based on the autograph fragment of Haydn's arrangement of "Dainty Davie," reasons that Haydn probably had only the song melodies and not the corresponding texts when he made the settings of Scottish songs for William Napier.

334. Hopkinson, Cecil, and C.B. Oldman. "Haydn's Settings of Scottish Songs in the Collections of Napier and Whyte." **Edinburgh Bibliographical Society Transactions** 3 (1948-55): 85-120.

Includes a brief essay on the historical context of Haydn's settings. Descriptions of editions; list of concordances in Thomson's collections; bibliography. Thematic catalogue.

* ————. "Thomson's Collections of National Song with Special Reference to the Contributions of Haydn and Beethoven."

Cited above as item 150.

335. Mies, Paul. "Joseph Haydns 'Abschiedslied'--von Adalbert Gyrowetz." **Haydn Yearbook** 2 (1963-64): 88-89.

Discusses the song "Abschiedslied," published as Haydn's but actually by Gyrowetz. It is possible that the song passed from its composer to Haydn when the two were in London in 1791-92.

336. Scott, Marion M. "Some English Affinities and Associations of Haydn's Songs." **Music and Letters** 25 (1944): 1-12.

Regards Haydn's songs as delightful when understood in their own terms, though more satisfying "as music than as songs." Haydn's German Lieder set to English words, his settings for William Napier, and his English canzonets are discussed, the latter individually. Melodic relationships may be traced between Haydn's themes and English music. His English acquaintances also influenced his writing of songs.

Michael Haydn
(1737-1806)

337. Ballam, Michael L. "The Life of Johann Michael Haydn and an

Examination of His Lieder Collections **Auserlesene Sammlung von Liedern mit Melodien** and **Aoide**." D.M. document,
Indiana University, 1976. viii, 168p.

Contains biographical material on the composer, a survey
of the background of Lied composition in the period, and
simple data on the songs in outline form. The twenty
portraits of Michael Haydn and his contemporaries are not
well reproduced in the photocopy. Bibliography. Appendices, including list of operas, oratorios, and dramatic
works; reproductions of the original prints of the two
collections.

Fanny Mendelssohn Hensel
(1805-1847)

338.   Citron, Marcia J. "The Lieder of Fanny Mendelssohn Hensel."
       The Musical Quarterly 69 (1983): 570-94.

Outlines the biographical context of Fanny Hensel's
songs, which made up the bulk of her compositions published
during her lifetime. The works are characterized in general, and several specific examples are discussed. Her style
is seen to be quite varied, and some of the settings are
judged to be superior to those by her brother Felix Mendelssohn of the same texts.

Heinrich von Herzogenberg
(1843-1900)

339.   Brusatti, Charlotte. "Das Liedschaffen Heinrich von
       Herzogenbergs." Ph.D. diss., University on Vienna, 1976.
       231p.

Not examined. According to the **RILM** abstract (76/2829),
gives biographical information, history of the songs, data
on the texts. Includes Herzogenberg's writings on harmony.
Bibliography; work-list.

John Hilton
(1599-1657)

340.   Chan, Mary. "John Hilton's Manuscript British Library Add.
       MS 11608." **Music and Letters** 60 (1979): 440-49.

Discusses the collection of songs compiled by the composer, probably in the 1640s and 1650s. Included are
Hilton's biblical and mythological dialogues, some solo
songs, and a separate section of catches. A table of the
contents of the manuscript is given. Plate showing Hilton's signature.

Paul Hindemith
(1895-1963)

341. Hepner, Steven Lorenz. "An Examination of the Sketches and
      Published Versions of Paul Hindemith's Songs for Solo
      Voice and Piano." Ph.D. diss., Northwestern University,
      1984. 598p.

      Not examined. The abstract (**Dissertation Abstracts** 45A
      [1985]: 1909a) indicates that the study illustrates Hinde-
      mith's compositional process. His approach to composing
      songs varied according to the seriousness of the texts.
      The effect of the text on musical construction is demon-
      strable.

342. Stephan, Rudolf. "Hindemith's **Marienleben:** An Assessment of
      Its Two Versions." **The Music Review** 15 (1954): 275-87.

      Compares the early (1922-23) and later (1948) versions of
      the cycle. Specific parallel passages from both are cited
      in music examples and critiqued. Stephan feels that in
      attempting to polish the composition Hindemith drained it
      of its spontaneity.

343. Truscott, Harold. "Hindemith and 'Das Marienleben'." **The
      Musical Times** 110 (1969): 1240-42.

      Argues that the later version of **Das Marienleben** is far
      superior to the earlier one. Overall, the loose set of
      songs was developed into an organic cycle by means of a new
      tonal plan. In several cases the singer's lines were made
      more vocal and satisfying. Each song is considered, with
      attention focused on those that were significantly revised.

Sidney Homer
(1864-1953)

344. Thorpe, Harry Colin. "The Songs of Sidney Homer." **The
      Musical Quarterly** 17 (1931): 47-73.

Surveys the composer's song oeuvre with comments on many
individual pieces. Thorpe praises Homer's choices of poetry for variety and quality. Characteristic of the music is
sincerity in styles ranging from the folksy to the serious
and introspective. Work-list.

Arthur Honegger
(1892-1955)

345. Fischer, Kurt von. "Arthur Honeggers erstes veröffent-
      lichtes Lied aus dem Jahre 1914." In **Musa-Mens-Musici, im
      Gedenken an Walther Vetter,** edited by Heinz Wegener, 383-
      88. Leipzig: VEB Deutscher Verlag für Musik, 1969.

      Finds in the youthful composer's setting of Fontainas's
      "Sur le basalte" evidence of the style of his predecessors,
      especially Debussy, as well as of his own mature style.

Alan Hovhaness
(b. 1911)

346. Gerbrandt, Carl James. "The Solo Vocal Music of Alan
      Hovhaness." D.M.A. diss., Peabody Conservatory of Music,
      1974. x, 273p.

      Not examined. The RILM abstract (76/10933) indicates
      that the study analyzes thirteen works for voice and in-
      struments other than the piano. The influence of Eastern
      musical styles on the composer is discussed. Facsimiles.
      Bibliography; work-list.

Sigismondo d'India
(ca. 1582-ca. 1629)

347. Joyce, John. "The Monodies of Sigismondo d'India." Ph.D.
      diss., Tulane University, 1975. xi, 423p.

      Analyzes d'India's songs, especially with regard to the
      treatment of words in the vocal parts, the harmonic style,
      and the use of ornamentation. Argues for a view of d'India
      as a mannerist of the Renaissance rather than as an early
      Baroque composer. Supplement of transcriptions of complete
      pieces. Work-list; bibliography.

348. Mompellio, Federico. "Sigismondo d'India e il suo primo

libro di **Musiche da cantar Sola." Collectanea historiae
musicae** 1 (1953): 113-34.

Discusses d'India's 1609 collection of monodies. Gives
general information on the history and contents of the
book. Describes the style of the music, including the
distinction between aria and madrigal types, the composer's
striking, expressive, melodic-harmonic devices, and the
role of the bass, which goes beyond mere harmonic support.
Provides some biographical details.

John Ireland
(1879-1962)

349. Lyle, Watson. "The Songs of John Ireland." **The Sackbut** 2
      (1921-22): 27-30.

Attributes the effectiveness of Ireland's songs to the
careful adherence to both the rhythmic phrasing and the
textual content of the poetry. Describes briefly a large
number of songs.

350. Yenne, Vernon Lee. "Three Twentieth Century English Song
      Composers: Peter Warlock, E.J. Moeran and John Ireland."
      D.M.A. diss., University of Illinois, 1969. 313p.

Not examined. According to the author's **RILM** abstract
(69/4297), relates the three composers to trends in the
English musical renaissance of 1915 to 1930.

Charles Ives
(1874-1954)

351. Copland, Aaron. "One Hundred and Fourteen Songs." **Modern
      Music** 11 (1934): 59-64.

Considers the significance of Ives's 1922 collection.
Copland emphasizes the variety among the songs, characterizing and categorizing a few of them. He regards the songs
of around 1900 as the first important ones, and those of
1919-20 as the most significant. The real point he wishes
to make is that the greatest need for the development of
American music is an attentive and critical audience.

352. Green, Douglass M. **"Exempli gratia**: A Chord Motive in
      Ives's **Serenity." In Theory Only** 4/5 (October 1978): 20-

21.

Not examined. According to the **RILM** abstract (78/6100), shows how a progression of two chords generates the song's structure and discusses word painting in the song.

353. Hitchcock, H. Wiley. "Charles Ives's Book of **114 Songs**." In **A Musical Offering: Essays in Honor of Martin Bernstein,** edited by Edward H. Clinkscale, 127-35. New York: Pendragon, 1977.

Presents an overview of the **114 Songs**. Outlines the history of the collection and places it in biographical context. Reviews Ives's aesthetic positions as represented in the Postface and in the music itself, emphasizing the allusion to both cultural and vernacular song traditions. Brief characterizations of many of the songs are included.

354. Newman, Philip Edward. "The Songs of Charles Ives (1874-1954)." Ph.D. diss., University of Iowa, 1967. 2 vols. 753p.

Not examined. The author's **RILM** abstract (69/4204) indicates that the songs are regarded as showing elements of Ives's style and philosophy, including his anticipation of twelve-tone and aleatory techniques, his choice and treatment of texts, and his general, personal philosophy. Information on the 205 individual songs studied is presented in outline by song title. Appendices, including work-list.

355. Schoffman, Nachum. "Charles Ives's Song 'A Vote for Names'." **Current Musicology** 23/1977: 56-68.

Presents a facsimile and offers a realization of Ives's sketch, which dates from 1912. The text and music satirize the United States electoral system.

356. ————. "The Songs of Charles Ives." Ph.D. diss., Hebrew University, Jerusalem, 1977. 456p.

Not examined. The **RILM** abstract (78/5359) indicates that the study gives analyses of twenty songs, discusses Ives's compositional methods, and evaluates his historical position.

357. Sear, H.G. "Charles Ives: Song Writer." **Monthly Musical Record** 81 (1951): 34-42.

A general essay on the **114 Songs**. Sear emphasizes the relation of the songs, taken as a body rather than individually, to Ives himself. The experimentalism of the music is seen to separate Ives's songs from the works of the nineteenth-century Lied composers and also from the public. A number of songs are given brief critiques, not always favorable; Sear objects particularly to the use of musical quotations, for example. On the whole, however, the article is appreciative of the songs.

Leoš Janáček
(1854-1928)

358. Acord, Thomas Wadsworth. "An Examination of Leoš Janáček's Compositions for Solo Voice and Piano." D.M.A. diss., University of Texas, Austin, 1981. 3v.

Not examined. According to the **RILM** abstract (81/2872), analyzes the songs and discusses Janáček's use of "speech-melody." Offers performance suggestions.

Adolf Jensen
(1837-1879)

359. Schweizer, Gottfried. "Das Liedschaffen Adolf Jensens." Ph.D. diss., Hessischen Ludwigs-Universität of Giessen, 1933. 149p.

Analyzes the songs in an attempt to identify the composer's style. The study is organized in sections dealing with melody, harmony and accompaniment, and form. The influences on the composer are traced to Schumann and Wagner and to the contrapuntal style associated with the Bach school. Music examples are relegated to an appendix. Tables, including a chronological overview of the songs.

Robert Jones
(fl. 1597-1615)

360. Fellowes, E.H. "The Text of the Song Books of Robert Jones." **Music and Letters** 8 (1927): 25-37.

Considers the problems of inaccuracies in the sources of Jones's works. Errors appear to have resulted from carelessness in transmission and must be corrected by modern editors.

Armin Knab
(1881-1951)

361. Lindlar, Heinrich. "Der Lyriker Armin Knab." **Zeitschrift für Musik** 112 (1951): 360-62.

Stresses Knab's compositions for solo voice and instruments other than piano. He turned to such scorings out of a sense that the piano accompaniment, which suited the Romantic Lied, was no longer appropriate to twentieth-century expression. Lindlar discusses particularly the 1940-41 "Knechtsballade" for tenor and string quartet.

Josef Martin Kraus
(1756-1792)

362. Bungardt, Volker. **Josef Martin Kraus (1756-1792): Ein Meister des klassischen Klavierliedes.** Kölner Beiträge zur Musikforschung 73. Regensburg: Bosse, 1973. 253, xxiip.

Discusses the songs of one of the less-known eighteenth-century Lied composers. Kraus worked principally in Sweden, but his background included the major poets and composers of the time. He set texts in German and in Swedish, as well as a few in other languages. Bungardt argues that Kraus developed a comparatively sophisticated style that anticipated that of Schubert. Appendices. Bibliography.

Christian Gottfried Krause
(1719-1770)

363. Edwards, John Richard. "Christian Gottfried Krause: Mentor of the First Berlin Song School." Ph.D. diss., University of Iowa, 1973. v, 243p.

Not examined. According to the abstract by the author in **RILM** (73/3436), discusses Krause's background, biography, aesthetics, and circle. An edition of the 1753 **Oden mit Melodien** is included. Bibliography.

Ernst Krenek
(b. 1900)

364. Schollum, Robert. "Anmerkungen zum Liedschaffen Ernst
Kreneks." **Oesterreichische Musikzeitschrift** 35 (1980):
446-52.

Makes general observations on Krenek's song style. While
he confronted the contemporary challenges to tonality, he
never failed to focus attention on the vocal line, the
text, and interpretation of the poetry through musical
symbols. Work-list.

Conradin Kreutzer
(1780-1849)

365. Peake, Luise Eitel. "Kreutzer's **Wanderlieder**: The Other
Winterreise." **The Musical Quarterly** 65 (1979): 83-102.

Studies Kreutzer's 1818 setting of Uhland's **Wanderlieder**.
The genre of the **Wanderlied** in general receives a very fine
treatment. Kreutzer's cycle is described. These songs are
credited with engendering numerous imitations, and they had
a clear influence on Wilhelm Müller's cycles and on Schubert, who greatly admired Kreutzer's works.

Adam Krieger
(1634-1666)

366. Osthoff, Helmuth. **Adam Krieger (1634-1666): Neue Beiträge
zur Geschichte des deutschen Liedes im 17. Jahrhundert.**
Leipzig: Breitkopf & Härtel, 1929. Reprint. Wiesbaden:
Breitkopf & Härtel, 1970. 107, vp.

Provides an overview of Krieger's output and his song
collections in particular, as well as a stylistic study of
the songs themselves, dealing first with the texts and then
with the music. A thematic index of the 1657 collection
Arien (insofar as it could be reconstructed) is included,
as well as a musical supplement giving complete songs with
critical notes. Additional notes update the reprint edition.

367. Schiørring, Nils. "Wiedergefundene Melodien aus der ver-
schollenen Adam-Krieger-Ariensammlung 1657." In **Festschrift Walter Wiora zum 30. Dezember 1966,** edited by

Ludwig Finscher and Christoph-Hellmut Mahling, 304-12. Kassel: Bärenreiter, 1967.

Reports the discovery of a manuscript copy of a set of psalm paraphrases compiled by the Danish preacher Anton Davidsen Foss, including some on previously unknown material from Krieger's 1657 publication. The source is in the Kongelige Bibliotek in Copenhagen, Ms. Thott, 4to, 457. The article cites several representative pieces, with comments on their style.

Franz Kugler
(1808-1858)

368. Hirschberg, Leopold. "Franz Kugler als Liederkomponist." **Die Musik** 2/2 (January-March 1903): 106-16.

Introduces the songs of Kugler, who was better known as an art historian, artist, and poet. The songs were generally published as musical supplements to collections of poetry. A list of the songs is appended.

Franz Lachner
(1803-1890)

369. Wagner, Günther. **Franz Lachner als Liederkomponist, nebst einem biographischen Teil und dem thematischen Verzeichnis sämtlicher Lieder.** Schriften zur Musik 3. Giebing: Katzbichler, 1970.   313p.

Not examined. According to the author's **RILM** abstract (70/2029), the study (a dissertation from Johannes Gutenberg University in Mainz 1969) places Lachner in a transitional position between Schubert and Brahms. Identifies the influences of Schubert and Mendelssohn in Lachner's song style, as well as elements traceable to his exposure to Bach's music. Facsimiles. Bibliography; thematic catalogue.

Michel L'Affilard
(ca. 1656-1708)

370. Schwandt, Erich. "L'Affilard's Published 'Sketchbooks'." **The Musical Quarterly** 63 (1977): 99-113.

Traces revisions in the songs used as musical examples in the successive editions of L'Affilard's **Principes très-faciles pour bien apprendre la musique** (1694-1747). A variety of degrees of revision is illustrated, and these reflect compositional improvements and particularly the emergence of the tonal system.

Nicholas Lanier
(1588-1666)

371. Duckles, Vincent. "English Song and the Challenge of Italian Monody." In **Words to Music: Papers on English Seventeenth-Century Song Read at a Clark Library Seminar, December 11, 1965,** by Vincent Duckles and Franklin B. Zimmerman, 1-42. Los Angeles: William Andrews Clark Memorial Library, University of California, 1967.

Examines the influence of the declamatory Italian style of English music, particularly on Lanier, whose **Hero and Leander** is included in full, and on Henry Lawes. These men created dramatic monodies in which the music responded sensitively to the dramatic and lyrical impulses of the texts.

372. Emslie, McD. "Nicholas Lanier's Innovations in English Song." **Music and Letters** 41 (1960): 13-27.

Credits Lanier with the invention of the declamatory ayre (as early as 1614), the first English recitative (**Hero and Leander,** 1628), and the first setting of English words in strophic-variation structure (Thomas Carew's "No more shall meads").

Eduard Lassen
(1830-1904)

373. Marx-Weber, Magda. "Die Lieder Eduard Lassens." **Hamburger Jahrbuch für Musikwissenschaft** 2 (1977): 147-85.

Not examined. The author's **RILM** abstract (77/2766) states that the article identifies Lassen's song style as a synthesis of the grace of the French romance and the warmth of the German Lied.

Henry Lawes
(1596-1662)

*   Duckles, Vincent. "English Song and the Challenge of Ital-
       ian Monody."

       Cited above as item 371.

374.   Hill, Georgia A. "Henry Lawes, the Orpheus and Aesculapius
       of English Music in the Seventeenth Century: A Study of
       the Literary, Historical, and Musical Significance of His
       Song Books." Ph.D. diss., University of Kentucky, 1967.
       254p.

       Not examined. According to the author's **RILM** abstract
       (69/859), finds in laudatory verse to Lawes evidence that
       his songs were regarded as having therapeutic, educational,
       religious, and nationalistic functions. His song books are
       judged to be superior to those of Playford. Facsimiles.
       Bibliography.

375.   McGrady, R.J. "Henry Lawes and the Concept of 'Just Note
       and Accent'." **Music and Letters** 50 (1968): 86-102.

       Places Lawes's style in relation to Caroline poetry,
       which was less emotional and more directed toward argument
       and poetic design than was the Elizabethan lyric. Lawes's
       contemporary poets, with whom he probably worked closely,
       are quoted to show that his style was highly regarded in
       his own time. The contents of his principal autograph
       manuscript, the "Cooper Smith Manuscript" (British Museum
       [i.e., Library] Loan 35), which seems to embody his style
       development from about 1630 to 1650, are described. The
       composer began in the tradition of the simple declamatory
       ayre but progressed to more intricate reflection of the
       rhythm and sense of the text in continuous and strophic-
       variation forms.

William Lawes
(1602-1645)

376.   Crum, M.C. "Notes on the Texts of William Lawes's Songs in
       B.M. MS. Add. 31432." **The Library,** 5th series, 9 (1954):
       122-27.

       Compares the texts of Lawes's songs with the versions
       known elsewhere. In some cases the Lawes versions have

considerable authority. Whére the readings diverge, there
are various causes, ranging from errors of transmission to
problems connected with musical settings.

Benjamin Lees
(b. 1924)

377. Westwood, Shirley Ann. "Poetic Imagery in the Songs of
Benjamin Lees." D.M.A. diss., University of Missouri,
Kansas City, 1980. 96p.

Not examined. According to the **RILM** abstract (80/4991),
explores the compositional techniques used by Lees in his
song cycles based on texts by Richard Nickson. Both poet
and composer were interviewed.

Thomas Linley
(1756-1778)

378. Beechey, Gwilym. "Thomas Linley, 1756-78, and His Vocal
Music." **The Musical Times** 119 (1978): 669-71.

Introduces the composer and his vocal works. Only a
handful of songs are attributed to Linley, and these are
preserved only in two-staff reduction of the original scoring for strings.

Franz Liszt
(1811-1886)

379. Cooper, Martin. "Liszt as Song Writer." **Music and Letters**
19 (1938): 171-81.

Surveys Liszt's songs, with close critical discussion.
About half of the works are by outstanding poets, and these
also contain the best music. The composer is judged to
succeed in suiting music to the emotions of the poetry,
when this is not carried to such an extreme that the song
is over-dramatic.

380. Dart, William J. "Revisions and Reworkings in the Lieder of
Franz Liszt." **Studies in Music** (Australia) 9 (1975): 41-
53.

Shows that Liszt was a disciplined and thoughtful reviser

of his own works. Among the concerns shown in his reworkings are the achievement of simplicity and economy in the
piano texture, word-setting, tightness of form, and harmony. The three Petrarch sonnets of 1861 are given special
discussion. List of revisions.

381. Goebel, Albrecht. "Franz Liszt, 'Die drei Zigeuner': Ein
     Beitrag zum Balladenschaffen im 19. Jahrhundert." **Musica**
     35 (1981): 241-45.

     Analyzes Liszt's setting of Nikolaus Lenau's poem. Sev-
     eral style traits stand out: free form, chromatic harmony,
     decisive text declamation, and such coloristic details as
     extreme intervals, rhythmic richess, and free, improvisa-
     tional ornamentation. The piece is representative of the
     late Romantic style and especially of the period's image of
     gypsy music.

382. Hughes, Edwin. "Liszt as Lieder Composer." **The Musical
     Quarterly** 3 (1917): 390-409.

     Describes Liszt's song output. His Lieder are regarded
     as belonging to the main body of the German tradition,
     strongly influenced by Schubert and leading to Wolf and
     Strauss. Characteristic of the style is a sense of drama,
     and uniquely evident in his songs is Liszt's humor. Exam-
     ples to illustrate the composer's Lied style are selected
     from a number of songs.

383. Kecskeméti, István. "Two Liszt Discoveries: 2: An Unknown
     Song." **The Musical Times** 115 (1974): 743-44.

     Reports the acquisition of a previously unknown setting
     by Liszt of the first stanza of a song from Victor Hugo's
     Marie Tudor, act 1, scene 5. The manuscript is catalogued
     as mus. 5.108 in the National Széchényi Library in Buda-
     pest; it was originally an album leaf, dated 28 May 1849.
     The song is in the style of a berceuse. Facsimile.

384. Montu-Berthon, Suzanne. "Un Liszt méconnu: Mélodies et
     Lieder." 2 vols. comprising numbers 342-44 and 345-46 of
     La Revue musicale. Paris: Richard-Masse, 1981. 198, 56p.

     Makes a biographical-historical and a systematic, stylis-
     tic study of Liszt's songs. Emphasis is placed on the
     diversity of stylistic traits and in particular on the
     conscious progressivism of the composer. Indexes. Biblio-
     graphy. The second volume contains the music examples for

the discussion in the first.

385. Turner, Ronald. "A Comparison of Two Sets of Liszt-Hugo
      Songs." **Journal of the American Liszt Society** 5 (June
      1979): 16-31.

      Compares early versions (1841-43) and revisions (pub-
      lished in 1860) of "Oh, quand je dors," "S'il est un
      charmant gazon," "Comment, disaient-ils," and "Enfant, si
      j'étais roi." The later versions eschew the excitement and
      virtuosity of the earlier ones, becoming instead more
      subtle, practical, sensitive to the texts, clear in form,
      and unified in both motivic material and mood.

386. Werba, Erik. "Franz Liszt und das Lied." **Oesterreichische
      Musikzeitschrift** 16 (1961): 412-15.

      Surveys Liszt's German songs. The poets whose texts
      Liszt chose are listed. Werba groups the pieces into
      ballads, monologues, and Lieder proper and characterizes
      them individually. In conclusion, possibilities for pro-
      graming and for research topics are suggested.

                         Carl Loewe
                        (1796-1869)

387. Althouse, Paul Leinbach, Jr. "Carl Loewe (1796-1869): His
      Lieder, Ballads, and Their Performance." Ph.D. diss.,
      Yale University, 1971. 350, 76p.

      A life-and-works study. The author first discusses the
      composer's biography, emphasizing his relative isolation
      from the mainstream of German musical life. There is a
      brief survey of the antecedents of Loewe's work. The
      extensive discussion of the music is organized by genre and
      by aspects of style. Althouse draws particular attention
      to Loewe's affinity for narrative poems and corresponding
      emphasis on musical depiction of text images. He argues
      that the composer's style was established by about 1820 and
      did not develop significantly thereafter. Appendices in-
      clude a list of poets whose texts Loewe set, a substantial
      discography, and reviews of Loewe's work.

388. Anton, Karl. "Aus Karl Loewes noch unveröffentlicher Lehre
      des Balladengesangs." **Zeitschrift für Musikwissenschaft** 2
      (1919-20): 235-39.

Collects statements by Loewe and recollections of his ideas by members of his circle on the singing of ballads. Emphasized are the importance of narrative objectivity, the necessity of maturity, attention to the text, and careful handling of expressive nuance.

389.   Bach, Albert B. **The Art Ballad: Loewe and Schubert.** 3rd ed. London: Kegan Paul, Trench, Trübner & Co., 1897. 215p.

The title is misleading--the book is really about Loewe. Bach begins with a brief introduction to the Lied, romance, and ballad. There is a biographical chapter on Loewe, an extremely cursory glance at Schubert, and an extended descriptive discussion of some of Loewe's ballads. List of Loewe's works, organized by publishers.

390.   Bulthaupt, Heinrich. **Carl Loewe, Deutschlands Balladenkomponist.** Berlin: Verlagsgesellschaft für Literatur und Kunst, 1898. 102p.

Recounts Loewe's biography, based on the composer's autobiography of 1870 and on other personal and family documents. Loewe's works are described, including a chapter on the ballads and another on his other works. Of broader interest is the book's first chapter, which discusses the nature of the ballad genre in both poetry and music. Illustrations; facsimiles of manuscript documents and music.

391.   Porter, E.G. "The Ballads of Carl Loewe." **The Music Review** 24 (1963): 134-38.

Evaluates the composer's ballad oeuvre. As compared to Schubert, Loewe was more masterful in dramatic sense and generally in establishing unity over long, narrative-form songs, while his purely musical gifts were more modest. Thus his talents and weaknesses suited him for the genre of ballads. Several pieces are described.

Witold Lutosławski
(b. 1913)

392.   Nordwall, Ove. "Fünf Iłłakowicz-Lieder von Witold Lutosławski." **Melos** 7 (1966): 212-16.

Describes the composer's cycle of five songs on poems of Kazimiera Iłłakowicz, composed for mezzo-soprano and piano in 1956-57 and re-scored for voice and thirty solo instru-

ments two years later. The discussion concentrates on the
scoring, from which Lutosŀawski obtains effects varying
from a lullaby to outbreaks of stormy drama.

Luzzasco Luzzaschi
(ca. 1545-1607)

393. Kinkeldey, Otto. "Luzzasco Luzzaschi's Solo-Madrigale mit
Klavierbegleitung." **Sammelbände der Internationalen
Musik-Gesellschaft** 9 (1907-8): 538-65.

Places these pieces in their music-historical context.
Describes the publication itself and the style of the
music. The madrigals are important evidence of the orna-
mental manner of performance in the late sixteenth century
and represent a contrast to the Florentine declamatory
style.

394. Racek, Jan. "Les Madrigaux à voix seule de Luzzasco Luzzaschi." **La Revue musicale** 13/2 (1932): 11-23.

Examines the Luzzaschi madrigals, particularly with regard to the vocal and the keyboard styles. Concludes that
these works represent a step in the direction of homophonic
conception, since the vocal lines become clearly separated
from the accompanying keyboard parts, which in turn are
reduced to a supporting role.

Alma Mahler
(1879-1964)

395. Schollum, Robert. "Die Lieder von Alma Maria Schindler-
Mahler." **Oesterreichische Musikzeitschrift** 34 (1979):
544-51.

Offers a general introduction to Alma Mahler's songs.
Biographical notes indicate that although Gustav Mahler
forbade his wife to compose, he respected her songs highly.
In general, her style was most strongly influenced by her
teacher Zemlinsky and by the harmonic ideas of Wagner as
well as the formal models of Brahms; it is comparable
therefore to the early songs of Schoenberg and Berg.
Schollum cites brief examples to illustrate the style.

Gustav Mahler
(1860-1911)

396. Adorno, Theodor W. "Zu einer imaginären Auswahl von Liedern
      Gustav Mahlers." In **Impromptus**, 30-38. Frankfurt am Main:
      Suhrkamp, 1968.

      Points out the subtlety with which Mahler's songs achieve
      the effect of simplicity through sophisticated devices.
      Adorno selects a few of Mahler's best-known songs with
      piano accompaniment to illustrate his penetrating observa-
      tions.

397. Agawu, V. Kofi. "The Musical Language of **Kindertotenlieder**
      No. 2." **The Journal of Musicology** 2 (1983): 81-93.

      Presents an analysis of the song from three points of
      view: generation of musical ideas from the text, melodic
      unity, and harmonic structure. Agawu first indicates how
      both foreground and long-range characteristics in the music
      reflect Rückert's poem. The organic development of the
      melodic material from a single scalar figure is then demon-
      strated. Finally, a linear analysis of the harmonic proce-
      dures in the song is offered. Supporting statements by
      Mahler are adduced.

398. Bruner, Ellen Carole. "The Relationship of Text and Music
      in the Lieder of Hugo Wolf and Gustav Mahler." Ph.D.
      diss., Syracuse University, 1974.   383p.

      Contrasts the songs of these two contemporary Viennese
      composers. Wolf's songs are more oriented toward intimate,
      poetically controlled, and sophisticated interpretations;
      Mahler was inclined to a more extroverted, musically struc-
      tured, and folk-derived style. The discussion centers on
      the style elements of melodic text treatment, harmony,
      accompaniment, and form. Form diagrams. Bibliography.

399. Dargie, E. Mary. **Music and Poetry in the Songs of Gustav
      Mahler.** European University Studies, Series 1, German
      Language and Literature, 401. Berne: Peter Lang, 1981.
      349p.

      After introductory chapters on the aesthetic problems and
      history of nineteenth-century song setting, discusses the
      relationships of poems and music in individual songs. Con-
      cludes that rather than reflecting surface features of the
      poems Mahler's music exploits the poetry to establish musi-

cal structures and atmosphere.

400. Diether, Jack. "Notes on Some Mahler Juvenilia." **Chord and Discord** 3/1 (1969): 3-100.

The middle section of this extended study, "Mahler and Heine" (pp. 65-76), treats two incomplete settings. One of these, Heine's "Im wunderschönen Monat Mai," appears to have been abandoned because the first strophe was set so languishingly that it could not be followed up. The other song, on a folksong text, may have presented a musical problem that the young Mahler could not yet solve. Both fragments already show the traces of the composer's later style.

401. Fischer, Jens Malte. "Das klagende Lied von der Erde: Zu Gustav Mahlers Liedern und ihren Texten." **Zeitschrift für Literaturwissenschaft und Linguistik** 9 (1979): 55-69.

Argues that Mahler's choice of texts was more focused than those of his contemporaries and followed a sensible development. Examines his changes in the texts.

402. Fischer, Kurt von. "Bemerkungen zu Gustav Mahlers Liedern." **Musikoloski Zbornik** 13 (1977): 57-67.

Deals with several aspects of Mahler's songs. The Wunderhorn texts and Mahler's free treatment of them are discussed. The influence of Schubert on the **Lieder eines fahrenden Gesellen** is noted, as is that of Berlioz in the orchestration of songs. The change of Mahler's style with the **Kindertotenlieder** to a more polyphonic, chamber-music-like texture is addressed. Finally the relation of the songs to the symphonies is discussed.

403. ————. "Gustav Mahlers Umgang mit Wunderhorntexten." **Melos/Neue Zeitschrift für Musik** 4 (1978): 103-7.

Clarifies aspects of Mahler's treatment of the Wunderhorn poetic material. Unlike the usual process in song composition, Mahler treated the text as material with which he could work as part of the composition process. His alterations and expansions of the poems allowed him to intensify their expressive effect and to make personal, subjective statements.

404. Gerlach, Reinhard. "Mahler, Rückert und das Ende des Liedes: Essay über lyrisch-musikalische Form." **Jahrbuch**

des staatlichen Instituts für Musikforschung 1975 (1976):
7-45.

Not examined. According to the entry in RILM (76/16326)
discusses relationships between poetry and music not only
in the area of form but also in rhythmic diction and
meaning.

405.   Hamm, Peter. "'Von Euch ich Urlaub nimm'. . .': Zu den von
       Gustav Mahler vertonten Texten." **Akzente** 24 (1977): 159-
       67.

Discusses Mahler's use of texts, concentrating on the
Wunderhorn texts. Stresses that Mahler's music is more
indissolubly bound to the texts than that of other composers and that the Lied serves as the core of all his
work. Gives special consideration to the significance of
traditional texts as material for music in current style.

406.   Kalisch, Volker. "Bemerkungen zu Gustav Mahler's **Kinder-
       totenliedern**--dargestellt am Beispiel des zweiten." **Muzi-
       koloski zbornik** 16 (1980): 30-51.

Analyzes the second song from **Kindertotenlieder** in technical terms, as well as discussing Mahler's philosophical
concern with the subject of death and the hereafter.

407.   Kravitt, Edward F. "Mahler's Dirges for His Death: February
       24, 1901." **The Musical Quarterly** 64 (1978): 329-53.

Proposes that a group of Mahler's songs--"Um Mitternacht," "Der Tambourg'sell," "Ich bin der Welt abhanden
gekommen," and **Kindertotenlieder**--reflect autobiographi-
cally the composer's own confrontation with potentially
fatal illness. The concept of immortality by the birth of
children was particularly important to Mahler. The music
of **Kindertotenlieder** is analyzed to show how Mahler's ideas
of death and the renewal of life are conveyed. Facsimiles.

408.   Pamer, Fritz Egon. "Gustav Mahlers Lieder." **Studien zur
       Musikwissenschaft** 16 (1929): 116-38; 17 (1930): 105-27.

An abridgement of Pamer's 1922 dissertation (subtitled
"Eine stilkritische Studie," University of Vienna), represents a major early study of Mahler's songs. A thorough
survey is made of the sources of the poetry and the alterations Mahler made in it, as was his general practice. The
musical style is described systematically in the areas of

formal structures, melody, rhythm, harmony, accompaniment.
Pamer stresses Mahler's roots in folk idiom.

409.   Rölleke, Heinz. "Gustav Mahlers 'Wunderhorn'-Lieder: Text-
       grundlagen und Textauswahl." **Jahrbuch des Freien
       Deutschen Hochstifts** (1981): 370-78.

       Not examined. The author's **RILM** abstract (81/3892) re-
       ports that the editions Mahler used for his texts are
       identified. The choices he made show his intuitive affin-
       ity for genuine folk poems rather than the more heavily
       adapted ones of the Wunderhorn anthology.

410.   Roman, Zoltan. "Bar Form in Mahler's Songs: Omission and
       Misconception." In **International Musicological Society,
       11th Congress Report, Copenhagen 1972**, 617-22.

       Regards Mahler as an important proponent of the revival
       of the Bar form. Seven of his vocal works are identified
       as utilizing the form; two, "Ich ging mit Lust" and "Der
       Einsame im Herbst," are analyzed. Analysis also shows that
       two works earlier considered to exemplify Bar form do not
       actually employ it, the fourth movement of the Third Sym-
       phony and the first movement of **Das Lied von der Erde.**

411.   ———. "The Pianoforte and Orchestral Manuscripts of
       Mahler's **Lieder eines fahrenden Gesellen:** Compositional
       Process as a Key to Chronology." **Bericht über den Inter-
       nationalen Musikwissenschaftlichen Kongress Berlin 1974,**
       402-4.

       Not examined. According to the author's **RILM** abstract
       (80/794), attempts to trace the compositional history of
       the songs by relating them to the Symphony no. 1. Focuses
       on the second song.

412.   ———. "Structure as a Factor in the Genesis of Mahler's
       Songs." **The Music Review** 35 (1974): 157-66.

       Attempts to show by analysis of the forms of the songs
       that Mahler achieved a balance between musical and literary
       principles. Takes issue with the common judgment that
       Mahler was extensively influenced by folksong. Roman finds
       that Mahler's songs are strongly dominated by variation
       forms and variation technique, which he interprets as indi-
       cating an avoidance of the musically governed strophic,
       Bar, and arch forms on the one hand, or text-controlled
       through-composition on the other.

413. Waeltner, Ernst-Ludwig. "Lieder-Zyklus und Volkslied-Meta-
      morphose: Zu den Texten der Mahlerschen Gesellenlieder."
      **Jahrbuch des Staatlichen Instituts für Musikforschung
      1977** (1978): 61-95.

      Not examined. The **RILM** abstract (78/791) indicates that
      the article contends that the folk element in Mahler's
      texts and music is only superficial.

Joseph Marx
(1882-1964)

414. Sims, Charles Kessler. "The **Italienisches Liederbuch** of
      Joseph Marx." Ph.D. diss., Indiana University, 1976.
      90p.

      Not examined. According to the **RILM** abstract (76/2991),
      deals principally with matters of performance. Bibliogra-
      phy.

415. Werba, Erik. "Italienische Liederbücher von Hugo Wolf und
      Joseph Marx." **Oesterreichische Musikzeitschrift** 25
      (1970): 600-607.

      Compares the two composers' settings of songs from
      Heyse's collection. The history of each set is recounted,
      Wolf's having occupied him from 1890 to 1896 and Marx's
      dating from 1912. In contrasting the styles of the two
      sets, Werba regards Wolf as a painter of characteristic
      detail and Marx as concerned with the general impression of
      the text.

Jules Massenet
(1842-1912)

416. Dorminy, Wendell Larry. "The Song Cycles of Jules
      Massenet." D.M.A. diss., Indiana University, 1977.   98p.

      Not examined. The author's abstract in **RILM** (77/652)
      indicates that the study has two components, a discussion
      of musical style and consideration of performance matters.

417. d'Udine, Jean. **L'Art du Lied et les mélodies de Massenet.**
      Paris: Heugel, 1931.   34p.

      Passionately defends Massenet's songs against detraction

and neglect.   Insists that the songs maintain the great
artistic values of the genre, such as concentration of
materials, judiciousness, and balance of elements.

Arnold Mendelssohn
(1855-1933)

418.   Werner-Jensen, Arnold. **Arnold Mendelssohn als Liederkomponist.** Winterthur: Amadeus, 1976.

Not examined.   Originally the author's Ph.D. dissertation
(Frankfurt am Main, 1974) and abstracted in **Die Musikforschung** 28 (1975): 332-33, places Mendelssohn (who has
been neglected since the Nazi period) in his proper context
in the development of song style.   Emphasizes the relationship of text and music, melody and accompaniment, form,
harmony, and preludes and postludes.   Regards Mendelssohn
as having extended the Classic-Romantic song tradition.
Bibliography; work-list.   Index of names.

419.   ————. "Erinnerung an Arnold Mendelssohn." **Melos/Neue
Zeitschrift für Musik** 3 (1977): 19-22.

Gives a general characterization of some of the stylistic
forces operating in Mendelssohn's songs.   Mendelssohn be-
longed to the generation of Wolf, Strauss, Pfitzner, and
Reger, and shared their exploration of the harmonic limits
of the tonal system.   The author illustrates the composer's
use of ballad style, folksong style, and large-scale,
through-composed style, as well as the exploration of chromaticism in Mendelssohn's late works.

Felix Mendelssohn Bartholdy
(1809-1847)

420.   Geck, Martin. "Sentiment und Sentimentalität im volkstümlichen Liede Felix Mendelssohn Bartholdys." **Hans Albrecht
in Memoriam: Gedenkschrift mit Beiträgen von Freunden** und
Schülern, edited by Wilfried Brennecke and Hans Haase,
200-206. Kassel: Bärenreiter, 1962.

Distinguishes between the Biedermeier sentimentality
which can be found in some of Mendelssohn's songs, and true
Romantic sentiment, which others evidence.   The genuine,
sincere sentiment is illustrated by a thorough examination
of "Gruss," op. 19, no. 5.

421. Stoner, Thomas. "Mendelssohn's Lieder not Included in the
      Werke." **Fontes artis musicae** 26 (1979): 258-66.

      Gives an annotated list of songs, citing locations and
      descriptions of the manuscript sources, dates and places in
      which they were composed, and identification of poets, as
      well as other comments. The list includes five unpublished
      songs that survive in autograph manuscripts, fourteen songs
      actually published but omitted from the **Werke**, five frag-
      ments, four songs for which no musical sources have been
      located, and seven songs that have not been authenticated.

422. ————. "Mendelssohn's Published Songs." Ph.D. diss., Uni-
      versity of Maryland, 1972. 428p.

      Not examined. According to the author's **RILM** abstract
      (72/582), places the seventy-three songs in historical,
      social, and biographical perspective. Examines each song.
      Mendelssohn's work in this genre is held to represent the
      transition from Classic to Romantic approaches. Work-list,
      bibliography; discography. Index.

423. Werba, Erik. "Der Lyriker Felix Mendelssohn-Bartholdy."
      Oesterreichische Musikzeitschrift 15 (1960): 17-21.

      "Leafs through" the Mendelssohn songs, noting the general
      spirit and quality of each one. At the end of the article
      are several suggestions for groupings of Mendelssohn's
      songs on recital programs. Werba hits the nail on the head
      when he suggests that the somewhat neglected composer has a
      well-deserved place in the history of the Lied beside
      Schumann and between Schubert and Brahms.

                          E.J. Moeran
                          (1894-1950)

*   Yenne, Vernon Lee. "Three Twentieth Century English Song
      Composers: Peter Warlock, E.J. Moeran and John Ireland."
      D.M.A. diss., University of Illinois, 1969. 313p.

      Cited above as item 350.

                       Claudio Monteverdi
                         (1567-1643)

424. Godt, Irving. "A Monteverdi Source Reappears: The

'Grilanda' of F.M. Fucci." **Music and Letters** 60 (1979): 428-39.

Reports the recovery of this source, which includes Monteverdi's "Lamento d'Arianna" and the "Lamento d'Erminia" attributed to him but probably spurious, as well as works by other composers. The manuscript collection now belongs to the Conservatorio di Musica "Benedetto Marcello" in Venice; its provenance is discussed in the article. The "Lamento d'Erminia" is printed, as is a facsimile of the manuscript's title page.

Thomas Morley
(1557 or 1558-1602)

425. Davie, Cedric Thorpe. "A Lost Morley Song Rediscovered." **Early Music** 9 (1981): 338-39.

Reports the discovery of Morley's "White as lillies" in a manuscript copy dating from the seventeenth century. The music, consisting of vocal line and bass, is printed with the article. The source also allows the correction of the text of verse 8, known previously in a corrupt version preserved in a copy of a setting by Dowland.

426. Greer, David. "The Lute Songs of Thomas Morley." **The Lute Society Journal** 8 (1966): 25-35.

Considers the music of **The First Book of Airs** of 1600. In general the songs reflect Morley's background as a madrigalist through their extensive and contrapuntally conceived lute parts, which sometimes depict or interpret the texts. Seven of the fourteen songs in the single, partially preserved exemplar are discussed. The texts also set by Dowland and Jones are compared (favorably) to those other settings.

Lawrence K. Moss
(b. 1927)

427. Barkin, Elaine. "Lawrence K. Moss: Three Rilke Songs from 'Das Stundenbuch' (1963)." **Perspectives of New Music** 6/1 (Fall-Winter 1967): 144-52.

Presents an analysis of the songs, describing in particular how Moss employs pitch-phoneme correspondences to ge-

nerate pitch content. Also treated are matters of rhythmic
planning, texture, and shaping.

Wolfgang Amadeus Mozart
(1756-1791)

428. Ballin, Ernst August. **Der Dichter von Mozarts Freimaurer-
lied "O heiliges Band" und das erste erhaltene deutsche
Freimaurerleiderbuch.** Tutzing: Hans Schneider, 1960.
vii, 44, 95p.

Discusses in model scholarly fashion the poet Ludwig
Friedrich Lenz (1717-1780) and his works, especially the
collection **Freimäurer-Lieder. Im Jahr 1746.** The complete
collection of nine Lieder is included in a facsimile reproduction. The book then considers Mozart's setting of "O
heiliges Band" and concludes that his text came from the
edition published in Regensburg in 1772. Appendices treat
the models for Lenz's song text "Lied derer Lehrlinge" and
the transmission of the poet's text in later Masonic song
books. Bibliography.

429. ─────. "Die Klavierlieder Mozarts." Ph.D. diss., Rheinische Friedrich-Wilhelms Universität of Bonn, 1943.
355p.

A thorough, critical study of Mozart's songs. Examines
history, texts, formal structure, and expressive means.
Concludes that the composer's music-dramatic skill made it
possible for him to charge his songs with a uniquely true-
to-life character. Bibliography.

430. ─────. **Das Wort-Ton-Verhältnis in den klavierbegleiteten
Liedern Mozarts.** Schriftenreihe der Internationalen
Stiftung Mozarteum 8. Kassel: Bärenreiter, 1984. 153p.

Shows how the composer interpreted his texts. The body
of the book (developed from the author's dissertation, item
430) consists of examination of the individual songs. The
pieces are grouped into types by form and style. The
opening and closing chapters place Mozart's songs in biographical and historical context. A special index lists
musical formulas the author considers important. Bibliography.

431. ─────. "Zu Mozarts Liedschaffen: Die Lieder KV 149-151, KV
52 und Leopold Mozart." **Acta Mozartiana** 8/2 (1961): 18-

24.

Applies the evidence of the manuscript sources to determining the authenticity of four songs generally attributed to Wolfgang Mozart. Concludes that in three cases ("Die grossmütige Gelassenheit" K. 149/125d, "Geheime Liebe" K. 150/125e, and "Die Zufriedenheit im niedrigen Stande" K. 151/125f) the pieces are by Leopold Mozart. The fourth song, "Daphne, deine Rosenwangen" K. 52/46c, is actually a piano transcription with a new text of the aria "Meiner Liebsten schöne Wangen" from **Bastien und Bastienne** and may be the work of either Leopold or Wolfgang Mozart.

432. Brown, Maurice J.E. "Mozart's Songs for Voice and Piano." **The Music Review** 17 (1956): 19-28.

Makes an excellent general survey of Mozart's song output. The compositional and publication history of these works is outlined. Analytical discussion concentrates on structural matters.

433. Friedlaender, Max. "Mozarts Lieder." In **Festschrift zum 90. Geburtstage Rochus Freiherrn von Liliencron**, 81-86. Leipzig: Breitkopf & Härtel, 1910. Reprint. Westmead, Farnborough, Hants.: Gregg, 1970.

Provides an overview of Mozart's songs. The problems of the authentic canon are discussed. Friedlaender places the Lieder in context, relating them to the song-like opera arias and citing some of the influences on their style. The music is successful when it partakes of the dramatic kind of expression developed in Mozart's operas and in finding a balance between the voice and the accompaniment. "Das Veilchen" receives special mention; it is regarded as the first "classical" Lied and the foundation of the genre of German art song.

434. Moser, Hans Joachim. "Mozart als Liederkomponist." **Oesterreichische Musikzeitschrift** 11 (1956): 90-94.

Summarizes Mozart's production of Lieder in chronological order. Although he wrote songs only sporadically, partly because they were inspired as occasional works and partly because the genre itself was not a major one, these Lieder constitute a valuable heritage.

435. Nettl, Paul. "Das Lied." In **Mozart Aspekte**, edited by Paul Schaller and Hans Kühner, 205-27. Olten: Otto Walter,

1956.

Examines the background of Mozart's songs and the development of their style. There is an extensive discussion
of "Das Veilchen," in which Mozart's setting is compared to
those of other composers.

436.   ————. "'Das Veilchen': Geschichte eines Liedes." **Mozart
Jahrbuch** 1955: 158-69.

A purely historical rather than analytical study. The
history of the text, from Goethe's play **Erwin und Elmira**,
and of its various settings is traced. Mozart's work is
placed in the context of the composition of songs in Vienna
at the time. In discussing Mozart's composition, Nettl
takes issue with the common notion that Mozart did not
actually know the identity of the poet. The history of the
sources is outlined. Mozart's situation at the time of the
composition is described.

437.   Reichert, Ernst. "Das Mozart-Lied." **Osterreichische Musikzeitschrift** 13 (1958): 161-62.

Commends Mozart's songs for study, arguing that the songs
remain too little known. Although not all of them are
appropriate for modern concert use, they may make useful
teaching pieces, and they represent the full range of song
styles of Mozart's time.

438.   Reijen, Paul-W. van. "Mozarts Lied 'An Chloe' in der
Fassung Wilhelm Gottlieb Hauffs." **Acta Mozartiana** 19
(1972): 60-70.

Not examined. The author's abstract in **RILM** (72/3271)
indicates that Hauff (ca. 1755-1817) wrote out an embel-
lished version of Mozart's song. The manuscript is in the
Toonkunst-Bibliothek in Amsterdam.

439.   Tenschert, Roland. "Rund um Mozarts 'Veilchen'." **Oesterreichische Musikzeitschrift** 15 (1960): 22-23.

Points out that unlike other composers who set "Das
Veilchen" Mozart used a through-composed design rather than
simple, folk-like, strophic form. Thus he was able to
respond to the subtleties of the text. Although Goethe
probably would have been opposed to the freedom of form,
Mozart opened the door directly to the new style of Schubert.

440. Werba, Erik. "Das Mozart-Lied in der Aufführungspraxis der
     Gegenwart." **Oesterreichische Musikzeitschrift** 22 (1967):
     452-56.

     Proposes applications of Mozart songs to specific voice
     types for modern recital use. The songs are related to
     Mozart opera roles to indicate which ones best suit partic-
     ular voices.

Modest Petrovich Musorgsky
(1839-1881)

441. Fedorov, Vladimir. "Sur un manuscrit de Moussorgskii: Les
     différentes éditions de ses Lieder." **Revue de musicologie**
     13 (1932): 10-23.

     Discusses an autograph manuscript collection containing
     seventeen of Musorgsky's songs and one arrangement, held in
     the Library of the Paris Conservatory. Discrepancies be-
     tween these and the published versions of the same songs
     are noted. Fedorov urges a new, scholarly edition of all
     of Musorgsky's songs.

442. Fox, Andrew C. "Evolution of Style in the Songs of Modest
     Mussorgsky." Ph.D. diss., Florida State University, 1974.
     iii, 139p.

     Divides Musorgsky's song oeuvre into three periods, re-
     spectively covering the years 1857-66, 1866-72, and 1874-
     79. Fox holds that Musorgsky's style developed in the
     direction of impressionism. Bibliography.

443. Lehmann, Dieter. "Satire und Parodie in den Liedern Modest
     Mussorgskis." **Beiträge zur Musikwissenschaft** 9/3 (1967):
     105-11.

     Not examined. The abstract by the author in **RILM**
     (68/2088) indicates that the article argues that the music
     not only satirizes but also reflects Russian culture.

444. Sydow, Brigitte. "Untersuchungen über die Klavierlieder
     M.P. Musorgskijs." Ph.D. diss., University of Göttingen,
     1974. 128p.

     Not examined. According to the author's abstract in **RILM**
     (75/3798), finds Musorgsky's search for "musical truth"
     illustrated in the songs, particulary those of his middle

period, which depart most sharply from the traditional
romance. Bibliography.

445. Walker, James. "Mussorgsky's **Sunless** Cycle in Russian Crit-
      icism: Focus of Controversy." **The Musical Quarterly** 67
      (1981): 382-91.

      Summarizes the criticism of Musorgsky's problematic song
      cycle. The songs represent the expression of a period of
      change in the composer's personal and artistic life. The
      critics have disagreed both on the quality of the cycle and
      on its significance for the understanding of Musorgsky's
      later years.

                    Christian Gottlob Neefe
                        (1748-1798)

446. Neely, James Bert. "Christian Gottlob Neefe's Early Vocal
      Style as Reflected in **Oden von Klopstock** (1776) and
      Serenaten beim Klavier zu singen (1777)." D.M.A. diss.,
      Indiana University, 1977. 256p.

      Not examined. According to the **RILM** abstract (77/582) by
      the author, deals with style, the composer's place in the
      history of the Lied, and his relationship to Beethoven.
      Includes an edition of the music. Work-list; bibliography.

                      C. Hubert H. Parry
                        (1848-1918)

447. Colles, H.C. "Parry as Song-Writer." **The Musical Times** 62
      (1921): 82-87.

      Surveys Sir Hubert Parry's song output, with descriptive
      and critical evaluations of a number of pieces. Parry is
      regarded as having achieved a personal style early and
      maintained it quite consistently through his career. His
      ability to adapt to a great variety of poetic subjects and
      styles is praised.

                        Jacopo Peri
                        (1561-1633)

448. Carter, Tim. "Jacopo Peri (1561-1633): Aspects of His Life
      and Works." **Proceedings of the Royal Musical Association**

105 (1978-79): 50-62.

Evaluates Peri's significance from the point of view of his monodies, represented particularly in the 1609 (reprinted 1619) collection **Le varie musiche.** Peri is judged to have been a well-trained and highly capable but somewhat conservative composer, who was finally unsuccessful in adapting to the rapidly changing style of his time.

Hans Pfitzner
(1869-1949)

449. Diez, Werner. **Hans Pfitzners Lieder: Versuch einer Stilbetrachtung.** Forschungsbeiträge zur Musikwissenschaft 21. Regensburg: Bosse, 1968. [iv], 126p.

Studies the style of Pfitzner's songs by comparison to those of other important Lied composers as well as in their own terms. The composer's works are divided into three style periods--an early period (to about 1890) in which Schumann seems to have been a strong influence; a middle phase (1901-ca. 1922) of fragmentation of the composer's style in search of an original synthesis; and a final, mature stage (from ca. 1922) in which unity is achieved among a polyphonic texture, declamation that is faithful to the text, and singable melody. List of Pfitzner's published songs by opus number. Indexes of songs and poets.

450. Lindlar, Heinrich. **Hans Pfitzners Klavierlied.** Würzburg: Triltsch, 1940.

A style-critical study, was the author's dissertation at the University of Cologne. The songs are grouped into five style periods: youth (1884-87), student and travel years (1888-89, 1894-95), mastery (1901-9, 1916), fulfillment (1922-24), and "Abgesang" (1931). Lindlar believes that in his fully developed style Pfitzner achieved a symbiosis of poetry and music. Brief bibliography; work-list.

451. Moser, Hans Joachim. "Hans Pfitzner als Liederkomponist" **Hellweg** 4/1 (1924): 192-96.

Surveys Pfitzner's Lied style in general, with brief characterizations of many songs. Notes the composer's affinity for the poetry of Eichendorff. Concludes by observing that Pfitzner's music is not self-consciously progressive and ranges from traditional to new and original

types of expression.   Precisely in that it is not "modish,"
the composer's oeuvre may have some claim to timelessness.

Ildebrando Pizzetti
(1880-1968)

452.   Antcliffe, Herbert. "Pizzetti as a Song Writer." **The
Chesterian**, new ser. 3 (1921-22): 108-11.

Discusses the seven songs of Ildebrando Pizzetti published between 1908 and 1918. The texts are described as
carefully reflective of the declamation of the spoken
words, while the mood is portrayed in the piano parts,
which seem to approach the orchestral in the use of leit-
motiv-like technique, sonorous effects, and in some cases,
difficulty.

453.   Gatti, Guido M. "Le **liriche** di Ildebrando Pizzetti." **Rivista musicale italiana** 26 (1916): 192-206.

After general discussion of aesthetic values in song,
discusses Pizzetti's work. On the whole, the composer is
praised for his choice of texts that suit his own artistic
inclinations and for the result that his melodies seem to
have been conceived together with the words. The accompaniments are kept in perfectly balanced relation to the
vocal lines, i.e., they seem to arise from the melody.
Several individual works are discussed in particular, more
in terms of their spirit than in regard to technical details.

John Playford
(1623-1686)

454.   Schleiner, Louise. "The Composer as Reader: A Setting of
George Herbert's 'Altar'." **The Musical Quarterly** 61
(1975): 422-32.

Discusses Herbert's poem, from **The Temple** of 1633, and
the setting, most probably by Playford. The composer both
matched the pictographic layout of the text and reflected
the poetic imagery of hard and soft in his composition.

Francis Poulenc
(1899-1963)

455.   Bernac, Pierre. **Francis Poulenc: The Man and His Songs.**
       Translated by Winifred Radford. London: Gollancz, 1977.
       233p.   Published in French as **Francis Poulenc et ses
       mélodies.** Paris: Buchet/Chastel, 1978.   220p.

       Includes a list of Poulenc's songs and brief biographical
       and critical chapters which profit from the authoritative
       voice of Bernac, one of the composer's close associates and
       collaborators.   The bulk of the text consists of song-by-
       song discussions of the repertoire from the point of view
       of performance interpretation.   Complete texts with paral-
       lel-column translations are provided.   (The French version
       does not include the texts.)   Indexes of songs by titles
       and first lines.

456.   Lockspeiser, Edward. "Francis Poulenc and Modern French
       Poets." **Monthly Musical Record** 7 (1940): 29-33.

       Regards Poulenc as especially successful in interpreting
       surrealist poetry, in particular that of Guillaume Apol-
       linaire, Max Jacob, and Paul Eluard.

457.   Wood, Vivian Lee Poates. **Poulenc's Songs: An Analysis of
       Style.** Jackson, Mississippi: University Press of Missis-
       sippi, 1979.   xiii, 173p.

       Offers detailed analytical treatment of melody, harmony,
       form, and piano accompaniment.   The author argues that
       Poulenc's style is generally based on conventional musical
       language, used eclectically and always adapted to the exi-
       gencies of text expression.   Form diagrams.   Bibliography;
       catalogue of published songs.   Indexes.

Sergei Prokofiev
(1891-1953)

458.   Evans, Robert Kenneth. "The Early Songs of Sergei Prokofiev
       and their Relation to the Synthesis of the Arts in
       Russia, 1890-1922." Ph.D. diss., Ohio State University,
       1971.   302p.

       Not examined.   According to the author's abstract in **RILM**
       (71/2550), places the poetry and the music in cultural and
       ideological context.   Prokofiev's songs, which respond to a

variety of artistic styles represented by their texts, are
held to stand out as the culmination of Russian song
against the stagnation of the genre in the Soviet socialist
climate. Translations are provided. Bibliography.

Henry Purcell
(1659-1695)

459. Rohrer, Katherine Tinley. "The Energy of English Words: A
      Linguistic Approach to Henry Purcell's Methods of Setting
      Texts." Ph.D. diss., Princeton University, 1980. 278p.

      Not examined. The author's abstract in **Dissertation
      Abstracts** (41A [1980]: 846-A) indicates that the study
      proposes a system, based on contemporary evidence, for
      analysis of text settings by Purcell and applies that
      system to discussion of a number of works. Especially
      relevant here are Chapters 6 and 7, which deal with the
      songs in particular.

460. Rose, Gloria. "A New Purcell Source." **Journal of the Ameri-
      can Musicological Society** 25 (1972): 230-36.

      Reports on Yale University, Beinecke Rare Book and Manu-
      script Library, Osborn Collection, MS 9, which contains
      vocal parts only for a number of songs, including nine
      (some from theatrical works) by Purcell. The songs were
      copied by 1692 for the use of a singer and include written-
      out ornaments and indications of inequality. These reflect
      contemporary performance practice and taste. Facsimile
      reproductions of two pages of Purcell songs.

461. Zimmerman, Franklin B. "Sound and Sense in Purcell's
      'Single Songs'." In **Words to Music: Papers on English
      Seventeenth-Century Song Read at a Clark Library Seminar,
      December 11, 1965,** by Vincent Duckles and Franklin B.
      Zimmerman, 43-90. Los Angeles: William Andrews Clark
      Memorial Library, University of California, 1967.

      Establishes the historical context for Purcell's songs
      with regard to the principles of text setting during his
      era. Purcell's earlier songs are more strictly based on
      musical paralleling of the prosody of the texts, while in
      later works he added to this more freedom to apply illus-
      trative figures and generate thematic unity. In his last
      years he also contributed to a pseudo-folksong style.
      Tables. Representative song texts.

Roger Quilter
(1877-1953)

462. Banfield, Stephen. "Roger Quilter: A Centenary Note." **The
      Musical Times** 118 (1977): 903-6.

      An honest, critical view of Quilter's work. Banfield
      suggests that although much of Quilter's work lacks great
      depth, the facility and sentimentality of expression in
      many of the songs may be attributed to a counterbalance of
      the composer's painful personal life. Nevertheless, sev-
      eral songs--not always the most popular--do display pro-
      found feeling.

463. Goddard, Scott. "The Art of Roger Quilter." **The Chesterian**
      6 (1925): 213-17.

      Praises Quilter warmly but undermines the praise by the
      critical details of the discussion. Extols the composer as
      "the last reputable upholder of the best traditions of the
      English drawing-room song." He is criticized for the
      choice of trivial texts and the unimaginative treatment of
      his best texts. Quilter's work falls short in comparison
      to that of true art song composers. Regarded as successful
      are his grateful writing for the voice and his effective
      harmony and piano textures.

464. Hold, Trevor. **The Walled-In Garden: A Study of the Songs of
      Roger Quilter (1877-1953).** Bibliographical Series 8.
      Rickmansworth: Triad, 1978. 71p.

      Surveys the songs of Quilter. A brief biographical out-
      line is provided, together with observations on the style,
      and a chronological overview of the music. The author
      recognizes Quilter's limitations but argues for a more
      favorable judgment than Quilter has generally received.
      Music examples are placed on separate pages at the back of
      the book. Appendices include checklists of songs and poets
      whose texts Quilter set. Bibliography; discography. Index
      of names.

465. Raphael, Mark. "Roger Quilter, 1877-1953: The Man and His
      Songs." **Tempo** 30 (1953-54): 20.

      Concentrates on the virtues of Quilter's song style:
      flowing melody that is grateful to the singer and to the
      poetry, pianistic accompaniments, and conservative harmony.

Sergei Vassilievich Rachmaninov
(1873-1943)

466. Brewerton, Erik. "Rachmaninov's Songs." **Music and Letters**
15 (1934): 32-36.

Criticizes Rachmaninov's songs as too self-indulgent in
musical gesture. The author argues that, at least for
English tastes, the music seems to lack restraint in both
vocal and keyboard parts, and to overwhelm the poems. A
few songs are spared this criticism--mostly the brief, more
introverted ones.

467. Simpson, Anne. "Dear Re: A Glimpse into the Six Songs of
Rachmaninoff's Opus 38." **College Music Symposium** 24/1
(Spring 1984): 97-106.

Deals with the relationship between Rachmaninov and the
writer Marietta Sergeyevna Shaginian (1888-1982). She was
a close friend of the composer and conversed and corresponded with him on artistic matters. She also gathered
texts which he set as songs in his op. 34 and the Six Songs
for Soprano, op. 38. The op. 38 songs are discussed briefly, with notes on the poets and a characterization of each
piece. Portraits of Rachmaninov and Shaginian.

Francesco Rasi
(1574-after 1620)

468. Einstein, Alfred. "Ein Emissär der Monodie in Deutschland:
Francesco Rasi." In **Musikwissenschaftliche Beiträge:
Festschrift für Johannes Wolf zu seinem sechzigsten Ge-
burtstage**, edited by Walter Lott, Helmuth Osthoff, and
Werner Wolffheim, 31-34.

Points out the importance of Rasi's transmission of the
Italian monodic style to German territory. Brief remarks
are made on his life and musical style. A manuscript
collection of his works prepared for the Prince Arch-
bishop's court in Salzburg and owned by the Proske Library
in Regensburg seems to represent the first appearance of
monody in the German-speaking world.

469. MacClintock, Carol. "The Monodies of Francesco Rasi." **Journal of the American Musicological Society** 14 (1961): 31-
36.

Discusses Rasi's two collections of monodies, **Le vaghezze di musica** of 1608 and **Madrigale di diversi autori** 1610, totaling thirty-six songs. They include strophic arias, madrigals, and strophic variations. The songs show Rasi to have been an especially gifted melodist. Both books show ornaments, the earlier one more completely.

Maurice Ravel
(1875-1937)

* Böhmer, Helga. "Alchimie der Töne: Die Mallarmé-Vertonungen von Debussy und Ravel." **Musica** 22 (1968): 83-85.

  Cited above as item 257.

470. Gronquist, Robert. "Ravel's Trois Poèmes de Stéphane Mallarmé." **The Musical Quarterly** 64 (1978): 507-23.

  Gives the compositional history of the songs, as well as an extended description and critique of each setting. Mallarmé's symbolist texts evoked a colorful harmonic and sonorous language from the composer. The structure is governed by a tripartite conception with clear links among the songs. The progress of ideas seems to follow a plan from relative clarity to the brink of absurdism.

* Hirsbrunner, Theo. "Zu Debussys und Ravels Mallarmé-Vertonungen." **Archiv für Musikwissenschaft** 35 (1978): 81-103.

  Cited above as item 265.

Max Reger
(1873-1916)

471. Wehmeyer, Grete. "Der Liederkomponist Reger in seiner Zeit." In **Max Reger in seiner Zeit,** edited by Siegfried Kross, 45-49. Bonn: Rheinische Friedrich-Wilhelms Universität, 1973.

  Places Reger's Lied composition in historical perspective. The composer began in the period of tension between the New German School and the conservative style, and ultimately emerged into a neo-Classic style. Most characteristic for Reger, however, is his middle period (opp. 55-104) which featured a declamatory vocal style and keyboard parts that are quite independent.

472.   ————. **Max Reger als Liedkomponist: Ein Beitrag zum Prob-
        lem der Wort-Ton-Beziehung.** Kölner Beiträge zur Musik-
        forschung 8. Regensburg: Bosse, 1955. 331p.

Makes a stylistic study of Reger's nearly three hundred
songs. The discussion deals with four matters: vocal declamation, piano accompaniments, textual and musical form,
and the musical response to poetic content in general.
Facsmiles of song manuscripts. Lists of works, poets.
Bibliography.

473.   Wirth, Helmuth. "Max Reger und seine Dichter." In **Reger-
        Studien 1: Festschrift für Ottmar Schreiber zum 70.
        Geburtstag am 16.** Februar 1976, edited by Günther
        Massenkeil and Susanne Popp, 47-57. Schriftenreihe des
        Max-Reger-Instituts Bonn-Bad Godesberg 1. Wiesbaden:
        Breitkopf & Härtel, 1978.

Not examined. According to the **RILM** abstract (78/6387)
considers a number of aspects of Reger's choices of poets.
He employed both prominent authors of earlier years and his
contemporaries. Special attention is given to his use of
texts of Christian Morgenstern, and to political topics.

                    Johann Friedrich Reichardt
                         (1752-1814)

474.   Pauli, Walther. **Johann Friedrich Reichardt: Seine Leben und
        seine Stellung in der Geschichte des deutschen Liedes.**
        Musikwissenschaftliche Studien 2. Berlin: Ebering, 1903.
        228p.

Devotes itself mostly to Reichardt's biography, with a
briefer second part on his works. He is regarded as a link
between the First Berlin School and Schubert. A single
chapter concisely but cogently describes the style of his
songs, noting the year 1779 as the watershed between his
early and mature works. Index.

475.   Salmen, Walter. **Johann Friedrich Reichardt: Komponist,
        Schriftsteller, Kapellmeister und Verwaltungsbeamter der
        Goethezeit.** Freiburg: Atlantis, 1963. 363p.

Surveys the composer's life and accomplishments. Besides
outlining the biography, Salmen discusses separately each

of the fields in which the versatile Reichardt worked and his philosophical positions. Considerable attention is given to his musical compositions in all genres. As a song composer, he is judged to have been the most substantial link between the continuo-Lied and the Romantic Lied. Bibliography. Index of names.

Hermann Reutter
(b.1900)

476. Reutter, Hermann. "Meine Lieder-Zyklen auf Gedichte von Lorca." **Melos** 9 (1963): 283-91.

Describes the **Spanischer Totentanz** of 1953, **Drei Zigeu-nerromanzen** of 1956 , **Kleine Requiem** of 1961, **Andalusiana** of 1962. Emphasizes the variety of musical styles employed.

Ned Rorem
(b. 1923)

477. Miller, Philip Lieson. "The Songs of Ned Rorem." **Tempo** 127 (December 1978): 25-31.

Characterizes Rorem as a conservative, with illustrations of his musical style. He uses standard materials with craftsmanship and unusual sensitivity to poetry.

478. Pilar, Lillian Nobleza. "The Vocal Style of Ned Rorem in the Song Cycle **Poems of Love and the Rain.**" Ph.D. diss., Indiana University, 1972. 96p.

Not examined. According to the author's **RILM** abstract (72/2033), gives biography, excerpts of Rorem's writings, and analyses covering melody, rhythm, harmony, tonality, form, text-setting. Identifies influences of neo-Classic and neo-Baroque style, jazz, Satie, Poulenc. Work-list.

Philip Rosseter
(1567 or 1568-1623)

479. Fortune, Nigel. "Philip Rosseter and His Songs." **Lute Society Journal** 7 (1965): 7-14.

Gives a biography of Rosseter and a general stylistic

description of his lute songs. The author believes that
Rosseter wrote both texts and music. His style is harmoni-
cally simple but lively in rhythm and melody.

Luigi Rossi
(ca. 1597-1653)

480. Caluori, Eleanor. **The Cantatas of Luigi Rossi: Analysis and
Thematic Index.** 2 vols. Studies in Musicology 41. Ann
Arbor, Mich.: UMI Research Press, 1981. 303, 212p.

Is a revision of the author's 1972 Ph.D. dissertation
(Eleanor Caluori Venables) from Brandeis University.
Volume 1 discusses texts and structures of the cantatas,
concentrating on the **ariette corte.** Volume 2 consists of
an annotated thematic index, giving source locations. Bibliography. Index.

481. ————. **Luigi Rossi (ca. 1598-1653).** Wellesley Edition
Cantata Index Series 3. Wellesley College, 1965.

Gives textual and musical incipits, concordances to previous catalogues, and sources. There are two fascicles; 3a
gives cantatas reliably attributed to Rossi, 3b those for
which the grounds for attribution are unreliable. Appendices.

Edmund Rubbra
(b. 1901)

482. Banfield, Stephen. "Rubbra's Songs." In **Edmund Rubbra:
Composer--Essays,** edited by Lewis Foreman, 89-95. Rick-
mansworth, Herts.: Triad, 1977.

Emphasizes the unique character of Rubbra's songs, which
contrast with those of his immediate predecessors and
which, over the development of his career, take on a more
modern style and aesthetic approach. "Orpheus" is discussed in detail as a "touchstone of musical sensitivity."

Joseph Boulogne Saint-Georges
(ca. 1739-1799)

483. de Lerma, Dominique-René. "Two Friends within the Saint-
Georges Songs." **The Black Perspective in Music** 1 (1973):

115-19.

Identifies two items from a manuscript collection of
Saint-Georges's songs. One is a setting of the poem "Dans
un bois solitaire," also used by Mozart. The other is a
song from Beaumarchais's **Le Barbier de Seville**, set by
Antoine Laurent Baudron and arranged by Saint-Georges. The
complete musical and poetic texts of both Saint-Georges
songs are included, as well as Baudron's song.

Othmar Schoeck
(1886-1957)

484. Corrodi, Hans. "Othmar Schoeck's Songs." **Music and Letters**
29 (1948): 129-39.

Divides Schoeck's song-composing career into three
periods with turning points at 1918 and 1944. The first
period is that of Schoeck's attainment of compositional
maturity and is characterized by optimism; the second is
pessimistic and confessional; the third is introspective.
A number of representative songs are described. Discography.

485. Hirsbrunner, Theo. "Othmar Schoeck: Zwischen Romantik und
Moderne." **Musica** 35 (1981): 246-49.

Considers Schoeck's position in the historical development of musical style, illustrating with examples from the
songs. Schoeck was conscious of the progress of style, and
Hirsbrunner attempts to show that his harmonic and tonal
language was not simply conservative. In rhythm, however,
he seems to be more traditional. Facsimile of part of the
autograph of "Sommernacht" on Hesse's text, op. 44.

486. Isler, Ernst. "Othmar Schoecks Frühlied: Eine Studie zur
Entwicklungsgechichte des Komponisten." In **Othmar
Schoeck: Festgabe der Freunde zum 50. Geburtstag**, edited
by Willi Schuh, 92-119. Erlenbach-Zurich: Eugen Rentsch,
1936.

Discusses the composer's fifty-nine songs written from
1903 to 1909. Isler identifies the poets whose works
Schoeck set, the forms he used (mostly through-composed),
and the influences of other Lied composers. He then takes
up a large number of the songs individually.

487.   Puffett, Derrick. **The Song Cycles of Othmar Schoeck.** Pub-
       likationen der Schweizerischen Musikforschenden Gesell-
       schaft, Ser. II, vol. 32. Bern: Paul Haupt, 1982. viii,
       482p.

       Presents a critical analysis of Schoeck's cycles. After
       outlining their biographical and historical context,
       Puffett discusses each of the cycles in turn. He concludes
       that the composer's music reflects aspects of his biogra-
       phy, and he views Schoeck as combining the nineteenth-
       century traditions of Lied composition with a twentieth-
       century technical language. Appendices provide a chronol-
       ogy of Schoeck's early songs and a list of texts set by
       Schoeck and by other composers. Bibliography, discography.
       Indexes.

488.   Tiltmann-Fuchs, Stefanie. **Othmar Schoecks Liederzyklen für
       Singstimme und Orchester.** Kölner Beiträge zur Musik-
       forschung 86. Regensburg: Bosse, 1976. 182p.

       Not examined. The author's **RILM** abstract (76/11242)
       states that four cycles, opp. 36, 40, 66, and 70, are
       analyzed. Includes biography of Schoeck.

489.   ———. **Wesenszüge von Othmar Schoecks Liedkunst.** Zurich:
       Juris, 1950. 230p.

       First establishes a background for Schoeck's songs in
       relation to the principles of song composition, the influ-
       ences on the composer, and his poets and poetry. The
       discussion of the music begins with the melodic style,
       which is viewed as governed more by musical principles than
       by text-painting. Vogel then deals with the "ostinato
       technique" whereby a brief musical unit becomes a model
       that is continued and developed over the course of the
       song. Work-list; bibliography. Index of names.

Arnold Schoenberg
(1874-1951)

490.   Adorno, Theodor Wiesengrund. "Situation des Liedes." **An-
       bruch** 10 (1928): 363-69.

       Claims that the model for Lied composition after the end
       of Romanticism is Schoenberg. Schoenberg's objectification
       of the genre represents for Adorno the most satisfactory
       solution to the problems confronted by song composers of

the day. The George songs are cited as exemplary. Other
song composers are briefly mentioned.

491. Brinkmann, Reinhold. "Schönberg und George: Interpretation
eines Liedes." **Archiv für Musikwissenschaft** 26 (1969): 1-
28.

Analyzes Schoenberg's setting of Stefan George's poetry
in op. 15, no. 4. There is a detailed analysis of the text
following George's cue that the components of poetry are
"Ton, Bewegung, Gestalt." An extremely thorough discussion
of the music occupies the body of the article. Brinkmann
reasons that the setting of George's texts helped Schoenberg in this period of atonal composition to achieve unity
of tonal material, perfection of structure, and concentration of expression.

492. ————. "Schönberg's Lieder." In **Arnold Schönberg**, edited
by Carl Dahlhaus, 44-50. Berlin: Akademie der Künste,
1974.

Summarizes and discusses the history of Schoenberg's
Lieder and offers critical remarks on the oeuvre and on
individual works. Special attention is given to the importance of the settings of texts by George, with whose ideas
Schoenberg found himself in sympathy. In setting these
poems the composer made significant musical progress.

493. Dahlhaus, Carl. "Schoenbergs Lied 'Streng ist uns das gluck
und spröde'." In **Neue Wege der musikalische Analyse**, 45-
52. Veröffentlichungen des Instituts für neue Musik und
Musikerziehung Darmstadt 6. Berlin: Merseburger, 1967.

Offers a detailed analysis of Schoenberg's setting of
George's poem. Dahlhaus argues that the song falls into
the category of "narrative" rather than "lyrical" style.

494. Dean, Jerry Mac. "Evolution and Unity in Schoenberg's
George Songs op. 15." Ph.D. diss., University of Michigan, 1971. 209p.

Not examined. The abstract in **RILM** (71/3943) states that
the study reveals the evolution of Schoenberg's tonal language and the diversity of style in the George songs. Pre-
serial means of achieving unity in atonal music are illustrated.

495. ————. "Schoenberg's Vertical-Linear Relationships in

1908." **Perspectives of New Music** 12 (1973-74): 173-80.

Demonstrates by excerpts from the **Georgelieder,** op. 15, nos. 6, 2, and 11 that as early as 1908 Schoenberg had begun to develop a technique in which groups of unordered pitch classes with identical or similar interval-class vectors were used both vertically and horizontally. Diagrams.

496. Dill, Heinz J. "Schoenberg's **George-Lieder:** The Relationship between Text and Music in Light of Some Expressionist Tendencies." **Current Musicology** 17/1974: 91-95.

Points out Schoenberg's abandonment of traditional concepts of text-setting (i.e., the reflection of surface features of the poetic text in the music). Schoenberg rather redefined the relationship of words and music, dissolving George's tightly structured poetry into prose. This, in turn, liberates the "real content" of the work.

497. Domek, Richard. "Some Aspects of Organization in Schoenberg's **Book of the Hanging Gardens,** Opus 15." **College Music Symposium** 19/2 (Fall 1979): 111-28.

Shows that in the songs of this set the music is highly, if subtly, concentrated. Illustrates how harmony is focused on specific chords and "normal" progressions, how coherence is achieved by contrapuntal and melodic use of motives and by linear motion, and how melodic motion is deliberately planned. Includes specific analysis of structural unifying techniques in song 8.

498. Dümling, Albrecht. "Oeffentliche Einsamkeit: Untersuchungen zur Situation von Lied und Lyrik um 1900 am Beispiel **des Buches der hängenden Gärten** von Stefan George und Arnold Schönberg." Ph.D. diss., Technische Universität, Berlin, 1978. 2 vols., 580p.

Not examined. According to the **RILM** abstract (78/6362) takes an aesthetic, sociological, and cultural-history approach. (This approach sets the study apart from the substantial number of more technical, analytical treatments of op. 15.) Bibliography.

499. Ehrenforth, Karl Heinrich. **Ausdruck und Form: Schönbergs Durchbruch zur Atonalität in den George-Liedern Op. 15.** Abhandlungen zur Kunst-, Musik-, und Literaturwissenschaft 18. Bonn: Bouvier, 1963. [iv], 161p.

Analyzes the George-Lieder in terms of literary-musical relationships. Ehrenforth argues that the George-Lieder represent the culmination of the Romantic song cycle tradition as well as a progressive leap into modern, atonal style. In the sense that Schoenberg seems to have been seeking a balance between musical ideals of form/restraint (the Brahms tradition of the late nineteenth century) and expression/freedom (the Wagner-Wolf tradition), the study suggests that it is inadequate to categorize these songs as "expressionist." Bibliography.

500.   ————. "Schönberg und Webern: Das XIV. Lied aus Schönbergs Georgeliedern op. 15." **Neue Zeitschrift für Musik** 126 (1965): 102-5.

Attempts to clarify Schoenberg's complex aesthetic position. The song "Sprich nicht immer vom dem Laub, Windesraub" is seen as exceptional among the songs of the George set. In its compact and abstract style it suggests the influence of Webern, who was in close contact with Schoenberg through the years just preceding its composition. The difference between the two composers is that for Schoenberg miniatures served as stepping-stones to larger works, whereas Webern conceived miniatures as ends in themselves.

501.   Kaufmann, Harald. "Struktur in Schoenbergs Georgeliedern." In **Neue Wege der musikalische Analyse,** 53-61. Veröffentlichungen des Instituts für neue Musik und Musikerziehung Darmstadt 6. Berlin: Merseburger, 1967.

Analyzes the first song of the George-Lieder, "Unterm schütz vom dichten blättergründen," with regard to both pitch structure and the rhythmic declamation of the vocal line. The author concludes that although no abstract theoretical system is applied in these compositions, they manifest a satisfactory practical approach to musical construction.

502.   Lessem, Alan Philip. **Music and Text in the Works of Arnold Schoenberg: The Critical Years, 1908-1922.** Studies in Musicology 8. Ann Arbor, Michigan: UMI Research Press, 1979. vii, 247p.

From the author's 1973 University of Illinois dissertation, investigates text-music relationships in all the vocal works between the dissolution of tonality and the twelve-tone system. Of these works, only the George-Lieder belong to the tradition of the Lied, and they are given

substantial treatment. The set is considered to be both
the closure of the nineteenth-century song cycle and the
opening of a new style. Each song is discussed separately.
Bibliography. Index.

503. Lewin, David. "Toward the Analysis of a Schoenberg Song
(Op. 15, No. XI)." **Perspectives of New Music** 12 (1973-
74): 43-86.

Offers a highly detailed analysis of various levels of
musical activity in the song, from elements of its melodic,
harmonic, and rhythmic construction to its overall shape.
These suggest musico-dramatic interpretations. The complete song is included.

504. Neumann, Peter Horst. "Schönberg, George, Petrarca: Zur
Textwahl von Opus 8 bis Opus 24." In **Bericht über den 1.
Kongress der Internationalen Schönberg-Gesellschaft, Wien
4. bis 9. Juni 1974,** edited by Rudolf Stephan, 140-46.
Publikationen der Internationalen Schönberg-Gesellschaft
1. Vienna: Elisabeth Lafite, 1978.

Investigates the reasons for Schoenberg's selection of
specific texts for the works of the first part of his
atonal period and for the beginning of the use of twelve-
tone technique. Neumann argues that the texts of the two
poets share with Schoenberg's music a special quality of
nobility and intellectuality.

505. Neuwirth, Gösta. "Schönbergs George-Lieder op. 15: Die
Entwürfe zum XIV. Lied." In **Bericht über den 1. Kongress
der Internationalen Schönberg-Gesellschaft, Wien 4. bis
9. Juni 1974,** edited by Rudolf Stephan, 147-58. Publikationen der Internationalen Schönberg-Gesellschaft 1.
Vienna: Elisabeth Lafite, 1978.

Studies the two drafts for the song, which show the
composer's compositional process. The two do not represent
successive stages in a course toward the completed song but
two different approaches each of which contributes something to the final product.

506. Ruf, Wolfgang. "Arnold Schoenbergs Lied 'Herzgewächse'."
Archiv für Musikwissenschaft 41 (1984): 257-73.

Contemplates the uniqueness of "Herzgewächse," op. 20,
for soprano, celesta, harmonium, and harp. A penetrating
analysis of both text and music leads to the conclusion

that the song constitutes the key work in Schoenberg's
expressionist phase. It is significant that the piece
first appeared in conjunction with the essay "Das Verhältnis zum Text," as a sort of practical demonstration of the
ideas propounded there.

507. Stein, Leonard. "Toward a Chronology of Schoenberg's Early
      Unpublished Songs." **Journal of the Arnold Schoenberg
      Institute** 2 (October 1977): 72-80.

      Based on research with the sources, compiles a working
      chronological list of thirty-three songs dating from 1893
      to 1900. The list gives dates, titles and first lines,
      authors' names, and sources.

508. Stroh, Wolfgang Martin. "Schoenberg's Use of Text: The Text
      as a Musical Control in the 14th **Georgelied,** Op. 15."
      Perspectives of New Music 6/2 (Spring-Summer 1968): 35-
      44.

      Analyzes the song to show how Schoenberg incorporated the
      text into the compositional structure of the song. The
      individual words control the form rather than the content
      of the music. Stroh argues that the text is not merely an
      external substitute for musical coherence but a source of
      musical growth.

509. Weber, Horst. "Schönbergs und Zemlinskys Vertonung der
      Ballade 'Jane Grey' von Heinrich Ammann: Untersuchungen
      zum Spätstudium der Tonalität." **International Musicologi-
      cal Society, Report of the Eleventh Congress, Copenhagen
      1972,** 705-14.

      Contrasts the two composers' approaches to the dissolu-
      tion of tonality, using settings of the same text from the
      same time. Schoenberg's ballad is seen as progressive,
      forming part of the transition to atonality, while
      Zemlinsky's explores the limits of the tonal sytem without
      giving up reliance on it.

                          Franz Schreker
                          (1878-1934)

510. Budde, Elmar. "Ueber Metrik und Deklamation in den **Fünf
      Gesängen** für tiefe Stimme." In **Franz-Schreker-Symposium,**
      edited by Elmar Budde and Rudolf Stephan, 37-48.
      Schriftenreihe der Hochschule der Künste Berlin 1.

Berlin: Colloquium, 1980.

Not examined. According to the author's abstract in **RILM** (80/859), suggests that Schreker's melodic style tends to be similar to that of Schoenberg, while his treatment of rhythm resembles Webern's.

Franz Schubert
(1797-1828)

SURVEYS

511. Bauer, Moritz. **Die Lieder Franz Schuberts.** Vol. 1. Leipzig: Breitkopf & Härtel, 1915. Reprint. Walluf bei Wiesbaden: Sändig, 1972. x, 258p.

Seeks to demonstrate how Schubert's style varied according to the poets whose texts he set. The brief introduction outlines the chronological divisions of Schubert's song oeuvre and discusses the stylistic features of his Lieder in general. The author then turns to brief characterizations of each of the songs. The body of the study was organized according to groups of poets; only volume 1 was published, covering the older poets Schubert set-- Herder, Klopstock, the Göttinger Hainbund, and their contemporaries up to Schiller--and Goethe. Table listing songs (by poet), dates of composition, and forms.

512. Bell, A. Craig. **The Songs of Schubert.** Lowestoft: Alston Books, 1964. ix, 163p.

Discusses briefly a large number of what the author considers the best of Schubert's songs. Introductory chapters cursorily outline the earlier history of song and the composer's style in general. The songs are presented in chronological order. Appendices include a note on performance, a list of all Schubert's songs, and a list of poets. Facsimile details from the autograph manuscript of **Winterreise.** Indexes.

513. Brown, Maurice J.E. **Schubert Songs.** BBC Music Guides 9. London: British Broadcasting Corporation, 1967; Seattle: University of Washington Press, 1969. 62p.

Gives a brief, style-critical survey of Schubert's

Lieder, organized by poets.

514. Capell, Richard. **Schubert's Songs.** London: Benn, 1928.
      Reprint. New York: Da Capo, 1977. xi, 294p. (2nd ed.
      London: Benn, 1957; 3rd. ed. London: Pan Books, 1973.)

      After initial chapters on Schubert, his texts, and his
      style, attempts a survey of all the songs. Capell provides
      brief comments on each song, and these range from perfunc-
      tory description to insightful criticism. This is a sig-
      nificant work in the Schubert literature, which continues
      to be cited in more recent studies. Appendices; indexes.

515. Curzon, Henri de. **Les Lieder de Franz Schubert.** Paris:
      Fischbacher, 1899. 113p.

      Makes a very quick survey of Schubert's songs in an essay
      that touches variously on Schubert's poets, sources, and
      the character or quality of some songs. A concluding
      section discusses the reception of Schubert's Lieder in
      France. Worklist; very cursory and dated bibliography.

516. Fischer-Dieskau, Dietrich. **Auf den Spuren der Schubert-
      Lieder: Werden-Wesen-Wirkung.** Wiesbaden: F.A. Brockhaus,
      1971; also published in English translation by Kenneth S.
      Whitton as **Schubert: A Biographical Study of his Songs**
      (London: Cassell, 1976) and as **Schubert's Songs: A Bio-
      graphical Study** (New York: Knopf, 1977), and in French
      translation by Michel François Demet as **Les Lieder de
      Schubert** (Paris: R. Laffont, 1979). The American edition
      was examined for the present bibliography.

      Traces Schubert's life, with comments on the songs as
      they appear in the course of the chronology. The biograph-
      ical material draws significantly on quotations from docu-
      ments. The songs are treated in various ways, ranging from
      criticism to characterization to performance suggestions.
      Concluding chapters discuss the reception of Schubert's
      songs after his death and some of the important interpre-
      tive artists. Indexes of songs, names.

517. Fox Strangways, A.H. "Schubert in His Songs." **Music and
      Letters** 9 (1928): 297-303.

      Establishes perspective on Schubert's life and work,
      emphasizing that the man is to be understood more through
      his works than through his biography. Schubert's style is
      described, beginning at the breakthrough in "Gretchen am

Spinnrade" and with citations of other familiar songs.

518. Georgiades, Thrasybulos G. **Schubert: Musik und Lyrik.**
Göttingen: Vandenhoeck & Ruprecht, 1967.   396p.

An important and often-discussed study in two parts. The
first part deals with Schubert's style in general and with
his place in music history. Georgiades regards Schubert as
the link between two distinct eras, one oriented toward
vocal music and lasting from the ninth century to the
nineteenth, and the other, constituting the modern era,
centered on instrumental music. The argument rests on
detailed analyses both of songs and of instrumental works,
as well as on comparison of Schubert to his predecessors
and contemporaries. The second half of the book is occupied by close analyses of the songs of **Die schöne Müllerin**
and several later songs. Diagrams. Indexes of works,
names. The detailed analysis of "Wandrers Nachtlied" in
Chapter 1 (pp. 17-31) is excerpted in English translation
by Marie Louise Göllner as "Lyric as Musical Structure:
Schubert's **Wandrers Nachtlied** ("Ueber allen Gipfeln," D.
768)," in **Schubert: Critical and Analytical Studies,** edited
by Walter Frisch, 84-103. Lincoln: University of Nebraska
Press, 1986.

519. LeMassena, C.E. with Hans Merz. **The Songs of Schubert: A
Guide for Singers, Teachers, Students and Accompanists.**
New York: Schirmer, 1928. vii, 184p.

Lists alphabetically about two hundred of Schubert's most
important songs, with notes on each. Entries include
poets, dates of composition, original keys, musical incipits, summaries of texts, descriptions of music, and notes
for performers. Indexes of English titles, poets. Lists
of songs by singer's gender, program suggestions by voice
type.

520. Levi, Vito. "Le arie e ariette di Schubert su testo ital-
iano." **Studien zur Musikwissenschaft** 25 (1962): 307-14.

Demonstrates that it is possible to define some development of the composer in his relatively sparse settings of
Italian texts that date from 1813 to 1827.

521. Mies, Paul. **Schubert, der Meister des Liedes: Die Entwicklung von Form und Inhalt im Schubertschen Lied.** Berlin:
Max Hesse, 1928. 428p.

Traces Schubert's progress as a song composer. Mies articulates six periods in Schubert's development: an early period (through 1814), a first apprenticeship year (1815), a second apprenticeship year (1816), a transitional period (through 1818), early maturity (1819-1823), and a final period of mastery. The penetrating remarks about style are supported by numerous music examples. Indexes of songs, topics, names.

522. Pfordten, Hermann v.d. **Franz Schubert und das deutsche Lied.** Leipzig: Quelle & Meyer, 1928. 160p.

Begins with a basic summary of Schubert's life and works, followed by general comments on the Lied. The treatment of Schubert's songs is organized by structural approaches, from simple strophic songs through free forms. Several prominent examples of each type are mentioned and in some cases dealt with in detail. Schubert's influence on the later history of the Lied is summarized. Work-list, organized by poets; very general and dated bibliography. Index of names.

523. Porter, Ernest G. **Schubert's Song Technique.** London: Dennis Dobson, 1961. viii, 152p.

Consists of a collection of essays on aspects of Schubert's Lieder. The first chapter discusses the formation of Schubert's style in his early songs. Chapters 2-6 isolate particular elements of the style--phrasing and form, key, harmony, modulation, expression markings and grace notes--and Chapter 7 deals with several aspects of his works, including the compositional process. The final chapters take up special topics: songs about death, in which the author traces the Romantic desire for happy release in death; the affinity of Schubert to the poems of Mayrhofer; and **Schwanengesang.** Portraits. Appendices. Indexes.

524. ———. **The Songs of Schubert.** London: Williams & Norgate, 1937. 159p.

Describes the most prominent songs, concentrating on the musical means of expression. After an introductory chapter demonstrating Schubert's procedures in general, the songs are discussed in groups, beginning with the ballads, then mostly by poets. A chapter is devoted to the cycles and another to the English songs. An appendix gives model English translations of some of the less-known songs; a

second appendix lists the publications of songs during and
immediately after Schubert's life.   Index of songs.

525. Reed, John. **The Schubert Song Companion.** Manchester: Manchester University Press, 1985. xii, 510p.

Lists the songs alphabetically by title or first line
(unfortunately, the cross-referencing is sketchy). The
entry for each song gives the poet, date, original key,
Deutsch catalogue number, editions, musical incipit, prose
translation of the text, critical notes, and bibliographic
references. A section gives brief notes on the poets whose
works Schubert set. Appendices suggest a variety of interesting topics, from the use of keys for expression to the
patterns of working in Schubert's song-composing career.

526. Robertson, Alec. "The Songs." In **The Music of Schubert,**
edited by Gerald Abraham, 149-97. New York: Norton, 1947.

Credits Schubert with bringing to the Lied a dramatic
approach combined with folklike melody and variety in the
piano parts that opened a chapter in the history of the
genre. The songs themselves are considered according to
the authors of the texts. The discussions are brief and
there is little technical analysis.

STYLE, ANALYSIS, CRITICISM

527. Blom, Eric. "His Favorite Device." **Music and Letters** 9
(1928): 372-80.

Discusses Schubert's use of alternation of mode between
major and minor, citing a number of instances from his
Lieder.

528. Chochlow, Jurij N. "Zur Frage vom Verhältnis der Musik und
des poetischen Textes in Schuberts Liedern." In **Schubert-
Kongress Wien 1978: Bericht,** edited Otto Brusatti, 353-
61. Graz: Akademische Druck- und Verlangsanstalt, 1979.

Examines Schubert's treatment of his texts in terms of
musical structure. The author recognizes that Schubert was
freer in his handling of the poetic forms of texts than his
immediate predecessors, subordinating the poetic form to
the influence of poetic content. The tension between
structural generalization and reflection of specific mat-

ters of content is the focus of the paper. Text repetition
receives specific discussion.

529. Downs, Philip. "On an Aspect of Schubert's Expressive
     Means." **Studies in Music** (Canada) 2 (1977): 41-51.

     Not examined. The **RILM** abstract (77/5706) indicates that
     the dactylic rhythm of "Erlkönig," "Der Wanderer," and "Der
     Tod und das Mädchen" is considered to be an emotionally
     expressive symbol.

530. Dräger, Hans Heinz. "Zur Frage des Wort-Ton-Verhältnisses
     im Hinblicke auf Schuberts Strophenlied." **Archiv für
     Musikwissenschaft** 11 (1954): 39-59.

     Discusses the relation between musical and linguistic
     structures as applied to the setting of songs, arguing that
     Schubert's ability to exploit structural parallels set him
     apart. Relates the expressive value of pitch patterns in
     music and speech. Develops a theory of the use of harmonic
     progression for expression.

531. Dressler, Erhart. "Zum Problem der Begriffsbestimmung
     'musikalische Deklamation' dargestellt an ausgewählten
     Liedern von Franz Schubert." Ph.D. diss., University of
     Vienna, 1974. 192p.

     Not examined. The **RILM** abstract (75/1137) states that
     types of declamation in Schubert's and earlier songs are
     considered. The study includes an analysis of **Winterreise.**
     Bibliography.

532. Dürr, Walther. "Schubert's Songs and Their Poetry: Reflec-
     tions on Poetic Aspects of Song Composition." In **Schubert
     Studies: Problems of Style and Chronology,** edited by Eva
     Badura-Skoda and Peter Branscombe, 1-24. Cambridge: Cam-
     bridge University Press, 1982.

     Elucidates some aspects of the composer's treatment of
     poetry. Shows that Schubert did not set texts randomly,
     but only when he perceived their particular suitability and
     often systematically. From analysis, Dürr argues that
     Schubert's settings achieve a balance of literary and
     musical principles in which the former serve as stimulus
     while the latter provide the expressive means. "Der
     Taucher" (D. 77), "Wer sich der Einsamkeit ergibt" (D.
     478), and "Der Stadt" (D. 957/11) receive detailed treat-
     ment.

533. Eggebrecht, Hans Heinrich. "Prinzipien des Schubert-
      Liedes." **Archiv für Musikwissenschaft** 27 (1970): 89-109.
      (Also printed in its original, shorter version as a
      conference paper under the title "Der 'Ton' als ein
      Prinzip des Schubert-Liedes." In **Colloquium Music and
      Word, Brno 1969,** edited by Rudolf Pečman, 234-57. Brno:
      International Musical Festival, 1973.)

      Seeks to show how Schubert's Lieder are based on core
      musical ideas (Ton) generated by images in their texts,
      which in turn generate musical substance throughout the
      songs. Also examines the composer's use of a return of the
      theme to suggest a colon in the text. Schubert's use of
      such a reprise technique is seen as a solution to the
      problem of justifying musical recapitulation in the nine-
      teenth century.

534. Federhofer, Hellmut. "Zur Analyse und Deutung des Schubert-
      Liedes." In **Schubert-Studien: Festgabe der Oesterreich-
      ische Akademie der Wissenschaften zum Schubert-Jahr 1978,**
      edited by Franz Grasberger and Othmar Wessely, 57-67.
      Vienna: Oesterreichische Akademie der Wissenschaften,
      1978.

      Tackles the problem of approaching structure and meaning
      in general by comparing the methods of Eggebrecht and
      Georgiades in discussing Schubert's songs. Argues that it
      is impossible to effect a distinct separation of form and
      content.

535. Feil, Arnold. "Zur Genesis der Gattung Lied wie sie Franz
      Schubert definiert hat." **Musikoloski Zbornik** 11 (1975):
      40-53.

      Places Schubert's work in sociological and stylistic
      context. The social position into which Schubert's songs
      entered was that earlier occupied by the oral, folk-song
      tradition. In the area of style, Schubert's creation of
      the fully participatory accompaniment brought the Lied into
      the mainstream of Western polyphonic art music.

536. Fischer, Kurt von. "Zur semantischen Bedeutung von Text-
      repetitionen in Schuberts Liederzyklen." In **Schubert-
      Kongress Wien 1978: Bericht,** edited by Otto Brusatti,
      335-42. Graz: Akademische Druck- und Verlagsantalt, 1979.

      Argues that text repetitions are important reflections of
      Schubert's readings of the poems he set. The works con-

sidered are the two Müller cycles and the Heine "cycle" included in **Schwanengesang**. Repetition of words, lines, and stanzas are considered respectively, as well as the significance of songs with no use of text repetition.

537. Flothuis, Marius. "Schubert Revises Schubert." In **Schubert Studies: Problems of Style and Chronology,** edited by Eva Badura-Skoda and Peter Branscombe, 61-84. Cambridge: Cambridge University Press, 1982.

Discusses Schubert's reworkings or re-settings of ten songs (D. 126, 149, 162, 388, 474, 534; 215 and 368, 259 and 296, 160 and 766, 52 and 636). In attempting to explain the nature of such revisions Flothuis comes to the conclusion that the later versions are generally musically superior but that it is reasonable also to regard the pairs of settings as reflecting different and equally viable interpretations of the same poems.

538. Gerstenberg, Walter. "Der Rahmen der Tonalität im Liede Schuberts." In **Musicae scientiae collectanea: Festschrift Karl Gustav Fellerer zum siebsigsten Geburtstag am 7. Juli 1972,** edited by Heinrich Hüschen, 147-55. Cologne: Arno Volk, 1973.

Considers the songs in which the opening tonality does not return at the conclusion. From the earliest instances in the tradition of the dramatic ballad, Schubert adapted the procedure to the expression of complexes of poetic ideas.

539. ————. "Schubertiade: Anmerkungen zu einigen Liedern." In **Festschrift Otto Erich Deutsch,** edited by Walter Gerstenberg, Jan LaRue, and Wolfgang Rehm, 232-39. Kassel: Bärenreiter, 1963.

Makes several points. The effectiveness of Schubert's song technique in discovering a particular musical gesture that dominates the entire song is illustrated by "Des Baches Wiegenlied" (D. 795/20) and "Ständchen" (D. 957/4). The rhythmic complexity of "Des Fischers Liebesglück" (D. 933) is discussed, leading to the conclusion that original sources can be crucial to analysis. The previously unknown autograph of "Greisen-Gesang" (D. 788) is reproduced.

540. Gray, Walter. "The Classical Nature of Schubert's Lieder." **The Musical Quarterly** 57 (1971): 62-72.

144 Studies of Individual Composers and Works

Argues for an understanding of Schubert's songs as Classical rather than Romantic. The author declines to define
the terms Classic and Romantic, but argues that Schubert's
Lieder are Classical because they attempt to maintain per-
fect balance among text, vocal line, and piano accompaniment. Gray also emphasizes the contrast of Schubert's
approach, which he regards as objective, to Schumann's,
which is taken as more subjective and therefore Romantic.
Rather unexpectedly, Gray proposes that the accompaniment
figures in Schubert's songs have less to do with tone-
painting than with reflection of internal feelings and thus
are Classical rather than Romantic.

541. Hallmark, Rufus, and Ann Clark Fehn. "Text Declamation in
      Schubert's Settings of Pentameter Poetry." **Zeitschrift
      für Literaturwissenschaft und Linguistik** 9 (1979): 80-
      111.

      Points out two paradigms by which Schubert adapted a
      poetic line of five metric feet to the musical convention
      of phrases in even-numbered measure patterns: elongation of
      the final foot in an essentially even setting, or compres-
      sion of two feet into the time of one. The principles are
      illustrated in an analysis of "Der Zwerg" (D. 771), and a
      table identifying the methods used in each of Schubert's
      pentameter settings.

542. Haas, Hermann. **Ueber die Bedeutung der Harmonik in den
      Liedern Franz Schuberts.** Abhandlung zur Kunst-, Musik-,
      Literaturwissenschaft 1. Bonn: Bouvier, 1957.

      Traces Schubert's musical interpretation of his texts
      through the chronological development of his song oevure
      (following the periodization of Mies). For each period,
      personal reasons for Schubert's choice of texts are pro-
      pounded, followed by detailed analytical discussion of the
      characteristic expressive uses of harmony in the songs of
      that period. Charts and music examples appear in the
      appendix.

543. Holländer, Hans. "Franz Schubert's Repeated Settings of the
      Same Song-Texts." **The Musical Quarterly** 14 (1928): 563-
      74.

      Argues that Schubert's revisions of his Lieder and mul-
      tiple settings of texts reveal the composer's self-critical
      revaluation of his own work. Holländer maintains that in
      early years the successive settings tend to be directed

toward "concentration" of expressive means, resolving
through-composed or ballad-like interpretations into strophic ones, while in a later period the process seems to be
one of "extension," whereby strophic settings are replaced
by ones employing expanded, interpretive forms--modified
strophic and through-composed.

544. Istel, Edgar. "Schubert's Lyric Style." **The Musical Quar-
      terly** 14 (1928): 575-95.

      Consists of a somewhat rambling discussion of major
      Lieder with limited analytical observations.

545. Kinderman, William. "Schubert's Tragic Perspective." In
      Schubert: Critical and Analytical Studies, edited by
      Walter Frisch, 65-83. Lincoln: University of Nebraska
      Press, 1986.

      Departs from Schubert's characteristic juxtaposition of
      major and minor, which is identified as expressing the
      contrast of external reality and internal imagination in
      several songs. Traces such harmonic dichotomy from the
      early Goethe settings to "Ihr Bild," which Kinderman re-
      gards as the culmination of this process in the Lieder. He
      extends this manner of analysis to instrumental music in a
      discussion of the F-minor Fantasy for piano duet.

546. Knepler, Georg. "Schuberts Goethelieder und Goethes Musik-
      verständnis." In **Aufsätze, Quellen, Berichte** zur
      deutschen Klassik und Romantik, edited by Walter Dietze
      and Peter Goldammer, 136-55. Berlin: Aufbau, 1978.

      Not examined. According to the **RILM** abstract (78/1992),
      attributes Goethe's failure to respond to Schubert's set-
      tings of his poems to the difference in their generations.

547. Kramer, Lawrence. "The Schubert Lied: Romantic Form and
      Romantic Consciousness." **Schubert: Critical and Analyt-
      ical Studies,** edited by Walter Frisch, 200-236. Lincoln:
      University of Nebraska Press, 1986.

      Considers the role and significance of harmony in Schu-
      bert's songs. The composer treats harmony in a dialectical
      fashion, setting harmonic innovation against Classic tonal
      polarity. This is concurrent with the dichotomies set up
      in Romantic poetry and Schubert's interpretative approach.
      Kramer focuses analyses on "Meeres Stille" (D. 216),
      "Pause" (D. 795/12), "Der Doppelgänger" (D. 957/13), and

"Ganymed" (D. 544).

548.   LaMotte, Diether de. "Gedicht und Komposition: Anmerkungen zu fünf Schubert-Lièdern." **Beiträge zur Musikwissenschaft** 21 (1979): 298-305.

Not examined. The author's **RILM** abstract (79/5824) states that the interaction of poem and music is analyzed in "Im Dorfe" (D. 911/17), "Die Liebe hat gelogen" (D. 751), "Der Tod und das Mädchen" (D. 531), "Am Strome" (D. 539), "Wohin" (D. 795/2).

549.   McNamee, Ann K. "The Introduction in Schubert's **Lieder**." **Music Analysis** 4 (1985): 95-106.

Demonstrates that even in cases in which the piano introduction is differentiated from the vocal part, the introduction and the vocal line are structurally similar on multiple levels. A Schenkerian analytical approach is taken for "Die Stadt" (D. 957/11), "Der Lindenbaum" (D. 911/5), "Erlkönig" (D. 328), "Ungeduld" (D. 795/7), "Am Feierabend" (D. 795/5), "Pause" (D. 795/12), and "Der Tod und das Mädchen" (D. 531). The primary note may actually be established in the introduction.

550.   Massin, Brigitte. "Sur l'Usage et la portée psychologique de certaines formules d'accompagnement dans le lied schubertien." In **Schubert-Kongress Wien 1978: Bericht,** edited by Otto Brusatti, 343-51. Graz: Akademische Druck- und Verlagsanstalt, 1979.

Identifies specific content associated with several piano-accompaniment figurations in Schubert's Lieder. Traces the use of one of these--the arpeggiated triad, which is linked to the idea of beneficent nature--through a variety of specific manifestations, including several that Massin believes significant in instrumental works.

551.   Mies, Paul. "Die Bedeutung des Unisono im Schubertschen Liede." **Zeitschrift für Musikwissenschaft** 11 (1928-29): 96-108.

Classifies the expressive value of unison passages in the songs. Unison writing can serve at fast tempos and forte dynamic levels as a pictorial symbol of power; in a variety of moods as a dramatic or pathetic gesture; in drinking songs as a structural device or symbol of unity; and in soft, slow songs as an evocation of the mysterious. Helpful tables summarize the classifications of types.

552. Salmen, Walter. "Zur Semantik von Schuberts Harfenspieler-
     gesängen." In **Schubert-Studien: Festgabe der Oesterreich-
     ische Akademie der Wissenschaften zum Schubert-Jahr 1978,**
     edited by Franz Grasberger and Othmar Wessely, 141-49.
     Vienna: Oesterreichische Akademie der Wissenschaften,
     1978.

     Indicates that although the harp in Schubert's time was
     actually used in domestic music-making and by street musi-
     cians, the composer conceived of harpers in his songs as
     romantic figures based in medieval bardic tradition. The
     harper represented the artist estranged from common soci-
     ety. Several of Schubert's pianistic imitations of the
     harp are illustrated.

553. Sams, Eric. "Notes on a Magic Flute: The Origins of the
     Schubertian Lied." **The Musical Times** 119 (1978): 947-48.

     Adduces parallel musical ideas between several Schubert
     Lieder and **Die Zauberflöte** as well as other Mozart works.
     Sams argues in general that Schubert was strongly influ-
     enced by Mozart, rather than a genius operating in isola-
     tion or a successor of Zumsteeg and the Second Berlin
     School.

554. Schnapper, Edith. **Die Gesänge des jungen Schubert vor dem
     Durchbruch des romantischen Liedprinzipes.** Berner Veröf-
     fentlichungen zur Musikforschung 10. Berne and Leipzig:
     Paul Haupt, 1937. 168p.

     Consists of a detailed stylistic examination of Schu-
     bert's early songs. A survey of his choice of texts re-
     veals three distinct approaches: the ballad, the lyrical-
     poetic, and the internal or metaphysical. The study of the
     music shows stylistic developments that parallel this. The
     vocal parts, accompaniments, and piano solo sections are
     examined. In each area, Schubert's debt to his predeces-
     sors can be established, but the roots of his individual
     artistic direction after 1815 are perceptible as well.

555. Schollum, Robert. "Grétry-Salieri-Schubert: Zur Rolle der
     Deklamation in der Liedkomposition." In **Schubert-Kongress
     Wien 1978: Bericht,** edited by Otto Brusatti, 363-71.
     Graz: Akademische Druck- und Verlagsantalt, 1979.

     Discusses Schubert's melodic style in the Lieder, arguing

that the personal style he developed came essentially from
an emphasis on poetic declamation espoused by the Classic
opera composers of the French school and passed on to
Schubert by Salieri. Music examples compare Reichardt's
and Schubert's settings of several texts. Schollum as-
sembles a large number of statements about the principles
and practice of text-setting.

556.   Schwarmath, Erdmute. **Musikalischer Bau und Sprachvertonung
in Schuberts Liedern.** Münchner Veröffentlichungen zur
Musikgeschichte 17. Tutzing: Hans Schneider, 1969.   198p.

Concentrates on detailed analyses of songs. The analyt-
ical method is based on a concept of structural framework
(Gerüstbau) developed from the theories of Riemann and
Georgiades. The first part examines several complete songs
("Erlkönig," D. 328; "Auf dem See," D. 543; "Die junge
Nonne," D. 828; "Gondelfahrer," D. 808; "Kriegers Ahnung,"
D. 957/2; "Die Sterne," D. 939; and "Wehmut," D. 772). The
second part concentrates on special structural areas: pre-
ludes and postludes, closings, and preparations for re-
prises. Bibliography.   Index of songs cited.

557.   Spirk, Arthur. "Theorie, Beschreibung und Interpretation in
der Lied-Analyse: Zu einer kritischen Würdigung des
Schubert-Analysen von Thrasybulos Georgiades." **Archiv für
Musikwissenschaft** 34 (1977): 225-35.

Reviews Georgiades's **Schubert: Musik und Lyrik** (item
519). While Spirk regards the book as important to scholars of the Lied and insightful in many ways, he objects to
the tendency to draw conclusions that are more far-reaching
than the arguments presented warrant.

558.   Steglich, Rudolf. "Das romantische Wanderlied und Franz
Schubert." In **Musa-Mens-Musici, im Gedenken an Walther
Vetter,** edited by Heinz Wegener, 267-76. Leipzig: VEB
Deutscher Verlag für Musik, 1969.

Argues that the Romantic notion of wandering is more
broadly and idealistically conceived than merely a walking
pace, rather representing a union of the spirit with the
fluctuating motion of nature. Schubert's **Wanderlieder**
capture this generalized rhythmic oscillation.

559.   Walker, Ernest. "Mystical Songs." **Music and Letters** 9
(1928): 325-29.

Identifies a number of songs that testify to Schubert's
feeling for and ability to express spiritual experience in
a broad sense.

560. Wildberger, Jacques. "Verschiedene Schichten der musikalischen Wortdeutung in den Liedern Franz Schuberts."
Schweizerische Musikzeitschrift 109 (1969): 4-9.

Not examined. The author's **RILM** abstract (69/2905)
states that the article illustrates by examples from Schubert songs various relationships between music and text.

INDIVIDUAL POETS AND SONGS

Mathias Claudius

561. Wolff, Christoph. "Schubert's 'Der Tod und das Mädchen':
Analytical and Explanatory Notes on the Song D 531 and
the Quartet D 810." In **Schubert Studies: Problems of
Style and Chronology,** edited by Eva Badura-Skoda and
Peter Branscombe, 143-71. Cambridge: Cambridge University
Press, 1982.

A detailed and exemplary study of both song and string
quartet. The article begins with a brief introduction to
the poem. The excellent analysis of the song reveals how
Schubert paralleled certain aspects of Claudius's text,
amplified the feelings of the interlocutors, and gave his
own musical shape to the song. Wolff further relates the
quasi-dramatic dialogue setting to opera and specifically
to the convention of psalmody-like setting for oracular
pronouncements. Finally the article discusses the permea-
tion of the quartet by the **topos** of the song.

Johann Wolfgang von Goethe

562. Blume, Friedrich. "Goethes Mondlied in Schuberts Komposi-
tionen." In **Der Bär: Jahrbuch von Breitkopf & Härtel,**
1928: 31-58. Reprinted in **Syntagma Musicologicum,** 813-33.
Kassel: Bärenreiter, 1963.

Describes the change in Schubert's approach to song composition that took place in 1815 in response to the poetry

of Goethe. At this point in his career Schubert began to
turn away from the simple strophic or quasi-dramatic styles
he had used in his early songs and to seek methods that
would be more suited to Goethe's lyrical poems. The composer's two settings of Goethe's "An den Mond," dating from
August (D. 259) and November (D. 296) of 1815 are compared
in order to illustrate the point. The first version is
simpler and is controlled by more abstract musical considerations, while the second is more responsive to the structural details and content of the text.

563. Brown, Maurice J.E. "Schubert's 'Wilhelm Meister'." **Monthly
      Musical Record** 88 (1958): 4-12.

      Describes and evaluates the composer's various settings
      of the songs from Goethe's novel **Wilhelm Meisters Lehr-
      jahre.** Of particular interest is the comparison of the
      multiple settings of these texts.

564. Deutsch, Otto Erich. **Die Originalausgaben von Schuberts
      Goethe-Liedern: Ein musikbibliographischer Versuch.**
      Vienna: V.A. Heck, 1926. 24p.

      Gives the texts of the title pages, dates, and diplomatic
      information for the first editions of Schubert's songs on
      Goethe texts. The editions are given in order of opus
      number, including their reprints. Index of texts.

565. Dickinson, A.E.F. "Fine Points in 'The Erl King'." **Monthly
      Musical Record** 88 (1958): 141-43.

      After a brief introduction identifying some of the effec-
      tive devices in Schubert's song, turns to a discussion of
      the development of the piece through its four versions.
      The variants are grouped in the areas of dynamics, rhythm,
      pitch, and the texture of the bass.

566. Dürr, Walther. "Aus Schuberts erstem Publikationsplan: Zwei
      Hefte mit Liedern von Goethe." In **Schubert-Studien: Fest-
      gabe der Oesterreichischen Akademie der Wissenschaften
      zum Schubert-Jahr 1978,** edited by Franz Grasberger and
      Othmar Wessely, 43-56. Vienna: Oesterreichische Akademie
      der Wissenschaften, 1978.

      Reconstructs Schubert's two volumes of Goethe songs
      planned in 1816 for publication. The first collection
      contained the more important text settings and was sent to
      the poet. The second volume included smaller-scale songs.

567. Flothuis, Marius. "Franz Schubert's Compositions to Poems
      from Goethe's 'Wilhelm Meister's Lehrjahre'." In **Notes on
      Notes: Selected Essays by Marius Flothuis,** translated by
      Sylvia Broere-Moore, 87-138. Amsterdam: Frits Knuf, 1974.

      Begins with general notes on Schubert's choices of texts,
      reasoning that he was not indiscriminate in this matter.
      The second section discusses the song texts in their con-
      texts within the novel. The essay then turns to a survey
      of Schubert's settings of the poems, evaluating them and
      discussing their position in the chronology of Schubert's
      works. Flothuis disagrees with Deutsch's datings in some
      cases.

568. Frisch, Walter. "Schubert's **Nähe des Geliebten** (D. 162):
      Transformation of the **Volkston.**" In **Schubert: Critical
      and Analytical Studies,** edited by Walter Frisch, 175-99.
      Lincoln: University of Nebraska Press, 1986.

      Narrates the pre-history of Schubert's setting of
      Goethe's poem. The text belongs to a tradition of "Ich
      denke dein" poems, since Goethe's work was based on an
      existing Zelter setting of a poem by Frederike Brun, in
      turn modeled on one by Friedrich Matthisson. Schubert's
      song appears to manifest problems arising from the tension
      between folklike structure and poetic content.

569. Larsen, Jens Peter. "Zu Schuberts Vertonung des Liedes 'Nur
      wer die Sehnsucht kennt'." In **Musa-Mens-Musici, im Ge-
      denken an Walther Vetter,** edited by Heinz Wegener, 277-
      81. Leipzig: VEB Deutscher Verlag für Musik, 1969.

      Considers Schubert's multiple settings of Mignon's song
      from Goethe's **Wilhelm Meisters Lehrjahre,** with emphasis on
      the contrasting idea "Ach, der mich liebt und kennt ist in
      der Weite. Es schwindelt mir, es brennt mein Eingeweide."
      and the problem of setting it in a song. Particular con-
      sideration is given to the setting D. 877, modeled on
      Schubert's earlier setting of "In's stille Land" by Salis-
      Seewis, but with new material inserted for the lines in
      question.

570. Mackworth-Young, G. "Goethe's 'Prometheus' and Its Settings
      by Schubert and Wolf." **Proceedings of the Royal Musical
      Association** 78 (1951-52): 53-65.

      Outlines the history of Goethe's projected drama on the

subject of Prometheus and his monologue of 1774, as well as
Schubert's 1819 and Wolf's 1889 settings. Mackworth-Young
judges Schubert to have captured Goethe's intention almost
perfectly, while Wolf failed, perhaps because he had in
mind Shelley's **Prometheus Unbound.** A section-by-section
comparison of the two settings is provided.

571. Müller-Blattau, Joseph. "Franz Schubert, der Sänger
      Goethes." In **Goethe und die Meister der Musik,** 62-80.
      Stuttgart: Klett, 1969.

      Discusses a number of the most important of Schubert's
      songs to Goethe texts. The relation of Goethe's aesthetic
      to Schubert's method of song composition is considered.
      Schubert's settings are contrasted to those of composers in
      Goethe's generation, especially Reichardt.

572. Seelig, Harry E. "Schuberts Beitrag 'zu besserem Verständ-
      nis' von Goethes Suleika-Gestalt: Eine Literarisch-
      Musikalische Studie der 'Suleika-Lieder' op. 14 und 31."
      Beiträge zur Musikwissenschaft 17 (1975): 299-316.

      Not examined. According to the **RILM** abstract (76/7491)
      shows how Schubert's musical technique mirrors central
      aspects of the content of Goethe's **West-östlicher Divan.**

Heinrich Heine

573. Goldschmidt, Harry. "Welches war die ursprüngliche Reihen-
      folge in Schuberts Heine-Liedern?" **Deutsches Jahrbuch der
      Musikwissenchaft für 1972** 27 (1974): 52-62. Reprinted in
      Um die Sache der Musik: Reden und Aufsätze, 141-54.
      Leipzig: Reclam, 1976.

      Argues that Schubert intended a different order for the
      six Heine songs of **Schwanengesang** from that in which they
      appear there, Heine's original order. The return to that
      sequence is proposed on source-critical, poetic, and musi-
      cal grounds. The songs would then form a coherent cycle.

574. Gruber, Gernot. "Romantische Ironie in den Heine-Liedern?"
      In **Schubert-Kongress Wien 1978: Bericht,** edited by Otto
      Brusatti, 321-34. Graz: Akademische Druck- und Verlags-
      anstalt, 1979.

      Argues that, contrary to most evaluations, Schubert's

settings of the Heine songs in **Schwanengesang** do express irony. Gruber suggests that the composer's means of achieving this are inherently musical and not primarily tied to the poetry.

575. Kerman, Joseph. "A Romantic Detail in Schubert's **Schwanengesang.**" **The Musical Quarterly** 48 (1962): 36-49. Reprinted with revisions in **Schubert: Critical and Analytical Studies,** edited by Walter Frisch, 48-64. Lincoln: University of Nebraska Press, 1986.

Discusses the musical device of a stressed auxiliary chord resolving to the tonic. Schubert used the device to illustrate specific details in some songs ("Gondelfahrer," "Die Stadt") or more generally to evoke the inward and arcane ("Geistesgruss," "Am Meer"). Similar examples are drawn from Schubert's instrumental music. In "In der Ferne" and in "Ihr Bild" the symbol, reduced to hollow and ambiguous bare octaves, is further abstracted. Facsimile of "Gondelfahrer."

576. Kramer, Richard. "Schubert's Heine." **19th-Century Music** 8/3 (Spring 1985): 213-25.

Argues that the Heine settings in **Schwanengesang** were originally intended to form a cycle, but that Schubert consciously rejected this plan. The argument for seeing the set as a cycle is supported by musical and textual evidence but contradicted by the order of the songs in the autograph. The autograph itself is the subject of an extensive postscript.

577. Porter, E.G. "Der Doppelgänger." **The Music Review** 21 (1960): 16-18.

Attempts to explain the unique character of this song. Both Heine and Schubert express themselves in an extraordinarily simple and condensed manner. The singer must have a genius for drama in order to succeed in this piece.

578. Schnebel, Dieter. "Klangräume--Zeiträume: Zweiter Versuch über Schubert." In **Aspekte der musikalischen Interpretation: Sava Savoff zum 70. Geburtstag,** edited by Hermann Danuser and Christoph Keller, 111-20. Hamburg: Wagner, 1980.

Not examined. The **RILM** abstract (80/5577) indicates that the article discusses tempo and dynamic problems in interpreting "Ihr Bild."

579. Schneider, Frank. "Franz Schuberts Heine-Lieder." **Sinn und Form** 31 (1979): 1059-64.

Suggests that the conjoining of the Heine songs to those on Rellstab texts in **Schwanengesang** has led to misinterpretation of their character. Sees the Heine settings as remarkable in their expression of irony and of public rather than intimate statement.

580. Stein, Jack M. "Schubert's Heine Songs." **Journal of Aesthetics and Art Criticism** 24 (1966): 559-66.

Argues that Schubert's settings do not interpret Heine's poems correctly, so that while they may succeed as songs they fail as literary criticism. Discusses the faults of each of the six songs in turn.

581. Thomas, J.H. "Schubert's Modified Strophic Songs with Particular Reference to **Schwanengesang**." **The Music Review** 24 (1973): 83-99.

Classifies the formal procedures Schubert used in his songs on strophic texts into five main types other than simple strophic form. The variety of forms reveals Schubert's tailoring of his music to the innate qualities of the poems within a firmly controlled form.

582. Thomas, Werner. "'Der Doppelgänger' von Franz Schubert." **Archiv für Musikwissenschaft** 11 (1954): 252-67.

Analyzes the song, dealing with the piano part, then with the vocal line, and finally relating both to each other. A special feature of the song is the coexistence of opposing tendencies within the music. Thomas emphasizes the connection of the style of the song to music of earlier periods.

Friedrich Gottlieb Klopstock

583. Michel, Christoph, and Winfried Michel. "Friedrich Gottlieb Klopstock: 'Cidli' (1752); Franz Schubert: 'Das Rosenband' (1815)." **Jahrbuch des freien deutschen Hochstifts** 1975: 102-23.

Recounts the history and incorporates a critical discus-

sion of Klopstock's poem, then examines Schubert's generally neglected setting. Emphasizes the songs's reference
to eighteenth-century keyboard accompaniment texture, and
its asymmetrical period structure. Problematic for the
singer is the necessity to achieve dynamic, rhythmic, and
coloristic variety.

Karl Gottfried von Leitner

584. Feil, Arnold. **"Des Fischers Liebesglück** di Franz Schubert:
      Considerazioni sull'analysi strutturale e sull'inter-
      pretazione." **Richerche musicali** 18/4 (May 1980): 71-80.

      Not examined. The **RILM** abstract (80/3799) states that
      the study's main concern is with rhythmic aspects of the
      song, D. 933.

Wilhelm Müller

585. Armitage-Smith, Julian. "Notes on **Winterreise."** **The Musical
      Times** 113 (1972): 766-67.

      Discusses differences in readings between scores for two
      songs, "Rückblick" and "Mut." In the case of the former,
      the author shows by reference to the manuscript fair copy
      that the 1895 Gesamtausgabe edition gives the correct read-
      ing of the penultimate measure, whereas the Peters edition,
      following the first edition, is incorrect. With regard to
      "Mut," the suggestion is advanced that the opening four
      measures might not be repeated after the first verse.

586. ————. "Schubert's **Winterreise,** Part I: The Sources of the
      Musical Text." **The Musical Quarterly** 60 (1974): 20-36.

      Compares the various sources of the first part of **Winter-
      reise**--the manuscript, engraver's copy, first edition,
      Peters edition (edited by Max Friedlaender), and Gesamt-
      ausgabe (edited by Eusebius Mandyczewski for Breitkopf &
      Härtel). The author's conclusions are that Schubert's
      intentions are generally more fully reflected in the auto-
      graph composition score, because Schubert either did not
      proofread for the first edition or did not do so ade-
      quately. He finds the Mandyczewski text more reliable than
      other published versions. (It is important to remember

that all these published editions precede the **Neue Schubert Ausgabe**.)

587. Baum, Günther. "Schubert-Müllers Winterreise--neu gesehen." **Neue Zeitschrift für Musik** 128 (1967): 78-80.

Explains how Schubert's ordering of the songs of **Winterreise** departed from Müller's plan, because Schubert first became acquainted with a selection of the poems rather than the entire set in order. Baum suggests that Müller's arrangement more strongly outlines the protagonist's psychological collapse, and he suggests that the cycle might be performed in the poet's order.

588. Brown, Maurice J.E. "Schubert's **Winterreise**, Part I." **The Musical Quarterly** 39 (1953): 215-22.

Discusses the copyist's manuscript of the first twelve songs of the cycle. The source makes it possible to clarify Schubert's intentions in a number of points in which his autograph and the original edition disagree.

589. Chailley, Jacques. **Le Voyage d'hiver de Schubert**. Paris: Leduc, 1975. 53p.

In the first section, provides a general historical and critical background to **Winterreise**, emphasizing the contrast between the two parts of the cycle. The second section discusses each song, giving a brief synopsis, German text and French translation, a few paragraphs of commentary, and form outlines. Index to selected stylistic characteristics.

590. ⸻. "Le 'Winterreise' et l'énigme de Schubert." **Studia musicologica Academiae scientiarum hungaricae** 11 (1969): 107-12.

Pursues the hypothesis that the content in Schubert's **Winterreise** is not simply that of lost love but of the journey of life itself, with atheistic and probably Masonic undertones. Also considered is the problem of the order of the songs; Schubert's order reflects his having first encountered the set piecemeal, before Müller had established the final plan.

591. Damian, Franz Valentin. **Franz Schuberts Liederkreis "Die schöne Müllerin"**. Leipzig: Breitkopf & Härtel, 1928. 212p.

Takes up first the poems by themselves, then the musical settings. For each poem there is a structural analysis and commentary on its explicit content and its deeper meaning. The autobiographical aspect of the cycle as a portrayal of Müller's relationship with Luise Hensel is explored in detail. In the second half of the book each song is subjected to a descriptive analysis. An appendix collates the observations in the form of an overview of the treatment of each element of musical style for the cycle as a whole. There is a brief bibliography somewhat more weighted toward Müller than toward Schubert.

592. Feil, Arnold. **Franz Schubert: Die schöne Müllerin, Winterreise.** Stuttgart: Philipp Reclam, 1975. 197p.

Offers analytical interpretations of the songs of Schubert's two cycles on Wilhelm Müller texts, with emphasis on analysis of rhythmic devices. After a historical introduction, Feil discusses three songs in detail as models ("Im Dorfe," "Rückblick," "Halt"). He then proceeds through the two cycles in order. The complete texts of Müller's cycles and an essay on the poet by Rolf Vollmann ("Wilhelm Müller und die Romantik") supplement Feil's main discussion. Bibliography. The detailed analysis of "Im Dorfe" is excerpted in English translation by Walter Frisch in **Schubert: Critical and Analytical Studies,** edited by Walter Frisch, 104-16. Lincoln: University of Nebraska Press, 1986.

593. Goldschmidt, Harry. "Schuberts 'Winterreise'." In **Um die Sache der Musik: Reden und Aufsätze,** 116-40. Leipzig: Reclam, 1976.

Gives general background and a discussion of the individual songs in order. Emphasizes the intensive and unusually sophisticated compositional working out of the musical materials. This is demonstrated in the analytical commentary, and its significance for Schubert's development as a composer is stressed.

594. Greene, David B. "Schubert's 'Winterreise': A Study in the Aesthetics of Mixed Media." **Journal of Aesthetics and Art Criticism** 29 (1970/71): 181-93.

Attempts to show how the musical structure of songs affects the semantic meaning of the words. The uses of antecedent-consequent, statement-echo, and appoggiatura-resolution are employed as examples. Also mentioned are

the metaphysical aspect of word painting and the specific
character given to words by the musical tones to which they
are set.

595.   Kretzschmar, Hermann. "Franz Schuberts Müllerlieder." In
       Gesammelte Aufsätze über Musik und Anderes. Vol. 1,
       Gesammelte Aufsätze über Musik aus den Grenzboten, 36-44.
       Leipzig: Breitkopf & Härtel, 1910.

       Discusses **Die schöne Müllerin.** Kretzschmar identifies
       Schubert's original contribution to the development of the
       Lied as the use of the piano to set the scene. In this
       cycle he finds this to be so particularly at the opening
       and the close. He defines the main units of the action,
       dividing the cycle into four groups of songs: 1-4, 5-10,
       11-13, and 14-20.

596.   Lewin, David. **"Auf dem Flusse:** Image and Background in a
       Schubert Song." **19th-Century Music** 6/1 (Summer 1982): 47-
       57. Reprinted in revised form in **Schubert: Critical and
       Analytical Studies,** edited by Walter Frisch, 126-52.
       Lincoln: University of Nebraska Press, 1986.

       Analyzes the song in detail, to support an interpretation
       of the questions in the poet's last stanza as sincere
       rather than rhetorical. This reading, which Lewin believes
       to have been Schubert's, he finds reflected in the music at
       many levels. A reductive analytical method differing from
       that of Schenker is employed, and this is discussed in an
       appendix. Table.

597.   Marshall, H. Lowen. "Symbolism in Schubert's **Winterreise.**"
       Studies in Romanticism 12 (1973): 607-31.

       Takes up the songs one by one, pointing out instances in
       which the author finds that the music expresses feelings or
       meanings deeper than those suggested by the texts alone.
       Concludes that the emotions of the cycle as a whole are
       symbolic in the sense that they have a universality through
       which they embody the general experience of disappointment
       and grief.

598.   McKay, Elizabeth Norman. "Schubert's **Winterreise** Recon-
       sidered." **The Music Review** 38 (1977): 94-100.

       Suggests that it is possible to interpret the end of the
       cycle as hopeful rather than as leading to madness or
       death. The texts are read as indicating that neither

insanity nor suicide can be achieved by the speaker. The
open-ended conclusion of the vocal line in "Der Leiermann,"
as opposed to the fateful recurring descending line in many
other songs, is adduced as evidence that the traveler's
future holds some promise.

599. Neumann, Friedrich. **Musikalische Syntax und Form im Lieder-
zyklus "Die schöne Müllerin" von Franz Schubert: Eine
morphologische Studie.** Tutzing: Schneider, 1978. 138p.

Not examined. According to the author's **RILM** abstract
(78/3997), analyzes **Die schöne Müllerin,** concentrating on
the construction and combination of phrase units.

600. Newcomb, Anthony. "Structure and Expression in a Schubert
Song: **Noch einmal** Auf dem Flusse **zu hören.**" In **Schubert:
Critical and Analytical Studies,** edited by Walter Frisch,
153-74. Lincoln: University of Nebraska Press, 1986.

Presents a detailed analysis of the song, disagreeing
with Lewin's analysis by interpreting the song as pessimistic rather than optimistic. Argues that the first part of
Winterreise is a twelve-song cycle in which "Auf dem
Flusse" stands at the crux.

601. Reed, John. "'Die schöne Müllerin' Reconsidered." **Music and
Letters** 59 (1978): 411-19.

Defends both Müller's texts and Schubert's settings of
them from the common criticisms that they are naive or
comparatively simple. The poems are placed in historical-
biographical context and judged to be rather ironic or
pessimistic and representative of the Romantic myth of
tragic conflict between the conventional world and personal
emotion. Reed argues that Schubert in 1823 found the poems
to reflect his own spiritual experience. Critical analysis
of selected musical details in the settings leads to the
conclusion that the songs embody a sophistication of style
that has been generally overlooked.

602. Reininghaus, Frieder. "**Winterreise** und Vormärz: Zu Wilhelm
Müllers/Franz Schuberts Liederzyklus." **Spuren: Zeitschrift für Kunst und Gesellschaft 78/1** (April 1978): 10-
13.

Not examined. The **RILM** abstract by the author (78/1997)
indicates that the poetic content of the songs is held to
reflect aspects of the **Zeitgeist** both of Vienna in its own

time and of East Germany in the 1960s. Musical matters discussed include variation principle, cyclicity, and Schubert's late style.

603. Schaeffer, Erwin. "Schubert's 'Winterreise'." **The Musical Quarterly** 24 (1938): 39-57.

Reports on the autograph manuscript. The two books that contain the cycle are described, then notes are provided on details of the readings and revisions within each song. Occasional remarks on the expressive qualities of the songs are sometimes added.

604. Seidel, Elmar. "Ein chromatisches Harmonisierungs-Modell in Schuberts **Winterreise**." **Archiv für Musikwissenschaft** 26 (1969): 285-96.

Demonstrates that the harmonic progression in measures 57-67 of "Der Wegweiser" reflects a tradition of chromatic harmonization for which models may be found in the Viennese Classics and earlier. The progression has roots in the Baroque figure of **pathopoeia.**

605. Souchay, Marc-André. "Zu Schuberts 'Winterreise'." **Zeitschrift für Musikwissenschaft** 13 (1930-31): 266-85.

Presents a detailed study of the forms of the songs in the cycle. Takes **Winterreise** as the model for Schubert's late style. In these songs Souchay sees the forms as going beyond either the through-composed/centrifugal or strophic variation/centripetal approach to texts applied in the earlier songs. Rather, they show more concern with absolute musical form and synthesize the two types of formal procedure.

606. Youens, Susan. "Poetic Rhythm and Musical Metre in Schubert's 'Winterreise'." **Music and Letters** 65 (1984): 28-40.

Traces in detail the way in which Schubert sets Müller's poetic meters into music. Musical decisions are partly determined by poetic rhythm, but also by interpretive reading of the text and by purely musical concerns. Only four different meters appear in the twenty-four songs of the cycle, so Schubert was faced with the problem of achieving adequate variety. The subtleties of each song are discussed.

607.   ———. "Retracing a Winter's Journey: Reflections on Schu-
       bert's **Winterreise**." **19th-Century Music** 9/2 (Fall 1985):
       128-35.

       Argues that the story of **Winterreise** treats of an art-
       ist's sense of alienation, confrontation with his calling,
       and acceptance of a new kind of life. The emphasis is on
       Müller's poetry rather than Schubert's music.

Ossian (James Macpherson)

608.   Kinsey, Barbara. "Schubert and the Poems of Ossian." **The
       Music Review** 34 (1973): 22-29.

       Describes Schubert's nine settings of Ossianic texts,
       dating from 1815 and 1816. Some historical background is
       given, followed by remarks on the songs individually. The
       pictorial and dramatic style of these ballads contributed
       to Schubert's mature style.

Friedrich Rellstab

609.   Hallmark, Rufus. "Schubert's 'Auf dem Strom'." In **Schubert
       Studies: Problems of Style and Chronology,** edited by Eva
       Badura-Skoda and Peter Branscombe, 25-46. Cambridge:
       Cambridge University Press, 1982.

       The most serious examination of an undervalued work,
       elucidates the relationships of poetry and music in the
       song, examines some of the divergences between the auto-
       graph manuscript and published edition, and employs musical
       and documentary evidence to suggest that "Auf dem Strom"
       was intended as a tribute to Beethoven.

Sir Walter Scott

610.   Deutsch, Otto Erich. "The Walter Scott Songs," translated
       by A.H. Fox Strangways. **Music and Letters** 9 (1928): 330-
       35.

       Describes the settings of Schubert inspired by the vogue
       of the medieval romance in Scott's works.

Zacharias Werner

611. Hoorickx, Reinhard van. "Franz Schubert (1797-1828): Im-
promptu (o. D.) **Nur wer die Liebe kennt.**" **Mitteilungen
des steirischen Tonkünstlerbundes** 61 (July-September
1974): 16-18.

Not examined. According to the **RILM** abstract (76/2899),
completes Schubert's fragmentary setting of Werner's text.

TEXTS

612. Berke, Dietrich. "Zu einigen anonymen Texten Schubertscher
Lieder." **Die Musikforschung** 22 (1969): 485-89.

A number of the poets of Schubert songs are unknown,
either because Schubert did not, as was his habit, place
their names at the end of the song (especially in fragmentary manuscripts) or because he did not know them himself.
The article identifies the authors of several songs, as
well as the sources for a number of Schubert's texts. Of
particular importance were the volumes of the almanac **Selam**
for 1813 and 1814.

613. Fiedler, H.G. "Schubert's Poets." **Music and Letters** 6
(1925): 68-77.

Brief biographical notes on several poets whose texts
Schubert set. In some cases some poems are mentioned; in
some, the poet's connection with Schubert is established.

614. Schochow, Maximilian, and Lilly Schochow, eds. **Franz
Schubert: Die Texte seiner einstimmig komponierten Lieder
und ihre Dichter.** 2 vols. Hildesheim: Olms, 1974. xi,
744p.

Prints the texts of all the poems Schubert set as songs,
arranged by authors and order of composition. Notes are
given on each poet and the sources for the texts, including
the original language versions of poems Schubert set in
translation. Mention is made of alterations between the
poets' and Schubert's versions of the texts. (This collection is criticized by Berke—see item 622 below—for not
having adequately traced Schubert's actual sources for his
literary material.) Index of songs by titles and first

lines.

615. Wilson, Steuart. "The Question of Taste." **Music and Letters**
      9 (1928): 322-24.

      Points out Schubert's apparent lack of discrimination in
      the selection of texts and suggests that it helped lead to
      the variety and simplicity in his songs.

PERFORMANCE

616. Dürr, Walther. "Schubert and Johann Michael Vogl: A Reap-
      praisal." **19th-Century Music** 3/2 (November 1979): 126-40.

      Evaluates the documented applications of embellishment in
      Schubert's songs, especially those by the composer's friend
      Vogl. Concludes that discreet improvised ornamentation was
      applied by Vogl and accepted by the composer and his cir-
      cle, and does not constitute "falsification" (see Fried-
      laender's article below, item 617).

617. Friedlaender, Max. "Fälschungen in Schuberts Liedern."
      Vierteljahrsschrift für Musikwissenschaft 9 (1893): 166-
      85.

      Laments the circulation of alterations of the composer's
      harmony and of added embellishments in the vocal parts of
      Schubert's songs. The former are attributed to Hütten-
      brenner and the publisher Diabelli, the latter to the
      singer Johann Michael Vogl. A list of errors and correc-
      tions in a number of the best-known songs is given.

618. Greene, H. Plunket. "Songs as the Singer Sees Them." **Music
      and Letters** 9 (1928): 304-18.

      Attributes Schubert's effectiveness as a song composer to
      his imagination, versatility, and humanity. Numerous songs
      are cited in support of these observations.

619. Heck, Thomas F. "I Lieder di Schubert per chitarra." **Il
      Fronimo** 6/24 (July 1978): 16-21, 6/25 (October 1978): 24-
      29.

      Cites the publication of Schubert's songs with guitar
      accompaniment during the composer's life as evidence that
      performance in such a scoring is justifiable. The appear-

ance of some of the guitar versions was simultaneous with
the piano settings, and some may even have come first. A
tabulation is included of all the publications of Lieder
which appeared in versions for guitar.

620.   Moore, Gerald. **The Schubert Song Cycles: With Thoughts on
       Performance.** London: Hamish Hamilton, 1975. xvi, 240p.
       (Also published in German as **Schuberts Liederzyklen.**
       Tübingen: Wunderlich, 1975.)

       Consists of comments on matters of interpretive feeling
       and technical details of performance, by one of the great-
       est Lied pianists. Such matters as the use of rhythmic and
       dynamic nuance, articulation, and pedaling are treated.
       The text takes up each song of **Die schöne Müllerin, Winter-
       reise,** and **Schwanengesang** in order. Index.

621.   Werba, Erik. "Historisches und Aktuelles zur Interpretation
       des Schubert-Liedes." **Oesterreichische Musikzeitschrift**
       27 (1972): 194-99.

       Mentions some of the important singers in the history of
       the performance of Schubert's songs. Emphasizes the ele-
       ment of individual interpretation in performing his music
       in the modern period. Notes on some of the stylistic
       factors that should be considered in the settings of Goethe
       texts are included.

SOURCES

622.   Berke, Dietrich. "Schuberts Liedentwurf 'Abend' D 645 und
       dessen textliche Voraussetzungen." In **Schubert-Kongress
       Wien 1978, Bericht,** edited by Otto Brusatti, 305-20.
       Graz: Akademische Druck- und Verlagsanstalt, 1979.

       Identifies the source for the unfinished song draft on
       Ludwig Tieck's poem "Abend" (D. 645) as the **Musenalmanach
       für das Jahr 1802.** The study discusses the problems of
       identifying Schubert's text sources in general, and argues
       that the composer used sources somewhat systematically in
       turn. In considering the reasons that the song was not
       completed, Berke hypothesizes that Schubert often thought
       of groups of songs as cyclical units and that "Abend" was
       launched as part of such a group (entitled **Der Besuch** in
       the **Musenalmanach**) but turned out to be too problematic to
       set and was abandoned.

623. Brown, Maurice J.E. "Die Handschriften und Frühausgaben von Schuberts 'Die Forelle'." **Oesterreichische Musikzeit-schrift** 20 (1965): 578-88.

Describes and explains the significance of the sources for "Die Forelle." The variant readings contribute to an understanding of Schubert's compositional practice and help to evaluate the validity of the different readings, particularly in regard to the piano introduction, which was a late addition to the song.

624. ———. "Some Unpublished Schubert Songs and Song Fragments." **The Music Review** 15 (1954): 93-102.

Discusses the sources of ten songs (D. 39, 216, 327, 344, 363, 396, 503, 512, 663, 896), of which some are complete, some are preserved only as fragmentary sources for songs that were completed, and others were never completed. The music is described, in some cases quoted, and evaluated.

625. ———. "The Therese Grob Collection of Songs by Schubert." **Music and Letters** 49 (1968): 122-34.

Reports on a collection of seventeen songs written by Schubert in 1816 for a singer with whom he was apparently in love. All but one are in the composer's autograph. Three of the manuscripts represent unique pieces (D. 344, 503, 512); the others contain variants from the known versions of Schubert's Lieder. Each manuscript is discussed briefly and placed in the perspective of its concordances.

626. ———. "Two Schubert Discoveries." **The Musical Times** 109 (1968): 801.

Reports the discovery of the previously unknown song "Die Wallfahrt" in a manuscript copy owned by Baron Christoph Cornaro in Brussels. Brown describes the piece and suggests a date of 1816 for it.

627. Campbell, Frank C. "Schubert Song Autographs in the Whittall Collection." U.S. Library of Congress. **Quarterly Journal of Current Acquisitions** 6/4 (August 1949): 3-8.

Describes manuscripts in the Library of Congress for seven songs: "Die Forelle," D. 550e; "Cora an die Sonn," D. 263; "Abendständchen, an Lina," D. 265; "Todtengräbern-Weise," D. 869; "Einsamkeit," D. 620; "Hoffnung," D. 295b;

and "Thekla: eine Geisterstimme," D. 595? (fragmentary).
Substantial discussion is given to the manuscript of "Die
Forelle," which is reproduced in facsimile.

628. Dürr, Walther. "Autograph-autorisierte Abschrift-Original-
      ausgabe: Zu Quellenlage und Quellenbewertung bei Schu-
      berts Liedern." In **Festschrift Georg Dadelsen zum 60.
      Geburtstag,** edited by Thomas Kohlhase and Volker Scher-
      liess, 89-100. Stuttgart: Hänssler, 1978.

      Not examined. According to the author's abstract in **RILM**
      (78/3925), explains why no single authentic source can
      suffice for an edition of Schubert's Lieder and that cor-
      rection must be provided based on study of all the sources.

629. ———. "Beobachtungen am Linzer Autograph von Schubert's
      Rastlose Liebe." Historisches Jahrbuch der Stadt Linz
      (1970): 215-30.

      Not examined. The **RILM** abstract by the author (73/3588)
      states that the Linz source, the first draft of the song,
      is compared to the fair copy and original edition.

630. Feil, Arnold, and Walther Dürr. "Kritisch revidierte
      Gesamtausgaben von Werken Franz Schuberts im 19. Jahr-
      hundert." In **Musik und Verlag: Karl Vötterle zum 65.
      Geburtstag am 12. April 1968,** 268-78. Kassel: Bären-
      reiter, 1968.

      Not examined. The authors report in their **RILM** entry
      (68/2042) that the Breitkopf & Härtel and Peters editions
      are critiqued. The attempt to combine critical and per-
      forming editions is shown to be misguided.

631. Holschneider, Andreas. "Zu Schuberts 'Frühlingsglaube'." In
      Festschrift Otto Erich Deutsch, edited by Walter Gersten-
      berg, Jan LaRue, and Wolfgang Rehm, 240-44. Kassel:
      Bärenreiter, 1963.

      Reports the discovery of an autograph manuscript for this
      song (D. 686) in the Vatican Library (Vat. lat. 14838).
      The manuscript is described and placed in context with the
      other existing sources; the Vatican manuscript, dated
      "Sept. 1820," is the earliest for the song. Facsimile of
      the manuscript.

632. Hoorickx, Reinhard van. "The Chronology of Schubert's Frag-
      ments and Sketches." In **Schubert Studies: Problems of**

Style and Chronology, edited by Eva Badura-Skoda and
Peter Branscombe, 297-325. Cambridge: Cambridge University Press, 1982.

Among the items listed are many that represent songs.

633. ———. "Un Manuscrit inconnu de Schubert." Revue belge de
musicologie 28-29-30 (1974-75-76): 260-63.

Reports the existence of the composer's manuscript of the
song "Ueber Wildemann" (D. 884). The source was used for
the first printing (posthumous) of the song in 1829. A
reproduction of the first page is included.

634. ———. "Notes on a Collection of Schubert Songs Copied
from Early Manuscripts around 1821-1825, Preserved in the
Spaun Family, in the Possession of Dr. Christoph von
Cornaro, Brussels." Revue belge de musicologie 22 (1968):
86-101.

Lists the Schubert holdings of the Cornaro family, related to the Spauns and Moritz von Schwind. Of particular
concern in this article is a group of three volumes of
songs, apparently copied within Schubert's circle. For
each song textual notes are provided.

635. ———. "A Schubert Song Rediscovered." The Musical Times
121 (1980): 97-98.

Reports the discovery of Schubert's setting of "Mein
Frieden" by C. Heine. The song was apparently published
privately, and a copy came into the hands of Schubert
collector Father Leopold Puschl and is owned by the Benedictine monastery of Seitenstetten in Lower Austria. A
facsimile is included.

636. ———. "Schubert: Songs and Song-Fragments Not Included in
the Collected Edition." The Music Review 38 (1977): 267-
92.

Lists eighteen complete songs, ten partially or entirely
lost songs, and nineteen unfinished songs and sketches.
Comments on each item. The setting of "Psalm XII," missing
only the last few measures, is printed.

637. ———. "Schubert's Earliest Preserved Song-Fragments."
Revue belge de musicologie 36-38 (1982-84): 145-61.

Proposes that Schubert attempted two settings of Gabriele
von Baumberg's "Lebenstraum," the fragments catalogued as
D. 1a and D. 39, in about 1809. Hoorickx includes a reading of the music of each fragment fitted to the words of
the poem.

638.   Kecskeméti, István. "Neu entdeckte Schubert-Autographe."
       Oesterreichische Musikzeitschrift 24 (1969): 564-68.

Reports the discovery among the holdings of the National
Széchényi Library in Budapest of autograph manuscripts of
seven songs: "Gesang: An Sylvia" (D. 891), "Heimliches
Lieben" (D. 922b), "Das Weinen" (D. 926), "Vor meiner
Wiege" (D. 927), "Eine altschottische Ballade" (D. 923),
"Wandrers Nachtlied II" (D. 768), and "Fischerweise" (D.
881b). The volume containing the manuscripts is catalogued
as Ms. mus. 4770. The materials are described and the
problems of their provenance discussed. Facsimiles.

639.   ————. "Eine wieder aufgetauchte Eigenschrift Schuberts."
       Oesterreichische Musikzeitschrift 23 (1968): 70-74.

Reports that the holograph of the Ossian song "Die Nacht"
(D. 534) is in the possession of the Hungarian National
Library (Ms. mus. 109). The provenance of the source is
clarified and a description provided. The manuscript is
important because it resolves questions about the correct
reading of the song. Facsimiles.

640.   Landon, Christa. "New Schubert Finds." The Music Review 31
       (1970): 215-31. (Translated from "Neue Schubert-Funde:
       Unbekannte Manuscripte im Archiv des Wiener Männergesang-
       Vereines." Oesterreichische Musikzeitschrift 24 [1969]:
       299-323.)

Discusses the papers of Heinrich Kreissle von Hellborn,
which contain a number of songs and song fragments, including two settings of Matthisson texts, previously
thought to have been lost, "Vollendung" and "Die Erde" (D.
579a and b). The latter is incomplete in this source but
was discovered in a complete manuscript copy in the
archives of the Gesellschaft der Musikfreunde in time to be
included in the English version of this article. Facsimiles (but not of the songs).

641.   Schofield, B. "Note on Autographs, British Museum." Music
       and Letters 9 (1928): 324-25.

Reports the possession of Schubert manuscripts by the British Museum (now British Library) from the collection of Ernst Perabo. The songs included are "Wandrers Nachtlied" (D. 224, reproduced in facsimile), "Der Fischer" (D. 225), three Italian songs (D. 902), and part of "Die Sehnsucht" (D. 636b).

642. Weinmann, Alexander. "Zwei neue Schubert-Funde." **Oester-reichische Musikzeitschrift** 27 (1972): 75-78.

Reports on the autograph manuscript of an early version of "Mut" from **Winterreise,** in a private collection in Vienna, and on a copy of a previously unknown choral set-ting of Salis-Seewis's "Das Grab," dated 1819.

MISCELLANEOUS STUDIES

643. Biba, Otto. "Franz Schubert und Niederösterreich." **Oester-reichische Musikzeitschrift** 33 (1978): 359-66.

Includes incidental information relating to some of the songs. The letter of thanks from Bishop Dankesreither for the dedication of the harper's songs from **Wilhelm Meister** (D. 478, 479, 480) is included. Reference is made to the legend that the linden tree at the "Höldrichsmühle" was connected to the song "Der Lindenbaum" (D. 911/5). Also connected with the Lieder was Johann Ladislaus Pyrker von Felsö-Eör, a churchman at one time active in Lower Austria, who was the dedicatee of the three Goethe songs op. 3 (D. 121, 216, 257) and author of the texts of the two songs of op. 79 (D. 851, 852; the latter is the well-known "Die Allmacht"). Autographs of three songs, "Geistes-Gruss" (D. 142), "Der Wanderer" (D. 489?), and "Der Alpenjäger" (D. 524?), were taken to Grafenegg castle by Schubert's pupil Countess Marie Esterhazy; they had disappeared after World War II. Finally, several residents of Lower Austria among the subscribers to the publication of **Schwanengesang** are listed.

644. Prod'homme, J.G. "Schubert's Works in France." **The Musical Quarterly** 14 (1928): 495-514.

Discusses the reception of Schubert's music in France, beginning in 1828. Prod'homme recounts the history of the first performances and publications of Schubert's music. Prominent proponents of Schubert included the singer

Adolphe Nourrit, Franz Liszt, the translator Bélanger, and the publisher Richault. The article includes excerpts from the critical literature of the Romantic period in France, quoting Fétis, Berlioz, and others.

645. Sandberger, Adolf. "Johann Rudolph Zumsteeg und Franz Schubert." In **Ausgewählte Aufsätze zur Musikgeschichte.** Vol. 1, 288-99. Munich: Drei Masken, 1921.

Considers the influence of Zumsteeg on Schubert, discussing both similarities and differences between their settings of a number of the same texts. Those of Zumsteeg represent the work of a more mature composer, while Schubert's youthful efforts show his greater talent.

Johann Abraham Peter Schulz
(1747-1800)

646. Hahne, Gerhard. "Johann Heinrich Voss' Versuch einer Gesamtausgabe der Lieder Johann Abraham Peter Schulz'." **Die Musikforschung** 20 (1967): 176-81.

Reports on and prints the complete texts of two letters from Voss, discussing a planned posthumous edition of Schulz's songs. The edition was never published.

647. Klunger, Carl. **J.A.P. Schulz in seinen volkstümlichen Liedern.** Leipzig: Oscar Brandstetter, 1909.

By way of introduction, clarifies Schulz's aesthetic position and his song style, which is credited to his own talent and its basis in folk music rather than to his precursors in the First Berlin School or to Hiller's Singspiellieder. The bulk of the study (Klunger's dissertation at the University of Leipzig, 1909) is occupied by brief descriptions of individual songs published in the three collections of **Lieder im Volkston** and in the **Gesänge am Klavier.**

Robert Schumann
(1810-1856)

648. Agawu, V. Kofi. "Structural 'Highpoints' in Schumann's **Dichterliebe.**" **Music Analysis** 3 (1984): 27-38.

Correlates analytical study with poetic shape and expe-

rience of climax in the **Dichterliebe** songs. Agawu identifies the characteristic moments of "reversal" in Heine's
poems and shows by analysis how those moments determine the
structures in Schumann's settings. The analysis focuses on
songs 7, 13, and 4, with consideration of modification of
the general principle in songs 1 and 11.

649. Ashley, Douglas Daniels. "The Role of the Piano in Schu-
        mann's Songs." Ph.D. diss., Northwestern University,
        1973. iv, 173p.

Proceeds from the idea that in Schumann's songs the
essence of the poetry is translated into musical language
and that the piano parts convey the composer's subjective
response to his text. The focus of the study is on the
piano's contributions in musical terms--melody, harmony,
rhythm, form, texture and color. Examples are copied as
whole pages from the collected edition and inconveniently
placed at the back of the text. Bibliography.

650. Benary, Peter. "Die Technik der musikalischen Analyse dar-
        gestellt am ersten Lied aus Robert Schumanns 'Dichter-
        liebe'." **Versuch musikalischer Analysen.** Veröffentlich-
        ungen der Institut für neue Musik und Musikerziehung 8
        (1967): 21-29.

Demonstrates by an analysis of "Im wunderschönen Monat
Mai" the premise that analysis should not merely be the
identification of structural types (Formtypen) but the
elucidation of structural forces (Formkräfte) that operate
in the music. The analysis deals with the poetic text,
vocal melody, accompaniment texture, harmony. An overview
of the tonal plan of Schumann's cycle is also given.

651. Conrad, Dieter. "Schumanns Liedkomposition--von Schubert
        her gesehen: Einwendungen zu Th. Georgiades, **Schubert.
        Musik und Lyrik.**" **Die Musikforschung** 24 (1971): 135-63.

Takes issue with Georgiades's separation of Schumann from
the musical principles of Schubert and assignment of Schumann to the modern period, a period Georgiades defines as
having departed from the vocal tradition in music. Conrad's argument is supported by substantial analyses of
Schumann songs ("Wandrers Nachtlied," op. 96, no. 1; "Ich
will meine Seele tauchen," op. 48, no. 5; and "So lasst
mich scheinen bis ich werde," op. 98a, no. 9). The conclusion suggests a reconsideration of the idea of expression
in music.

652. Cooper, Martin. "The Songs." In **Schumann: A Symposium,**
     edited by Gerald Abraham, 98-137. London: Oxford Univer-
     sity Press, 1952.

     General discussion of Schumann's songs. There is a very
     brief treatment of Schumann's song-writing career and the
     Liederjahr. Cooper discusses the composer's choice of
     poets, emphasizing that Heine had the closest spiritual
     affinity to Schumann, criticizing the Goethe songs as fail-
     ures, and citing the setting of Elisabeth Kulmann's poems
     as evidence of a lapse of judgement. He categorizes song
     sub-genres such as ballad and salon song. Elements of
     style are discussed, including harmony and piano accompani-
     ment in particular. Schumann's influence on the songs of
     Liszt and of Wolf is also examined.

653. Desmond, Astra. **Schumann Songs.** BBC Music Guides 22. Lon-
     don: British Broadcasting Corporation; Seattle: Univer-
     sity of Washington Press, 1972. 64p.

     Presents a brief, descriptive overview of Schumann's
     Lieder, in chronological arrangement. Indexes of songs and
     poets.

654. Dalmonte, Rossana. "Il **Nachtlied** di Goethe-Schumann: pro-
     posta e verifica di un metodo d'analisi." **Richerche musi-
     cali** 18/4 (May 1980): 81-111.

     Not examined. According to the **RILM** abstract (80/3954),
     proposes an analytical method which is demonstrated by
     application to the text and music and reveals their seman-
     tic congruence.

655. Draheim, Joachim. "Bedeutung und Eigenart der Maria-Stuart-
     Lieder, op. 135, von Robert Schumann." **Archiv für das
     Studium der neueren Sprachen und Literaturen** 214 (1977):
     325-27.

     Emphasizes that these songs were Schumann's last Lieder
     and last cycle before his illness. Points out the symmet-
     rical text plan and tonal outline. Briefly characterizes
     the songs.

656. ————. "Schumann und Shakespeare." **Neue Zeitschrift für
     Musik** 142 (1981): 237-44.

     Documents Schumann's familiarity with Shakespeare's
     works, his interest in them, and his musical responses.

Some attention is given to Schumann's only song on a Shakespeare text, the closing song of **As You Like It**, op. 127,
no. 5.

657. Felber, Rudolf. "Schumann's Place in German Song." **The
      Musical Quarterly** 26 (1940): 340-54.

Identifies the influences on Schumann, some characteristics of his style, and his legacy in the works of later
song composers. Schumann is viewed as having taken up
where Schubert left off and perfected that style, influenced also by folk song, Mendelssohn, Loewe, and Wagner.
The development of Schumann's style in melody and harmony
is discussed. His influence on Brahms, Wolf, Strauss,
Pfitzner, and Mahler is cited.

658. Feldmann, Fritz. "Zur Frage des 'Liederjahres' bei Robert
      Schumann." **Archiv für Musikwissenschaft** 9 (1952): 246-69.

Adopts a series of positions regarding the perennial
issue of why Schumann suddenly began composing songs in
1840. The influence of Clara Wieck is traced in several
areas--on Schumann's state of mind, by her piano playing,
and through her singing voice. The issue of Schumann's
earlier resistance to the genre of song and the relationship of the Lieder to his earlier preoccupation with piano
music are also discussed.

659. Friedlaender, Max. **Textrevision zu Robert Schumann's
      Lieder.** Leipzig: C.F. Peters, 1887. 31p.

Gives the sources of the texts which Schumann set as
songs and lists variants in the poems between the poets'
original versions and Schumann's songs. The songs are
ordered as they are found in the three volumes of the
Peters Edition (2383a, 2384, 2385).

660. Geissler, William. "Vergleichende Analyse zu Robert Schu-
      manns Vertonungen **Die Lotosblume** nach Worten von Heinrich
      Heine." **Schumann-Tage (1.) des Bezirkes Karl-Marx-Stadt
      1976: 1. Wissenschaftliche Arbeitstagung zu Fragen der
      Schumann-Forschung,** edited by Günther Müller and William
      Geissler, 34-41. Zwickau: Robert-Schumann-Gesellschaft
      der DDR, 1977.

Not examined. According to the author's **RILM** abstract
(77/668), reasons that the musical contrasts between the
composer's settings of the text as a piano Lied and as a

four-part male chorus reflect the difference in scoring and
not a re-interpretation of Heine's poem.

661.   Hallmark, Rufus Eugene. **The Genesis of Schumann's "Dichter-
        liebe": A Source Study.** Studies in Musicology 12. Ann
        Arbor, Michigan: UMI Research Press, 1979. xvi, 208p.

Developed from Hallmark's Ph.D. dissertation (Princeton
University, 1975), investigates in detail the compositional
process in **Dichterliebe** as represented in the composer's
manuscript material. Reveals that Schumann adopted a new
and more craftsmanly approach to his work in the songs than
he had employed in his earlier piano music. The author
argues that the composer's interpretation of Heine should
be reevaluated in light of the evidence of his compositional choices. Plates. Bibliography.

662.   ———. "The Sketches for **Dichterliebe.**" 19th-Century Music
        1/2 (November 1977): 110-36.

Traces the compositional process by which Schumann worked
out the cycle through the sources. Although the actual
procedure took only a very short time, Schumann's effort
seems to have been concentrated on the selection of the
texts. In addition, there was substantial revision of the
first complete version before the cycle's publication.
Sketch facsimiles; tables showing stages in selection of
poems.

663.   Hernried, Robert. "Four Unpublished Compositions by Robert
        Schumann." **The Musical Quarterly** 28 (1942): 50-62.

Discusses and prints four pieces, two of which are
Lieder, "Ein Gedanke" (1840) and "Frühlingsglaube" (1851).
The songs show a characteristic contrast of style, the
later one so far advanced that it is described by Hernried
as decadent. (The other two pieces are domestic, occasional works, a duet "Liedchen von Marie und Papa" and a
chorus "Bei Schenkung eines Flügels.")

664.   Horton, Charles T. "A Structural Function of Dynamics in
        Schumann's 'Ich grolle nicht'." **In Theory Only** 4/8 (Feb-
        ruary-March 1979): 30-46.

Not examined. According to the entry in **RILM** (79/1687),
indicates how Schumann employs dynamics to clarify the
structure of the song, with implications for performers.
Also suggests that Schumann preferred the use of the lower

notes in the passage where optional high notes are given.

665. Killmayer, Wilhelm. "Schumann und seine Dichter." **Neue
      Zeitschrift für Musik** 142/3 (1981): 231-36.

      Briefly surveys Schumann's settings of poems of Heine,
      Eichendorff, Mörike, and Lenau.

666. Knaus, Herwig. **Musiksprache und Werkstruktur in Robert
      Schumanns "Liederkreis": mit dem Faksimile des Auto-
      graphs.** Schriften zur Musik 27. Munich: Katzbichler,
      1974. 105p.

      Not examined. The entry in **RILM** (75/3744) states that
      Schumanns's op. 39 is analyzed, revealing musical expres-
      sion of poetic imagery in structure, harmony, and treatment
      of motivic materials in particular.

667. Mahlert, Ulrich. **Fortschritt und Kunstlied: Späte Lieder
      Robert Schumanns im Licht der liedästhetischen Diskussion
      ab 1848.** Freiburger Schriften zur Musikwissenschaft 13.
      Munich, Salzburg: Katzbichler, 1983. 227p.

      Proposes that Schumann's late songs should be understood
      not so much from the perspective of Romanticism as from
      that of the progressive school after the revolutionary
      crisis of 1848. The aesthetics of the Lied and the pro-
      gressive movement, particularly in regard to the relation
      of the music to the public, are examined. Analyses of
      representative songs from the **Spanisches Liederspiel** (op.
      74), the **Liederalbum für die Jugend** (op. 79), and the
      Wilhelm Meister settings (op. 98a) are adduced in support
      of the argument. Bibliography.

668. Mayeda, Akio. "Das Reich der Nacht in den Liedern Robert
      Schumanns." In **De ratione in musica: Festschrift Erich
      Schenk zum 5. Mai 1972,** edited by Theophil Antonicek,
      Rudolf Flotzinger, and Othmar Wessely, 202-27. Kassel:
      Bärenreiter, 1975.

      Considers the interpretation of the image of night in
      Schumann's songs, with some tentative applications to un-
      derstanding the expressive content of instrumental pieces.
      Characteristic of the Romantic poetic meaning of night is
      not only its darkness and mystery but also the awakening of
      fantasy associated with it. Schumann was particularly
      interested in the moon and in the world of dreams. Spe-
      cific musical gestures--melodic, rhythmic, and harmonic--

may be identified with poetic images related to night in the songs.

669. Moore, Gerald. **Poet's Love: The Songs and Cycles of Schumann.** New York: Taplinger, 1981. xii, 247p.

Recommends details of performance for each song. For each song a synopsis is given, a description of the emotional content, and specific suggestions for such matters as ensemble, tempos and rubato, breathing, and dynamic nuance. Indexes of names, songs.

670. Moss, Lawrence. "Text and Context in **Dichterliebe.**" **Ars lyrica** 2 (1983): 23-38.

Attempts to trace the textual and musical sequence of ideas through Schumann's cycle. The author adopts the hypothesis that the texts were chosen and the music composed to reflect the progression of feelings from happiness to an inevitable, growing despair, perhaps related to ambivalent emotions in Schumann about the events of the year 1840.

671. Rothgeb, John. "Comment: On the Form of 'Ich grolle nicht'." **In Theory Only** 5/2 (May/June 1979): 15-17.

Not examined. The **RILM** abstract (79/3736) indicates that the article takes issue with the analysis by Horton (see item 665 above), in that the song's form should be regarded as ternary rather than binary, on both textual and musical grounds.

672. Sams, Eric. "Schumann's Year of Song: A 125th Anniversary Contribution." **The Musical Times** 106 (1965): 105-7.

Suggests that Schumann's sudden interest in writing songs in 1840 may have been the result of the influence of Mendelssohn. Both biographical facts and a suggestion of an actual musical quotation of the **Midsummer Night's Dream** Overture in Schumann's setting of Feste's song from **Twelfth Night** (op. 127, no. 5) are cited as evidence.

673. ————. "The Songs." In **Robert Schumann: The Man and His Music,** edited by Alan Walker, 120-61. London: Barrie and Jenkins, 1972.

Places Schumann's Lieder in their historical perspective ("at the heart of the **Lied**"), summarizes his style, and

surveys the song output. Each cycle, collection, or group
of songs is discussed in turn, providing an overview of
Schumann's development as a song composer.

674.   ————. **The Songs of Robert Schumann.** New York: Norton,
        1969. xii, 293p.

        Very briefly discusses all the songs, giving poets, dates
        of composition, translations, cursory characterizations of
        the settings, and notes on technical details. An opening
        section discusses Schumann's song composition in general,
        emphasizing the characteristic symbolic motives he em-
        ployed, especially those related to Clara. Appendices
        include a list of the early songs, a note on Schumann's
        illness, and the sources of the song texts. Indexes.

675.   Schlager, Karlheinz. "Erstarrte Idylle: Schumanns Eichen-
        dorff-Verständnis im Lied op. 39/VII (Auf einer Burg)."
        Archiv für Musikwissenschaft 33 (1976): 119-32.

        Analyzes both text and music in some detail. Schlager
        concludes that Schumann did not merely compose the music to
        reflect the surface or narrate the poem, but interpreted in
        the composition the underlying ironic imagery and the Ro-
        mantic idea of isolation. The departure from the key
        indicates Schumann's Romantic inclination to allow subjec-
        tive content to override formal principles.

676.   Schneider, Anneliese. "Robert Schumann und Heinrich Heine:
        Eine historisch-ästhetische Untersuchung anhand der Ver-
        tonungen mit Berücksichtigung einiger Probleme der Lied-
        analyse." Ph.D. diss., University of Berlin, 1970. 300p.

        Not examined. According to the **RILM** abstract (70/3437),
        discusses Schumann's aesthetics, both in general and in
        regard to setting Heine's texts, and analyzes the musical
        responses to poetic meter and rhythm. Lists Schumann's
        writings about Heine and surveys Heine settings in the
        nineteenth and twentieth centuries.

677.   Schumann, Robert. **Dichterliebe: An Authoritative Score,
        Historical Background, Essays in Analysis, Views and
        Comments,** edited by Arthur Komar. Norton Critical Scores.
        New York: Norton, 1971, viii, 136p.

        Presents score for **Dichterliebe,** including the four songs
        that were originally composed for the cycle but eliminated

from the published version. An introductory essay discusses the history and text setting. The analyses, which
are by Schenker and later analysts using his approach, have
been criticized by Joseph Kerman ("How We Got into Analysis
and How to Get Out," **Critical Inquiry** 7 [1980]: 311-331).
A variety of excerpts of essays rounds out the volume,
among them some statements from Schumann on songs in general and on specific songs by his contemporaries. Bibliography.

678. Spitz, Charlotte. "Schumann's 'Mary Stuart Songs'." **Monthly
      Musical Record** 67 (1937): 153-55.

      Identifies the origins of the set of poems used by Gis-
      bert von Vincke for the German translations which Schumann
      set as his op. 135. The first song is considered more
      conventional in text and music than the others.

679. Thym, Jürgen. "The Solo Song Settings of Eichendorff's
      Poems by Schumann and Wolf." Ph.D. diss., Case Western
      Reserve University, 1974. vii, 440p.

      Contrasts the interpretations of Eichendorff's poetry by
      the two composers. Schumann tended to select poems that
      emphasize mystery and ambiguity through man's relationship
      with nature and to reflect their subtlety in the music.
      Wolf selected texts that are more realistic, representing
      characters with humor and irony. His settings emphasize
      accurate speech declamation and tone painting of details.
      An appendix gives the song texts, translations, notes on
      their publication, and remarks on their treatment by the
      composers. Bibliography.

680. ———. "Text-Music Relationships in Schumann's Frühlings-
      fahrt." **Theory and Practice** 5/2 (December 1980): 7-25.

      Not examined. According to the **RILM** abstract (80/5834)
      relates text and music in the areas of structure, imagery,
      and content.

681. Turchin, Barbara Pearl. "Robert Schumann's Song Cycles in
      the Context of the Early Nineteenth-Century **Liederkreis**."
      Ph.D. diss., Columbia University, 1981. 434p.

      Emphasizes the scope of the early nineteenth-century song
      cycle, and demonstrates that Schumann's models were not
      simply the cycles of Beethoven and Schubert. The early

Romantic cycles were generally unified by poetic content. Schumann expanded the principle of cyclical unification by musical means, specifically through tonal planning and continuity and through application of variation technique.

682. ————. "Schumann's Conversion to Vocal Music: A Reconsideration." **The Musical Quarterly** 67 (1981): 392-404.

Suggests that a complex of situations may have led Schumann to turn to composing songs in 1840. Particularly important were the need for public acceptance of his music and concrete financial reward.

683. ————. "Schumann's Song Cycles: The Cycle within the Song." **19th-Century Music** 8/3 (Spring 1985): 231-44.

Demonstrates that the opening songs in Schumann's cycles establish not only poetic but also motivic and tonal parameters for the cycles. **Frauenliebe und -leben, Dichterliebe,** and the Eichendorff **Liederkreis** are analyzed by way of illustration.

684. Vessels, William Allen. "A Performance Study and Transcription of Schumann's Eichendorff **Liederkreis,** Opus 39." Ph.D. diss., Indiana University, 1976. 154p.

Not examined. According to the author's **RILM** abstract (76/869), compares manuscript, early editions, and modern editions in regard to performance problems. Considers such matters as tempo, pedallings, the order of the songs in the cycle. Bibliography.

685. Walsh, Stephen. **The Lieder of Schumann.** New York: Praeger, 1971. viii, 128p.

Surveys Schumann's song output, with descriptions of style and critical commentary. Attributes Schumann's success to his ability to grasp and convey the underlying psychological character of a poem. No documentation references. Index of song by title.

686. Werba, Erik. "Das Schumann-Lied in der Gegenwart." **Oesterreichische Musikzeitschrift** 11 (1956): 212-16.

Attempts to identify the Schumann songs that have shown the most enduring value. Both the outstanding and the less long-lived songs are listed and briefly characterized. Werba observes evidence of a renaissance of interest in

Schumann's Lieder.

687.   Zimmermann, Hans-Joachim. **"Die Gedichte der Königin Maria Stuart:** Gisbert Vincke, Robert Schumann und eine sentimentale Tradition." **Archiv für das Studium der neueren Sprachen und Literaturen** 214 (1977): 294-324.

Not examined. The author's abstract in **RILM** (77/1836) states that the texts, only two of which were actually by Mary Stuart, belong to a tradition of sentimentality in which Vincke, their translator, holds a place. The correct sources of the poems are traced. Bibliography.

Reinhard Schwarz-Schilling
(b. 1904)

688.   Thym, Jürgen. "Die klavierbegleiteten Eichendorff-lieder von Reinhard Schwarz-Schilling." **Aurora** (1977): 77-86.

Not examined. The **RILM** abstract by the author (77/2961) indicates that the songs, for baritone and piano, were the product of the composer's contact with Eichendorff's texts during the period of the Second World War. Work-list.

Sperontes (Johann Sigismund Scholze)
(1705-1750)

689.   Spitta, Philipp. "Sperontes' 'Singende Muse an der Pleisse': Zur Geschichte des deutschen Hausgesanges im achtzehnten Jahrhundert." In **Musikgeschichtliche Aufsätze**, 175-295. Berlin: Paetel, 1894. Reprint. Georg Olms, 1976. (Originally published in **Vierteljahrsschrift für Musikwissenschaft** 1 (1885): 35-126.)

Discusses this important series of parodistic song collections, which helped to launch the Classic-Romantic Lied tradition. The source is described and the compiler identified as Scholze. The songs are placed in their musical, historical, and social context.

Wilhelm Speyer
(1790-1878)

690.   Speyer, Edward. **Wilhelm Speyer der Liederkomponist (1790-1878): Sein Leben und Verkehr mit seinen Zeitgenossen.**

Munich: Drei Masken, 1924.

A biography based on Speyer's sizeable collection of
correspondence from many of the leading musical figures of
the period and other documents. Two complete ballads, "Der
Trompeter," op. 31, and "Die drei Liebchen," op. 33, are
printed, as well as a facsimile of the manuscript of the
Lied "Rheinsehnsucht," op. 42, no. 2. Numerous plates
include portraits of many of the musicians whom Speyer
knew. Index.

Louis Spohr
(1784-1859)

691. Gorrell, Lorraine. "The Songs of Louis Spohr." **The Music
Review** 39 (1978): 31-38.

Suggests that Spohr's songs represent the general style
of the composer's time, as compared to more prominent and
familiar works by exceptional composers. The main interest
of the songs is concentrated in the vocal melody, while the
harmony is Romantically chromatic, sometimes to excess.
The piano parts are intended for amateur players.

692. Hirschberg, Leopold. "Spohr als Balladenkomponist." **Die
Musik** 11/4 (July-September 1912): 212-22.

Characterizes and evaluates the composer's ballads, which
are among his best songs. The pieces are influenced by the
ballads Spohr composed within the context of dramatic
works. The main barrier to popularity for these works was
that the melodies are too far removed from a folk style
that would give them mass appeal.

Sir Charles Villiers Stanford
(1852-1924)

693. Lee, E. Markham. "Some Stanford Songs." **Musical Opinion** 53
(1929): 722-23.

Describes and comments in passing on the performance of
the settings of Thomas Moore's "There's a Bower of Roses,"
Keats's ballad "La Belle Dame sans merci," and Moira
O'Neill's "The Fairy Lough."

694. Greene, Harry Plunket. "Stanford's Songs." **Music and**

Letters 2 (1921): 96-106.

Praises Stanford's songs for their directness and craftsmanship. "The Fairy Lough" is discussed in detail.

Margaret McClure Stitt
(b. 1886)

695. Woodward, Henry. "Four Songs by Margaret McClure Stitt."
      College Music Symposium 23/1 (Spring 1983): 124-42.

      Recounts the biography of the Ohio composer (with many
      reminiscences by Mrs. Stitt) and discusses in detail four
      of her numerous songs: "Lullaby," "My Gold Balloon," "Cir-
      cus Days," and "Song for Adele." The composer's style is
      quite varied and characteristically features freely varied
      strophes. Includes the complete music for "My Gold Bal-
      loon."

Richard Strauss
(1864-1949)

696. Baum, Günther. "Hugo Wolf und Richard Strauss in ihren
      Liedern." **Neue Zeitschrift für Musik** 130 (1969): 575-79.

      Briefly contrasts the lives, personalities, and song
      styles of the two contemporary composers. Musical compari-
      sons in the areas of melody, style and function of the
      piano parts, and harmony show that the two men conceived
      the genre differently.

697. Carner, Mosco. "Strauss's **Vier letzte Lieder.**" **Monthly
      Musical Record** 80 (1950): 172-77.

      A critical essay written shortly after the composition of
      the songs and the death of the composer, stresses that the
      freshness of Strauss's earlier style is replaced in these
      songs by introspection and subtlety of expression. Each
      song is described and evaluated.

698. Frank, Alan. "Strauss's Last Songs." **Music and Letters** 31
      (1950): 305-6.

      Briefly describes the songs. The set is characterized by
      spiritual depth and a sustained tone of serenity and resig-
      nation.

700. Guttmann, Alfred. "Richard Strauss als Lyriker." **Die Musik** 4/2 (January–March 1905): 93-101.

   Evaluates Strauss's song style up to the date of the article. Guttmann believes that Strauss found his distinctive manner of writing Lieder around 1894 when he first dealt with the problems of contemporary verse. He succeeded with these texts because he also abandoned the traditional structures of the Lied and applied the style of the New German School to the genre of song.

701. Jefferson, Alan. **The Lieder of Richard Strauss.** New York: Praeger, 1971. x, 134p.

   Surveys Strauss's Lieder, mainly according to topics treated in the poems set. Includes a biographical introductory chapter and appendices giving a bibliographical note, lists of songs, key to poems also set by other composers, and notes on Strauss's poets. Index.

702. Lienenlüke, Ursula. **Lieder von Richard Strauss nach zeitgenössischer Lyrik.** Kölner Beiträge zur Musikforschung 93. Regensburg: Bosse, 1976. 180p.

   Not examined. The author's abstract in **RILM** (76/7478) states that the study, her dissertation (University of Köln), provides analyses of songs from the composer's early and middle periods. Emphasized is the relationship between the composer's background and the content of the texts he chose.

703. Morse, Peter, and Christopher Norton-Welsh. "Die Lieder von Richard Strauss: Eine Diskographie." **Richard Strauss-Blätter** 5 (1974): 81-123.

   Not examined. The **RILM** abstract (76/8490) suggests that the discography is similar to one published earlier by Morse (first edition 1970, second edition 1973; Utica, N.Y.: Weber). Index.

704. Petersen, Barbara A. **Ton und Wort: The Lieder of Richard Strauss.** Studies in Musicology 15. Ann Arbor, Michigan: UMI Research Press, 1980. xvii, 254p.

   Approaches Strauss's songs from a variety of viewpoints: the poetry he chose to set, the style, the manuscript and printed sources, the problems in orchestration, the evidence from the composer's and his wife's performances of

the Lieder. Petersen argues that the songs are closely
related to the course of the rest of Strauss's oeuvre and
his life. Reproductions of title pages. Chronological list
of songs and list of incomplete vocal works; excellent and
extensive bibliography. Index.

704.   Schuh, Willi. "A Forgotten Goethe Song by Richard Strauss."
       Tempo 12 (Summer 1949): 20-21. Also "Ein vergessenes
       Goethe-Lied von Richard Strauss." **Schweizerisches Musik-
       zeitung** 89 (1949): 235.

       Presents the setting of "Durch aller Schall und Klang"
       from the **Westöstlicher Divan**, composed 11 June 1925
       (Strauss's birthday) and dedicated to Romain Rolland on the
       writer's sixtieth birthday, 29 January 1926. The music,
       which is given in full, is in a simple, chorale-like style.

705.   Schumann, Elisabeth. "Richard Strauss: 'Morgen,' a Master
       Lesson." **Etude** 69/2 (February 1951): 26, 56.

       Gives the performer suggestions on the singing of
       "Morgen" based on Schumann's experience and work with
       Strauss. Especially important are the breathing and
       legato, the relationship of the singer's with the pianist's
       part, and maintaining the mood.

706.   Tenschert, Roland. "Der 'Krämerspiegel' von Richard
       Strauss." **Oesterreichische Musikzeitschrift** 16 (1961):
       221-23.

       Recounts the history of the composer's relationships with
       his publishers and the publication of the set, and points
       out the textual and musical references in the **Krämerspiegel**
       to Strauss's other works.

707.   Urban, Erich. "Richard Strauss in neuen Liedern." **Die Musik**
       1 (1902): 2137-41.

       Rather poetically identifies Strauss's place in the his-
       tory of the development of the Lied. The influence of
       Liszt is cited, as is the contrast between Strauss and
       Wolf. Strauss's songs aim toward a combination of the
       declamatory principle with flowing melody.

Igor Stravinsky
(1882-1971)

708.   **"Exempli Gratia:** What You Hear Is What You Get." **In Theory
       Only** 2/1-2 (April-May 1976): 51-54.

       Presents a two-pronged analysis of Stravinsky's setting
       of Shakespeare's "Musicke to heare," from a serial and from
       a tonal perspective. The piece dates from the period at
       which the composer began to use serial technique and raises
       for the author questions about whether the listener might
       be able to hear the song as belonging to either style or
       both at the same time.

709.   Lindlar, Heinrich. "Die frühen Lieder von Strawinsky."
       Musica 23 (1969): 116-20.

       Surveys Stravinsky's song output before 1920, placing it
       is its context in relation to the composer's literary and
       musical environment. Russian folksong was an important
       source. A number of these pieces were scored for ensemble
       accompaniment.

Barbara Strozzi
(1619-after 1664)

710.   Rosand, Ellen. "Barbara Strozzi, virtuosissima cantatrice:
       The Composer's Voice." **Journal of the American Musicolog-
       ical Society** 31 (1978): 241-81.

       Recounts the career of the Venetian singer and song
       composer. Most of her texts are love lyrics in the
       Marinist style. She used both the cantata structure made
       up of series of sections in contrasting styles and the
       strophic aria form with considerable ingenuity.

Arthur Sullivan
(1842-1900)

711.   Poladian, Sirvart. **Sir Arthur Sullivan: An Index to the
       Texts of His Vocal Works.** Detroit Studies in Music Bib-
       liography 2. Detroit: Information Service, 1961. xviii,
       91p.

       Lists songs by titles and first lines. Authors of texts
       are indicated. Most of the volume is occupied with the

list of songs from dramatic works; art songs are grouped together with hymns and other small items.

Pyotr Il'yich Tchaikovsky
(1840-1893)

712. Engel-Braunschmidt, Annelore. **"Nur Du allein** von Ada Christen und P.I. Cajkovskijs Vertonung." In **Festschrift für Herrn Prof. Dr. D. Gerhardt,** 123-39. Amsterdam: Hakkert, 1972.

Not examined. According to the **RILM** abstract (76/724), the translator of the text, A.N. Pleshcheyev, an acquaintance of Tchaikovsky, enriched the original poem by Ada Christen.

Georg Philipp Telemann
(1681-1767)

713. Richter, Lukas. "Telemanns Lieder nach Hagedorn." In **Telemann und seine Dichter: Konferenzbericht der 6. Magdeburger Telemann-Festtage vom 9. bis 12. Juni 1977,** edited by Walther Siegmund-Schulze and Günther Fleischhauer, 87-97. Magdeburg: Rat der Stadt, 1978.

Not examined. According to the author's abstract in **RILM** (78/6377), the composer was the first to set Hagedorn's texts to music, and these settings helped to stimulate the development of the genre.

714. Zauft, Karin. **Telemanns Liedschaffen.** Magdeburger Telemann Studien 2. Magdeburg: Arbeitskreis "Georg Philipp Telemann," 1967. 24p.

Not examined. According to Wendelin Müller-Blattau's review in **Die Musikforschung** 21 (1968): 402-3, establishes the historical position of Telemann's Lieder and solos as the first such collection by a single author, indicates the composer's broad knowledge of literature, identifies the musical roots of the song style and Telemann's contribution to the history of the genre.

Francesco Paolo Tosti
(1846-1916)

715. Little, John Arthur. "Romantic Italian Song Style in the
      Works of Francesco Paolo Tosti and some of His Contempo-
      raries." D.M.A. diss., University of Illinois, 1977.
      vii, 150p.

      Not examined. According to the **RILM** abstract (77/4769),
      summarizes the styles of selected songs by Tosti, Luigi
      Denza, Augusto Rotoli, Ruggero Leoncavallo, and Giacomo
      Puccini. Compares Tosti's style to Italian folksong, Nea-
      politan song, and opera arias.

716. Ricci, Vittorio. "F.P. Tosti e la lirica vocale italiana
      nell'ottocento." **Revista musicale italiana** 24 (1917):
      491-500.

      Evaluates Tosti's songs and the situation in song compo-
      sition in nineteenth-century Italy in general. Tosti's
      main gift was for melody; he also developed an accompani-
      ment style that was more interesting than the usual
      "guitar" style. The roots of his style were in Abruzzi
      folk melody, he reached his greatest artistry in his second
      period, and he declined into a more popular vein in his
      late (English) years. Ricci also criticizes the Italian
      song of the time for having become too exclusively oriented
      to melody.

Hermann Unger
(1886-1958)

717. Heldt, Gerhard. "Hermann Ungers Klavierlieder: Versuch
      einer Standortsbestimmung des deutschen Liedes nach Max
      Reger." In **Reger-Studien: Festschrift für Ottmar
      Schreiber zum 70. Geburtstag am 16. Februar 1976,** edited
      by Günther Massenkeil and Susanne Popp, 135-58.
      Schriftenreihe des Max-Reger Instituts Bonn-Bad Godesberg
      1. Wiesbaden: Breitkopf & Härtel, 1978.

      Not examined. The author's **RILM** abstract (78/5271) indi-
      cates that Unger, a student of Reger, developed a folk-like
      style influenced by Reger, expressionism, and naturalist
      poetry.

Edgard Varèse
(1883-1965)

718.   Stempel, Larry. "Not Even Varèse Can Be an Orphan." **The**
       Musical Quarterly 60 (1974): 46-60.

       Discusses the 1906 setting of Verlaine's "Un grand som-
       meil noir" by Varèse. This early work reveals traces of
       the influence of Debussy on Varèse both in the general
       tonal language and specifically in reference to Debussy's
       setting of Verlaine's "L'Ombre des arbres."

Ralph Vaughan Williams
(1872-1958)

719.   Evans, Edwin. "English Song and 'On Wenlock Edge'." **The**
       Musical Times 59 (1918): 247-49.

       Praises Vaughan Williams's A.E. Housman cycle. The
       author finds that the composer is especially sensitive to
       the diction of the English language and successful in
       evoking the national character. He is more cautiously
       positive in his evaluation of the use of rhetorical means.
       He regards the music's greatest beauty as residing in its
       sensual appeal.

720.   Kimmel, William. "Vaughan Williams's Choice of Words."
       Music and Letters 19 (1938): 132-42.

       Groups the texts set by Vaughan Williams into three
       categories: folk, folk-style, and rustic poems; poems from
       the great ages of English literature with Chaucer and
       Shakespeare; and mystic poetry. Each type reveals an as-
       pect of the composer's personality, and each evoked a
       characteristic musical style.

721.   LaRue, Jan. "A Legacy from Vaughan Williams: Authentic
       Tempi for **On Wenlock Edge**." **The Music Review** 28 (1967):
       147-48.

       Reports that the composer wrote tempo and metronome indi-
       cations, as well as other performance suggestions, into the
       score of the tenor Rulon Robison. The markings are listed.

722.   Ould, Hermann. "The Songs of Ralph Vaughan Williams."
       English Review 46 (1928): 605-9.

Critiques the songs, from those that preceded the composer's development of an original, personal style through
"his most important contribution to song literature," **On
Wenlock Edge** of 1909, to the mid-1920s. Alludes to the
importance of folk style and spiritual mysticism in Vaughan
Williams's songs.

Peter Warlock (Philip Heseltine)
(1894-1930)

723. Avery, Kenneth. "The Chronology of Warlock's Songs." **Music
and Letters** 29 (1948): 398-405.

Corrects and updates the listing in Cecil Gray's 1934
biography of the composer. The works are grouped by cate-
gory--solo songs, unison choral works, and pieces for more
than one solo singer--and by year.

724. Cockshott, Gerald. "Some Notes on the Songs of Peter Warlock." **Music and Letters** 21 (1940): 246-58.

Characterizes and evaluates the songs, showing the influences of Delius (later abandoned), van Dieren, Vaughan
Williams, and the sixteenth- and seventeenth-century
English composers. Cockshott is particularly concerned to
defend the composer against the charge that his piano
writing and harmony overpower the vocal lines. The songs
are characterized as falling into three characteristic
styles: the introverted ("Heseltine"), the extroverted
("Warlock"), and those which combine elements of both of
the first two types.

*   Hold, Trevor. "Two Aspects of 'Sleep': A Study in English
Song-Writing." **The Music Review** 41 (1980): 26-35.

Cited above as item 325.

*   Yenne, Vernon Lee. "Three Twentieth Century English Song
Composers: Peter Warlock, E.J. Moeran and John Ireland."
D.M.A. diss., University of Illinois, 1969. 313p.

Cited above as item 350.

Anton Webern
(1883-1945)

725. Beckmann, Dorothea. **Sprache und Musik im Vokalwerk Anton Weberns: Die Konstruktion des Ausdruckes.** Kölner Beiträge zur Musikforschung 57. Regensburg: Bosse, 1970. 237p.

Seeks to show how the composer's musical response to texts was a determining factor in the development of his style. Webern moved in the direction of increasing intervallic distances in his vocal lines and more frequent and abrupt changes in melodic direction, creating a higher concentration of pitch accentuations. Although the detailed analysis concentrates on the vocal lines of the songs, there is also a chapter on the reflection of the texts in instrumental parts. Index of works discussed. Bibliography.

726. Brinkmann, Reinhold. "Die George-Lieder 1908/9 und 1919/23: Ein Kapitel Webern-Philologie." In **Oesterreichische Gesellschaft für Musik, Beiträge 1972/73: Webern-Kongress,** 40-50. Kassel: Bärenreiter, 1973.

Shows that the versions in which the songs of opp. 3 and 4 are known are not the originals but date from as late as revisions made from ten to fifteen years after the original compositions. Some of the changes constitute significant musical alterations and thus require reconsideration of the understanding of Webern's style development.

727. Budde, Elmar. "Metrisch-rhythmische Probleme im Vokalwerk Weberns." In **Oesterreichische Gesellschaft für Musik, Beiträge 1972/73: Webern-Kongress,** 52-60. Kassel: Bärenreiter, 1973.

Demonstrates that in Webern's vocal lines rhythms are produced by metrical considerations in the poetic texts, while individual text lines are set off by rests. In earlier works the process is more rigid, while in those of the composer's middle period it becomes more flexible. The settings of George's "Im Windesweben" (op. 3, no. 2) and Trakl's "Ein Winterabend" (op. 13, no. 4) are employed as illustrations.

728. Chittum, Donald. "Some Observations on the Row Technique in Webern's Opus 25." **Current Musicology** 12/1971: 96-101.

Demonstrates how in the **Three Songs** op. 25 Webern takes

advantage of elisions to link forms of his row, and argues
that he employs row-form pairs in a kind of tonic-dominant
function, and transposition analogously to key contrast in
tonal music.

729.   Escot, Pozzi. "Webern's opus 25, no. 1: Perception of
       Large-Scale Patterns." **Theory and Practice** 4/1 (March
       1979): 28-29.

       Not examined. According to the **RILM** abstract (79/1680),
       suggests that large-scale patterns are heard by coordi-
       nating the basic rhythmic content with dynamics and text.

730.   Gerlach, Reinhard. "Anton Webern, Ein Winterabend op. 13,
       Nr. 4: Zum Verhältnis von Musik und Dichtung, oder Wahr-
       heit als Struktur." **Archiv für Musikwissenschaft** 30
       (1973): 44-68.

       Makes a thorough analysis of the music and of the text.
       Argues that for Webern's music and Trakl's poem analysis of
       any single aspect of the work fails to show an effective
       coherence, but that in both cases all the component aspects
       together combine to produce a coherent artistic entity.
       Thus the text and music work together to elucidate each
       other as interlinear versions of each other.

731.   ———. "Die Dehmel-Lieder von Anton Webern: Musik und
       Sprache im Uebergang zur Atonalität." **Jahrbuch des Staat-
       lichen Instituts für Musikforschung Preussischer Kultur-
       besitz 1970,** edited by Dagmar Droysen, 45-100. Berlin:
       Merseburger, 1971.

       Regards Webern's Dehmel songs as crucial in the develop-
       ment of his style. Detailed analysis of the texts leads to
       the conclusion that the songs form a cycle based on the
       metaphor of light yielding to darkness, reality becoming
       unreality, and the dissolution of the self. The music
       correspondingly reflects these ideas in the gradual transi-
       tion from a more traditional (tonal, homophonic, metric,
       symmetrical) style to a new, progressive one (atonal, con-
       trapuntal, rhythmically free, asymmetrical). Tables, dia-
       grams. Bibliography.

732.   ———. "Die Funktion des Textes in Liedern Anton Weberns."
       In **Colloquium Music and Word, Brno 1969,** edited by Rudolf
       Pečman, 263-85. Brno: International Musical Festival,
       1973.

Presents a detailed analysis of the music and text (by
Georg Trakl) of Webern's 1918 orchestral song "Ein Winterabend," op. 13, no. 4. Gerlach demonstrates that the
function of the text is to serve as a kind of "interlinear"
parallel to the music, while the music functions in the
same manner in relation to the text. Bibliography.

733. ⸻. "Die Handschriften der Dehmel-Lieder von Anton
    Webern: Textkritische Studien." **Archiv für Musikwissen-
    schaft** 29 (1972): 93-114.

Lists and discusses the significance of some of the
notational aspects of the manuscript of the Dehmel songs.
The source differs in several respects from the published
edition by Leonard Stein. The manuscript shows Webern's
compositional technique and clarifies his aesthetic intentions.

734. ⸻. "Kompositionsniederschrift und Werkfassung am Bei-
    spiel des Liedes 'Am Ufer' (1908) von Webern." In **Oester-
    reichische Gesellschaft für Musik, Beiträge 1972/73:
    Webern-Kongress,** 111-26. Kassel: Bärenreiter, 1973.

Distinguishes between various types of manuscripts produced in the course of a composition and shows how ambiguous readings can be resolved in different ways. Gerlach
criticizes the edition of "Am Ufer" by Leonard Stein (New
York: Carl Fischer, 1966).

735. Holopova, Valentina. "Chromatische Prinzipien in Anton
    Weberns Vokalzyklus **Sechs Lieder nach Gedichten von G.
    Trakl,** op. 14." **Beiträge zur Musikwissenschaft** 17 (1975):
    155-69.

Not examined. The **RILM** entry (76/7176) indicates that
the atonal music of the cycle is structured by procedures
modified from the chromatic tonal idiom.

736. Metzger, Heinz-Klaus. "Analysis of the Sacred Song, op. 15
    no. 4." In **Die Reihe 2: Anton Webern,** edited by Herbert
    Eimert and Karlheinz Stockhausen, 75-80. Bryn Mawr, Pa.:
    Presser, 1958.

Argues for a "diagonal" hearing of certain elements in
the song, where vertical relationships are not presented as
actual simultaneities. In Webern's music the usual dichotomy of horizontal and vertical (melody and accompaniment)
is suspended.

737.   Moldenhauer, Hans. "Anton von Webern: Neue Sichten über
       einige posthume Werke." **Oesterreichische Musikzeitschrift**
       27 (1972): 114-21.

       Gives details of the compositional history of the **Drei
       Orchesterlieder** (1913-14) and four songs on texts of Stefan
       George (1908-9), among other works.

738.   ———. "Webern's Projected op. 32." **The Musical Times** 111
       (1970): 789-92.

       Reports that at the time of his death Webern was working
       on a setting of Hildegard Jone's **Lumen** poems. Both musical
       sketches and letters from the composer bear witness to his
       work on this project.

739.   Ringger, Rolf Urs. **Anton Weberns Klavierlieder.** Zürich:
       Juris, 1968. 60p.

       Not examined. The **RILM** entry (69/1824) indicates that
       the study, Ringger's Ph.D. dissertation (University of
       Zurich, 1968), demonstrates the development of essential
       characteristics of Webern's oeuvre in his five song cycles.
       Bibliography.

740.   ———. "Reihenelemente in Anton Weberns Klavierliedern."
       Schweizerische Musikzeitung 107 (1967): 144-49.

       Not examined. The abstract in **RILM** (67/1937) states that
       the development of Webern's serial methods is traced in
       opp. 3, 4, 12, 23, and 25. In the last two cycles serial-
       ism is extended from pitch to other elements.

741.   ———. "Sprach-musikalische Chiffern in Anton Weberns
       Klavierliedern." **Schweizerische Musikzeitschrift** 106
       (1966): 14-19.

       Groups Webern's musical treatments of textual meaning in
       three categories: illustrative, symbolic, and structural.
       Demonstrates each type with several music examples. In the
       course of the composer's development, he moved increasingly
       toward the use of textual motivation for structural deci-
       sions.

742.   ———. "Zur Wort-Ton-Beziehung beim frühen Anton Webern."
       Schweizerische Musikzeitung 103 (1963): 330-35.

       Presents an analysis of "Dies ist ein Lied," op. 3 no. 1,

on a text of Stefan George, despite the title of the article dealing with musical matters to the near exclusion of textual ones. The song is seen to be forward-looking in its anticipation of Webern's middle-period style, the serial technique, and even the styles of some later composers.

743. Schollum, Robert. "Stilistische Elemente der frühen Webern-Lieder." In **Oesterreichische Gesellschaft für Musik, Beiträge 1972/73: Webern-Kongress,** 127-34. Kassel: Bärenreiter, 1973.

Seeks to identify stylistic characteristics in the early songs in order to provide grounds for interpretations of the later works. In the course of these early songs Webern departed from the influence of Wagner and Strauss and began to achieve a model for the balance between textual and musical considerations in song composition.

744. Stein, Leonard. "Webern's **Dehmel Lieder** of 1906-8: Threshold of a New Expression." In **Anton von Webern: Perspectives,** compiled and edited by Hans Moldenhauer and Demar Irvine, 53-61. Seattle: University of Washington Press, 1966.

Identifies traits of Webern's personal style in these works that lead to his achievement of compositional maturity. Unlike Schoenberg, Webern was inclined to avoid development, linear chromaticism, and complex chords. He instead achieves simplicity, transparency, conciseness, and unity of construction.

745. Stephan, Rudolf. "Zu einigen Liedern Anton Weberns." **Oesterreichische Gesellschaft für Musik, Beiträge 1972/73: Webern-Kongress,** 135-44. Kassel: Bärenreiter, 1973.

Demonstrates both textual and musical connections between Webern's songs opp. 12 and 13 and Mahler's **Das Lied von der Erde,** which had made a striking impression on Webern at its 1911 premiere performance. Webern's unusually simple "Der Tag ist vergangen" (op. 12, no. 1), in turn influenced Hanns Eisler's song "Wiegenlied bei Mondschein zu singen," (op. 2, no. 1).

746. Westergaard, Peter. "On the Problems of 'Reconstruction from a Sketch': Webern's **Kunfttag III** and **Leise Düfte.**" **Perspectives of New Music** 11/2 (Spring-Summer 1973): 104-

21.

Discusses the problems of the relation of sketches to complete versions, using these two posthumous songs. To validate the attempt to construct Webern's intention from the sketch which is all that is extant of "Kunfttag III," Westergaard tries the procedure with "Leise Düfte", for which both sketch and score are available. The result is a version that diverges from Webern's in significant ways. The conclusions to be drawn are that the sketch does not necessarily represent the composer's ideas but only clues to them that would serve him, and also that his thoughts might change between the early stage and the final score.

747. Wilsen, William. "Equitonality as a Measure of the Evolution toward Atonality in the Pre-Opus 1 Songs of Anton Webern." Ph.D. diss., Florida State University, 1975. xii, 178p.

Compiles statistical data based on the total duration of each pitch class in the music to demonstrate a chronological progression in the direction of equal time for each pitch class. Tables, graphs. Appendices. Bibliography.

John Wilson
(1595-1674)

748. Crum, Margaret. "A Manuscript of John Wilson's Songs." **The Library,** 5th series, 10 (1955): 55-57.

Considers the history of Bodleian MS.Mus.b.1. The manuscript is not Wilson's autograph but a fair copy made for the composer in order for him to work on the songs further.

749. Henderson, Hubert Platt. "The Vocal Music of John Wilson." Ph.D. diss., University of North Carolina, 1962. 388p.

Not examined. The author's abstract in **Dissertation Abstracts** (23 [1963]: 4376-77) states that the study presents a style analysis based on a collection of all of Wilson's works. There are two main types of songs: the tuneful ayres based on dance rhythms, and the declamatory ayres in which the text exerts more control over the rhythm. The style in general reflects the influence of dance patterns on rhythm, the use of long phrases and chromaticism in melody, and the transitional period from modal to tonal harmony. Especially important is Wilson's

focus on the voice by reducing the lute's role from that of
partner to one of subordinate accompaniment.

Hugo Wolf
(1860-1903)

750.   Austin, Frederic. "The Songs of Hugo Wolf." **Proceedings of
       the Musical Association** 38 (1911-12): 161-69.

       Combines a brief biography of Wolf, critical commentary
       on the songs in general, and descriptive remarks on some
       individual songs. Austin attributes Wolf's style to his
       objective approach to the true expression of the emotion of
       the poetry, expressive concentration, and unifying motivic
       development.

*   Baum, Günther. "Hugo Wolf und Richard Strauss in ihren
       Liedern."

       Cited above as item 696.

751.   ————. "Zur Vor- und Entstehunsgeschichte des Mörike-
       Liederbuches von Hugo Wolf." **Neue Zeitschrift für Musik**
       132 (1971): 648-49.

       Presents the history of Wolf's interest in Mörike's poems
       from 1878, when he dated his copy of the poems, through the
       next decade, during which he composed four settings of
       Mörike's texts, to 1888, the year of the composition of the
       collection of fifty-three Mörike-Lieder.

752.   Bieri, Georg. "Hugo Wolfs Lieder nach verschiedenen
       Dichtern." **Schweizerische Musikzeitung** 75 (1935): 401-7.

       Supplements the author's major study of the songs (see
       item 753 below). Discusses Wolf's thirty independent
       Lieder, spanning his entire compositional career from 1877
       to 1897. Describes the variety of styles employed in these
       songs, explaining how the texts influence the settings and
       illustrating the development of Wolf's style. The author
       judges most of these independent songs to be the equals of
       those in the major collections.

753.   ————. **Die Lieder von Hugo Wolf.** Berner Veröffentlichungen
       zur Musikforschung 5. Bern: Paul Haupt, 1935. xxiv,
       269p.

Analyzes in detail the style of Wolf's Lieder. The text begins with a brief historical introduction. A study of Wolf's declamation in vocal lines shows that considerations of diction predominate over those of vocalism in melody and places Wolf in the circle of Wagner. Examination of the piano parts reveals that Wolf's concept of the piano's role in accompaniment is based on the style of Schubert, while the developmental writing of his postludes and the corresponding expansion of preludes and interludes derive from Schumann's works. Indexes.

754. Böschenstein, Bernhard. "Zum Verhältnis von Dichtung und Musik in Hugo Wolfs Mörikeliedern." **Wirkendes Wort** 19 (1969): 175-93.

Discusses Wolf's treatment of Mörike's poems in four songs: "Um Mitternacht," "Wo find' ich Trost?" "Im Frühling," and "Auf eine Christblume I." Structurally, the procedures Wolf employed vary from strophic to through-composed. Expressively, Wolf's treatments represent intensification of the poems, often achieved by means of chromaticism.

755. Boylan, Paul Charles. "The Lieder of Hugo Wolf: Zenith of the German Art Song." Ph.D. diss., University of Michigan, 1968. vii, 402p.

Emphasizes the responses of music to poetry in Wolf's Lieder. Fairly thorough analyses of style and musical text-setting procedures are given. Songs of Wolf are compared to settings by Schubert, Schumann, and Brahms of the same texts. The study concludes that Wolf's style was forward-looking in harmony and melody, but rooted in traditions of form inherited from earlier Lied composers.

*   Bruner, Ellen Carole. "The Relationship of Text and Music in the Lieder of Hugo Wolf and Gustav Mahler."

Cited above as item 398.

756. Carner, Mosco. **Hugo Wolf Songs.** BBC Music Guides. London: British Broadcasting Corporation, 1982. 72p.

Discusses Wolf's song production in chronological outline. An introductory chapter summarizes Wolf's approaches both from an aesthetic point of view--stressing his emphasis on the primacy of the text and on artistic realism--and from the point of view of style and style development--

proceeding from a subjective to an objective attitude.   The
bulk of the book is devoted to brief (but pithy) commentary
on the songs themselves.   Index of songs.

757.   Dahlhaus, Carl. "Ein Dilemma der Verskomposition." **Melos/
       Neue Zeitschrift für Musik** 3 (1977): 15-18.

       Illustrates by examples taken from the songs of Wolf
       Wagner's observation that in setting verse the composer
       either must sacrifice musical regularity to precise decla-
       mation, as in recitative, or vice versa, as in songs and
       arias.   Wolf employs both approaches.   He also coordinates
       the various musical means of effecting accent.

758.   Decsey, Ernst. **Hugo Wolf: Das Leben und das Lied.** Berlin:
       Schuster & Loeffler, 1919.   198p.

       Supersedes an earlier biography by Decsey (**Hugo Wolf.** 4
       vols. Leipzig and Berlin: Schuster, 1903-6).   After an
       extensive biography there is a separate section on the
       music.   The predominant characteristics of the songs are
       held to be the importance Wolf assigned to the texts,
       artistic realism, and the influence of Wagner.   His style,
       based on sophisticated compositional procedures, is con-
       trasted to the folk-based Lied style of Mahler.   Each of
       the collections is discussed briefly.   Work-lists; biblio-
       graphy.   Indexes.

759.   Egger, Rita. **Die Deklamationsrhythmik Hugo Wolfs in
       historischer Sicht.** Tutzing: Hans Schneider, 1963.   62p.

       Illustrates the relationships between vocal rhythm and
       poetic rhythm in Wolf's songs.   The numerous musical exam-
       ples are grouped in order from more or less straightforward
       "metrical" declamations to syncopated departures from sim-
       ple metrical arrangements.   The more direct style is usu-
       ally used for setting simple, Lied-style poems; the more
       complex poetic rhythms generally receive more varied treat-
       ments.   Wolf also employs the piano parts to articulate the
       regular structure of a poem, however, permitting a more
       flexible treatment of the vocal declamation.   A supplement
       gives comparable declamations by other composers.   Indexes.

760.   Fox Strangways, A.H. "Schubert and Wolf." **Music and Letters**
       23 (1942): 126-34.

       Gives singing translations for Wolf's settings of
       Goethe's "Prometheus," "Ganymed," and "Grenzen der

Menschheit." The music of Schubert and Wolf for these poems is compared. Wolf's setting are adjudged more dramatic, Schubert's more lyrical.

761. **Gesammelte Aufsätze über Hugo Wolf.** 2 vols. Edited by the Hugo Wolf-Verein of Vienna. Berlin: S. Fischer, 1898-99. xii, 98; 63p.

Comprises a valuable set of contemporary views, principally from non-music publications. Wolf is recognized as the leader of the New German School in the Lied, due to his belief in the primacy of text over music. The contributors are Dr. Grumsky, Michael Haberlandt, Karl Hallwachs, Edmund Hellmer, Emil Kauffmann, Paul Müller, Ernst Otto Nodnagel, and Joseph Schalk.

762. Grasberger, Franz. "Aus den Erinnerungen Irmina Köcherts: Wie Hugo Wolf's 'Epiphanias' enstand." **Oesterreichische Musikzeitschrift** 23 (1968): 339-41.

Recounts the history of Wolf's setting of Goethe's text. The song was written at Christmas time in 1888 and was first performed for Wolf's friend Melanie Köchert by her three daughters on the Feast of the Three Kings 1889, as a birthday surprise.

763. Hamburger, Paul. "The Interpretation of Picturesque Elements in Wolf's Songs." **Tempo** 48 (1958): 9-15.

Considers the singer's choices in performing songs in which the vocal lines illustrate images in the text. The issue is whether the performer ought in each case to support the illustrative gesture itself or maintain the position of the speaker for whom the image is attached to an emotional stance. Specific representative examples are discussed. Matters of phrasing and dynamic nuance are dealt with.

764. Hantz, Edwin. "**Exempli gratia:** Le dernier cri (?): Wolf's Harmony Revisited." **In Theory Only** 5/4 (May 1981): 29-32.

Not examined. According to the author's abstract in **RILM** (81/3668), discusses the harmonic concept of deceptive resolution in "Du denkst mit einem Fädchen mich zu fangen" from the **Italienisches Liederbuch.**

765. Kravitt, Edward F. "The Influence of Theatrical Declamation upon Composers of the Late Romantic Lied." **Acta musico-**

logica 34 (1962): 18-28.

Adduces evidence that the late Romantic Lied composers
intended their vocal lines to resemble theatrical declamation. Analyzes Wolf's "Prometheus" in comparison to the
setting by Schubert and to recordings of the poem as read
by two actors who were Wolf's contemporaries, Josef Kainz
and Alexander Moissi. Compares music examples to diagrams
of speech inflections.

766. Legge, Walter. "Hugo Wolf's Afterthoughts on His Mörike-
Lieder." **The Music Review** 2 (1941): 211-14.

Lists alterations and additions Wolf entered in a copy of
the first edition of the Mörike Lieder.

*   Mackworth-Young, G. "Goethe's 'Prometheus' and Its Settings
by Schubert and Wolf."

Cited above as item 570.

767. Sams, Eric. **The Songs of Hugo Wolf.** London: Methuen, 1961.
xii, 268p.

Briefly describes all the songs. An introductory chapter
discusses Wolf's style and attempts to identify recurrent
expressive musical gestures. Each song is dealt with individually in a cursory outline that includes date of
composition, translation of the text, a characterization of
the music, and notes on more technical musical details.
Indexes.

768. Schmalzriedt, Siegfried. "Hugo Wolfs Vertonung von Mörikes
Gedicht 'Karwoche': Realistische Züge im spätromantischen
Lied." **Archiv für Musikwissenschaft** 41 (1984): 42-53.

Identifies in Wolf's songs musical traits associated with
the aesthetics of Realism. These include the speech-like
declamation and prose-like construction of the melody, the
emancipation of the vocal part from metrical and tonal
constraints, expanded harmonic language, naturalistic tone-
painting, and the symbolic use of tones and keys.

769. Stein, Deborah J. **Hugo Wolf's Lieder and Extensions of
Tonality.** Studies in Musicology 82. Ann Arbor, Michigan:
UMI Research Press, 1985. x, 237p.

Based on a Schenkerian approach to analysis of the songs,

investigates harmonic ambiguity in Wolf's style. In particular, the discussion takes up the emphasis on the plagal
axis, third relations, and directed tonality. Although
recognizing the importance of the text in motivating these
expansions of traditional tonal syntax, Stein holds that
they are also justified by intrinsically musical principles. Bibliography. Index.

770. Stein, Jack M. "Poem and Music in Hugo Wolf's Mörike
      Songs." **The Musical Quarterly** 53 (1967): 22-38.

      Judges Wolf's settings of Mörike's poems to be the most
      advanced achievements in the synthesis of works and music
      in the nineteenth century. Stein's method, as always, is
      to test Wolf's interpretations against his own readings of
      the texts. Some of the songs, including "An eine Aeols-
      harfe" and "Verborgenheit," are considered failures;
      others, notably "Um Mitternacht," "Fussreise," and "In der
      Frühe," are adjudged masterpieces.

771. Tausche, Anton. **Hugo Wolf's Mörikelieder in Dichtung, Musik
      und Vortrag.** Vienna: Amandus, 1947. 207p.

      Addresses singers, with emphasis on performance. The
      opening chapter gives general advice on performing Lieder.
      Each of the fifty-three songs receives individual treat-
      ment. Tausche elucidates the content of each text and
      draws attention to what he considers the most important
      musical details. Specific recommendations are offered as
      to interpretation. An appendix lists transcriptions and
      translations into French.

772. Thürmer, Helmut. **Die Melodik in den Liedern von Hugo Wolf.**
      Schriften zur Musik 2. Giebing: Katzbichler, 1970. 239p.

      Classifies basic melodic types, shows how Wolf developed
      melodic structures, and examines the interaction of declam-
      atory and purely melodic tendencies. Argues that the com-
      mon pigeon-holing of Wolf's melodic style as declamatory is
      misleading. Bibliography, list of poets and cycles, work-
      list. Index.

*   Thym, Jürgen. "The Solo Song Settings of Eichendorff's
      Poems by Schumann and Wolf."

      Cited above as item 679.

773. Walker, Frank. "Wolf's Spanish and Italian Songs." **Music**

and Letters 25 (1944): 194-209.

Gives a pre-publication extract from Walker's major 1951
study of the composer (**Hugo Wolf: A Biography,** 2nd ed. New
York: Knopf, 1968). Comments in a general way on the
songs, covering each in a few lines.

774. Werba, Erik. "Der Hugo-Wolf Liederabend." **Oesterreichische
Musikzeitschrift** 28 (1973): 434-37.

Proposes an arrangement of the songs of the **Italienisches
Liederbuch** for performance, based on the order of their
composition.

775. ———. "Hugo Wolfs 'Italienisches Liederbuch': Anmerkungen
zur Reihung und Aufführungspraxis." **Oesterreichische
Musikzeitschrift** 10 (1955): 164-67.

Recommends an ordering of the songs of the **Italienisches
Liederbuch** for performance by male and female singers singing in alternation.

*   ———. "Italienische Liederbücher von Hugo Wolf und Joseph
Marx."

Cited above as item 415.

776. ———. "Der Lyriker Hugo Wolf." **Oesterreichische Musikzeitschrift** 15 (1960): 76-77.

Briefly runs through the history of Wolf's song compositions. Werba suggests that Wolf stands as a counterpart to
Schubert in the genre. Wolf's nationalistic inclinations
are also stressed.

777. Wiora, Walter. "Der musikalische Fortschritt und der 'Wilde
Wolf'." **Festschrift 1817-1967 Akademie für Musik und
darstellende Kunst in Wien,** 88-92. Vienna: Lafite, 1967.

Not examined. According to the **RILM** abstract (69/1494),
deals with Wolf and the idea of progress in music. His
critical writing reveals his thought on the subject, and
his Lieder show progressiveness in style by breaking away
from the declamatory principle.

778. Youens, Susan Lee. "'Alles endet, was entsteht': The Second
of Hugo Wolf's Michaelangelo-Lieder." **Studies in Music**
(Australia) 14 (1980): 87-103.

Presents a motivic analysis of the song. The working out
of the central figure, a cambiata featuring pairs of half-
steps, leads to the brink of the dissolution of tonality.
The musical technique is generated from the text, in which
death and life, and past, present, and future mingle.

Felix Wolfes
(1892-1971)

779. Rectanus, Hans. "Unsterbliche Melodie: Die Lieder von Felix
Wolfes." **Mitteilungen der Hans-Pfitzner-Gesellschaft**
28(1972): 18-22.

Not examined. According to the author's abstract in **RILM**
(72/2046) surveys the songs of Wolfes, a student of Pfitzner, and discusses several representative ones in detail.

Carl Friedrich Zelter
(1758-1832)

780. Barr, Raymond Arthur. "Carl Friedrich Zelter: A Study of
the Lied in Berlin during the Late Eighteenth and Early
Nineteenth Centuries." Ph.D. diss., University of Wiscon-
sin, 1968. 290p.

Sets the background of the two Berlin Song Schools,
outlines Zelter's biography, and establishes his position
as a key figure in the development of the Lied. Explains
Zelter's procedures in composing Lieder and comments on
individual songs. Index of Lieder.

781. Moser, Hans Joachim. "Karl Friedrich Zelter und das Lied."
Jahrbuch der Musikbibliothek Peters 39 (1932): 43-54.

Describes and illustrates Zelter's song style. Moser
finds Zelter's melody graceful and his harmonic language
expressive. He suggests, quite reasonably, that the composer ought not to be judged harshly by the accomplishments
of his successors.

782. Wittmann, Gertraud. **Das klavierbegleitete Sololied Karl**
Friedrich Zelters. Giessen: Triltsch & Huther, 1936.
108p.

Describes the style of Zelter's songs. Introductory
material offers a historical and biographical context for

the music and discusses the texts Zelter set. The analytical approach is systematic, covering form, melodic style,
and accompaniment and harmony. Wittmann argues that Zelter
was not merely a successor to the tradition of the Second
Berlin School but a forerunner of the Romantic approach to
Lied composition, particularly in the areas of form and
harmony. Bibliography.

Alexander von Zemlinsky
(1871-1942)

*   Weber, Horst. "Schönbergs und Zemlinskys Vertonung der
      Ballade 'Jane Grey' von Heinrich Ammann: Untersuchungen
      zum Spätstudium der Tonalität."

      Cited above as item 509.

783.   ———. "Zemlinskys Maeterlinck-Gesänge." **Archiv für Musik-
        wissenschaft** 29 (1972): 182-202.

        Presents a very detailed analysis of op. 13, no. 1, "Die
        drei Schwestern." The structure of the song, like the
        meaning of the text, is open-ended, and this opens the way
        to the connection of the six songs into a cyclical whole.

Johann Rudolf Zumsteeg
(1760-1802)

784.   Landshoff, Ludwig. **Johann Rudolf Zumsteeg (1760-1802): Ein
        Beitrag zur Geschichte des Liedes und der Ballade.**
        Berlin: S. Fischer, 1902. vii, 214p.

        Landshoff's dissertation (University of Munich, 1900),
        concentrates on placing the songs in the context of the
        composer's biography rather than on style. An extensive
        appendix relates Zumsteeg's early songs to the melodrama.
        Work-list. Facsimile. Musical supplement.

785.   Maier, Gunter. **Die Lieder Johann Rudolf Zumsteegs und ihr
        Verhältnis zu Schubert.** Göppingen: Kümmerle, 1971.

        Maier's dissertation (University of Tübingen, 1970),
        examines the Lieder, as distinguished from ballads. Among
        the sources studied were forty-four previously neglected
        pieces. The poets are identified. The main body of the
        study deals with the character of the settings in general,

in regard to melody, rhythm, declamation, harmony, piano
accompaniment, and form. Among the major influences on
Zumsteeg were Jomelli, Benda, and Mozart; his manner of
text treatment is, however, quite original. Zumsteeg's
influence on Schubert is evident not only in the form of
the latter's early ballads, but in melodic ideas extending
into late works. A list of parallel settings by the two
composers is provided. Comparison of six of these shows
both Schubert's debt to Zumsteeg and the differences between their approaches. An appendix gives four previously
unpublished letters. Chronological index of Lieder and
ballads.

786. Porter, E.G. "Zumsteeg's Songs." **Monthly Musical Record** 88
(1958): 135-40.

Makes a general survey of Zumsteeg's songs. His style is
described as charming, but thin in texture (often in two
parts notated on two staves) and simple in harmony, while
the treatment of the texts is imaginative and often quite
varied within even a single short piece. Some songs are
described, others listed. In comparing the settings of the
same texts by Zumsteeg and Schubert, Porter finds that each
excels in some instances.

*   Sandberger, Adolf. "Johann Rudolph Zumsteeg und Franz Schubert." In **Ausgewählte Aufsätze zur Musikgeschichte.** Vol.
1, 288-99.

Cited above as item 645.

787. Szymichowski, Franz. "Johann Rudolph Zumsteeg als Komponist
von Balladen und Monodien." Ph.D. diss., Johann Wolfgang
Goethe-Universität, Frankfurt am Main, 1932. ix, 107p.

Studies the ballads and monodies of Zumsteeg in general.
A classification into sub-types is offered, with a survey
of the forms of the pieces. Szymichowski then discusses
the musical style in various areas, especially regarding
the influence of the texts on compositional choices. Zumsteeg is placed in historical perspective, particularly in
relation to Loewe. Finally there is a section of commentary on each song individually. An appendix gives analytical tables.

III

STUDIES OF INDIVIDUAL POETS AND TEXTS

Rafael Alberti
(b. 1902)

788. Curtis, Brandt B. "Rafael Alberti and Chilean Composers."
D.M.A. diss., Indiana University, 1977. 104p.

Not examined. According to the author's abstract in **RILM**
(77/806), analyzes settings of Alberti's poetry by Juan
Orrego-Salas and Carlos Riesco. Provides information on
the art song in Chile and on the poet and the two composers. Gives English translations of the songs. Bibliography.

Achim von Arnim
(1781-1831)

789. Sams, Eric. "Notes on a Magic Horn." **The Musical Times** 115
(1974): 556-59.

Defines the nature of the poems in **Des Knaben Wunderhorn**
and its reception by composers from Weber to Webern. Sams
stresses that the texts were not genuine folk poems, but
adaptions by Achim von Arnim. Their appeal to composers
was not the genuineness of folk style but the fecundity of
Romantic imagination they manifest. List of major settings.

Georg Friedrich Daumer
(1800-1875)

790. Otto, Eberhard. "Georg Friedrich Daumer und Johannes
Brahms: Ein fränkischer Dichter und seine Komponist."

Musik in Bayern 21 (1980): 11-18.

Not examined. According to the author's **RILM** abstract
(80/3965), emphasizes the importance of Daumer's religious
thought.

Walter de la Mare
(1873-1956)

791. Beechey, Gwilym. "Walter de la Mare: Settings of His
      Poetry--A Centenary Note." **The Musical Times** 114 (1973):
      371-73.

      An appreciation of de la Mare with notes on settings of
      his poems by Armstrong Gibbs, Arthus Bliss, Herbert
      Howells, Benjamin Britten, Ivor Gurney, and Lennox
      Berkeley.

Philippe Desportes
(1546-1606)

792. Verchaly, André. "Desportes et la musique." **Annales musi-
      cologiques** 2 (1954): 271-345.

      Covers the influence of the poet on music in general,
      including airs, polyphonic vocal pieces, and psalms. His
      poetry was employed by the composers of lute airs until
      about 1650 when tastes began to change. List of published
      musical settings by collections in chronological order;
      alphabetical list of of texts; musical appendix including
      two lute songs.

John Donne
(1572-1631)

793. Duckles, Vincent. "The Lyrics of John Donne as Set by His
      Contemporaries." In **International Musicological Society
      Kongressbericht, Köln 1958,** 91-93. Kassel: Bärenreiter,
      1959.

      Lists the seventeenth-century settings of lyrics by or
      attributed to Donne, with their sources. There are alto-
      gether only twenty-nine settings. Donne's poetry, while
      much of it was intended for music, presents problems to
      composers.

794. Hanscombe, Gillian. "John Donne and the Writing of Lyrics."
      Studies in Music (Australia) 6 (1972): 10-26.

      Attempts to explain how Donne's poetry is non-lyrical.
      The poems "The Triple Foole" and "Song, 'Sweetest love I do
      not goe'" are analyzed, together with the musical setting
      of the letter in MS 1018 f.44b from St. Michael's College.
      Donne's texts are distinct from lyrics in their speech-like
      rhythms and in their concentration on social action. When
      they are set to music, Donne's texts and the musical struc-
      tures interfere with each other.

                     Joseph, Freiherr von Eichendorff
                              (1788-1857)

795. Busse, Eckart. "Die Eichendorff-Rezeption im Kunstlied:
      Versuch einer Typologie anhand von Kompositionen Schu-
      manns, Wolfs und Pfitzners." Ph.D. diss., Marburg Univer-
      sity, 1973. 250p. Würzburg: Eichendorff-Gesellschaft,
      1975.

      Not examined. According to the author's abstract in **RILM**
      (74/4061), associates contrasting styles in the music with
      specific poetic types.

796. Speer, Gotthard. "Eichendorffs Lyrik in Vertonungen."
      Aurora 34 (1974): 52-64.

      Not examined. The author's abstract in **RILM** (75/4583)
      states that the study identifies a renaissance of interest
      in Eichendorff among composers, demonstrates the musicality
      of his poetry, and classifies the poems into folksong, art
      song, and cyclic types. Specific, representative works are
      examined.

797. Valentin, Hans Erich. "'Schläft ein Lied in allen Dingen':
      Eichendorff in der Musik." **Aurora** 35 (1975): 35-44.

      Not examined. According to the abstract in **RILM** (76/
      4322), deals with settings by a number of the most promi-
      nent Lied composers.

                       Johann Wolfgang von Goethe
                              (1749-1832)

798. Blume, Friedrich. **Goethe und die Musik**. Kassel: Bären-
      reiter, 1948. 101p.

Discusses Goethe's thought on music in general. Considerable attention is given to his ideas on the Lied, particularly as he expressed them in his correspondence with Karl Friedrich Zelter, his favorite composer of his own texts. There are no chapter divisions; the Lied is discussed mostly on pp. 30-44.

799. Düring, Werner-Joachim. **Erlkönig-Vertonungen: Eine historische und systematische Untersuchung.** Kölner Beiträge zur Musikforschung 69. Regensburg: Bosse, 1972. 140, xxip.

Provides a survey of settings of Goethe's ballad "Der Erlkönig." Düring first gives a historical overview of the treatments of the text, of which 131 are listed. The bulk of the study is made up of a discussion, based on 69 settings, of the variety of ways in which the poem has been handled, covering the use of text variants, content and inner meaning, structure, style, and performance setting. Bibliography. Appendices.

800. Forbes, Elliot. **"Nur wer die Sehnsucht kennt:** An Example of a Goethe Lyric Set to Music." In **Words and Music: The Scholar's View—A Medley of Problems and Solutions Compiled in Honor of A. Tillman Merritt,** edited by Laurence Berman, 59-82. Harvard University: Department of Music, 1971.

Analyzes and evaluates settings of Mignon's Lied by Zelter, Beethoven, and Schubert. Forbes regards Zelter's and Beethoven's settings as reflecting Goethe's own aesthetic values for song composition, Schubert's as perfectly balancing text and music. Complete scores for several settings.

801. Friedlaender, Max. "Goethes Gedichte in der Musik." **Goethe-Jahrbuch** 17 (1896): 176-94.

Provides lists of songs based on two dozen of Goethe's most often set texts, with brief notes on some of the outstanding pieces.

802. Holle, Hugo. **Goethes Lyrik in Weisen deutscher Tonsetzer bis zur Gegenwart: Eine stilkritische Studie.** Munich: Wunderhorn-Verlag, 1914. 111p.

Groups a handful of representative texts into three categories--**volkstümliche** Lieder, art lyrics, and ballads--and compares a number of settings of each text. For the folk-

like texts strophic form is adopted automatically. The
art-song type evoked increasingly substantial application
of variation to the strophic structure. The ballads show
how strongly the composers can be influenced by the texts.

803. Mies, Paul. "Goethes Harfenspielergesang 'Wer sich der
     Einsamkeit ergibt' in den Kompositionen Schuberts, Schu-
     manns und H. Wolfs: Eine vergleichende Analyse." In **Zur
     Musikalischen Analyse**, edited by Gerhard Schuhmacher,
     349-62. Darmstadt: Wissenschaftliche Buchg., 1974.

     Not examined. The editor's abstract in **RILM** (74/2573)
     indicates that the three composers' handling of the text is
     discussed.

804. Moser, Hans Joachim. "Goethes Dichtung in der neuen Musik."
     Jahrbuch der Goethe-Gesellschaft 17 (1931): 261-81.

     Discusses Goethe settings from the time of Loewe and
     Schubert through the 1920s. Emphasizes the variety of
     approaches, reflecting both the composers' artistic person-
     alities and the wide range of styles and ideas within
     Goethe's own oeuvre.

805. Musioł, Karol. "Goethe und die Polnische Musik." **Die Musik-
     forschung** 31 (1978): 1-15.

     Goethe's texts have appealed to Polish composers. In
     particular, they were used by Stanisław Moniuszko, whose
     setting of "Kennst du das Land" from 1846 represents a peak
     in Polish song composition.

806. Neumann, Peter Horst. "Zur musikgeschichtlichen Bedeutung
     Goethescher Gedichte." In **Dichtung und Musik: Kaleidoskop
     ihrer Beziehungen**, edited by Günter Schnitzler, 122-33.
     Stuttgart: Klett-Cotta, 1979.

     Treats the position of Goethe's poetry in the poet's own
     perspective and its treatment as song texts from his time
     to the twentieth century. Stresses the whole history of
     relations between text and music in settings and Goethe's
     emphasis on texts and on strophic treatment. As examples,
     settings of "Kennst du das Land" by Reichardt, Beethoven,
     Schubert, and Schumann are discussed. Neumann points out
     that later composers were more interested in Goethe's poems
     for their value for song settings than in his aesthetic
     theories. Even much later settings, based on aesthetics
     very different from those of the poet and his time, may,

nevertheless, achieve a satisfactory wedding of words and music.

807. Schuh, Willi, comp. **Goethe-Vertonungen: Ein Verzeichnis.** Zurich: Artemis, 1952. 95p.

Lists Goethe poems by first line, with the composers who set each one. For titled poems, titles are given with cross-references to first lines. Also lists dramatic works set to music. Index by composers.

808. Siddons, James. "The Works and Music of the **Erlking.**" **Music Analysis** 1/2 (Summer 1972): 27-38.

Not examined. According to the **RILM** abstract (72/1851) by the author, the several literary forms of the story and the various musical settings of Goethe's text are covered. The songs of Schubert and Loewe are compared.

809. Stein, Jack M. "Musical Settings of the Songs from **Wilhelm Meister.**" **Comparative Literature** 22 (1970): 125-46.

Critiques settings by Lied composers from Reichardt to Wolf. Judges that the composers from Schubert onward lost touch with the context of the novel, and that the texts were "so multifaceted that it seems to have been impossible for any nineteenth-century composer to express their true essence," as the later composers imposed their own readings on the poetry.

810. Sternfeld, Frederick W. **Goethe and Music: A List of Parodies** and **Goethe's Relationship to Music, a List of References.** New York: New York Public Library, 1954. Reprint. New York: Da Capo, 1979.

Consists of two separate bibliographic studies. The first half of the book contains a sizeable essay on the parody and Goethe's use of it, with a detailed list of the parodies and critical notes on each. The second portion of the book is a bibliography (with scattered annotations) of literature on Goethe and music. Index.

811. Termini, Olga. "Five Settings of Goethe's 'Mailied' in Relation to His Concept of the German Lied." In **Festival Essays for Pauline Alderman: A Musicological Tribute,** edited by Burton L. Karson, 169-86. Provo, Utah: Brigham Young University Press, 1976.

Suggests that ideas similar to Goethe's about the setting
of songs have been adopted for new reasons in the twentieth
century, in particular in connection with the **Jugendmusik**
movement. The development of the song aesthetic is illustrated by analyses of settings of "Mailied" by Reichardt,
Christian August Gabler, Beethoven, Schoeck, and Knab.

Heinrich Heine
(1797-1856)

812. Brauner, Charles S. "Irony in the Heine Lieder of Schubert
      and Schumann." **The Musical Quarterly** 67 (1981): 261-81.

      Examines treatments of irony in a variety of ways. Fol-
      lowing recent theories in literary criticism, irony in the
      texts is divided into covert and overt types. The musical
      requirements of the two types are different. Covert irony
      in a poem requires ironic expression in music if the irony
      is to be carried into the song, whereas overt irony in the
      text may be treated in different ways by the music. In
      addition to numerous songs of Schubert and Schumann, set-
      tings by Mendelssohn and Franz (of "Allnächtlich im
      Traume") are discussed.

813. Eckhoff, Annemarie, comp. **Dichterliebe: Heinrich Heine im
      Lied.** Hamburg: Oeffentliche Bücherhalle, 1972. 88p.

      Lists song settings of Heine's texts by titles and first
      lines (including titles given by the composers), and by the
      composers. There is an introductory essay by Lutz Lesle,
      and reproductions of the title page of Robert Franz's six
      Heine songs op. 25 and the autograph manuscript of Mendels-
      sohn's setting of "Allnächtlich im Traume seh ich dich,"
      op. 86, no. 4, are included.

814. Mühlhäuser, Siegfried. "'... Kaum wage ich das Bekenntnis--
      ich verstehe keine Note...': Ein bisher ungedruckter
      Brief Heinrich Heines an Eduard Marxsen--Ein Beitrag zur
      Frage der Vertonung Heinescher Gedichte." **Die Musik-
      forschung** 26 (1973): 63-69.

      Prints a letter of thanks from the poet to Marxsen, dated
      18 November 1830, on the occasion of the dedication to
      Heine of Marxsen's settings of some Heine poems. Discusses
      the settings, praised in Heine's letter, of the poet's
      texts by Josef Klein. Heine was also aware of Schubert's
      settings (D. 957/8-13), although he had not heard them.

815. Westrup, Jack. "Some Settings of Heine." In **Festival Essays
      for Pauline Alderman: A Musicological Tribute**, edited by
      Burton L. Karson, 187-94. Provo, Utah: Brigham Young
      University Press, 1976.

      On the whole, takes Romantic and post-Romantic Lied com-
      posers to task for failing to do justic to Heine's texts,
      though several songs are praised. The discussion naturally
      centers on Schumann's songs, with attention also given to
      those of Franz and Liszt and brief mentions of those of
      Wolf and Strauss. Notably, Schubert's Heine songs meet
      with approval, in contrast to many critiques.

                          Friedrich Hölderlin
                             (1770-1843)

816. Kelletat, Alfred. "Bibliographie der Vertonungen von Dicht-
      ungen Hölderlins." **Hölderlin-Jahrbuch** 7 (1953): 119-35.

      Lists settings of Hölderlin's texts in all genres, orga-
      nizing them alphabetically by composers. Entries include
      scoring, publishers, dates. Index of texts.

817. Komma, Karl Michael. **Lieder und Gesänge nach Dichtungen von
      Friedrich Hölderlin.** Schriften der Hölderlin-Gesellschaft
      5. Tübingen: J.C.B. Mohr [Paul Siebeck], 1967. xxxviii,
      99p.

      Not examined. According to the author's abstract in **RILM**
      (68/1272), gives an overview of settings of Hölderlin's
      poetry, as well as analyzing a number of specific songs in
      the areas of form, word-tone relationships, and identifica-
      tion of archaic references.

818. Schuhmacher, Gerhard. **Geschichte und Möglichkeiten der
      Vertonung von Dichtungen Friedrich Hölderlins.** For-
      schungsbeiträge zur Musikwissenschaft 18. Regensburg:
      Bosse, 1967. iii, 456p.

      Examines the fate of the poet's work in musical settings.
      The Romantic composers did not often adopt Hölderlin's
      texts, for they did not suit the musical style of the time.
      With the development of more prose-like musical structures
      and especially the twelve-tone method, the poems appear
      more frequently in music. Schuhmacher appends a number of
      statements in letters and interviews by composers on the
      matter of setting Hölderlin's words. Appendices include

list of settings, index of poems, musical supplement.
Plates. Bibliography. Indexes.

A.E. Housman
(1859-1936)

819. Curtis, Brandt B. "A Comparison of Early Musical Settings
      of Four Poems by A.E. Housman." D.M.A. diss., Indiana
      University, 1977. 134p.

      Not examined. According to the author's **RILM** abstract
      (77/1821), compares settings of texts from **A Shropshire Lad**
      by George Butterworth, E.G. Moeran, C.W. Orr, Arthur Somer-
      vell, Cecil Armstrong Gibbs, Alan de Beer, and Vaughan
      Williams.

Henry Hughes
(fl. 17th century)

820. Maynard, Winifred. "Henry Hughes: A Forgotten Poet." **Music
      and Letters** 33 (1952): 335-40.

      Draws attention to the little-known poet of a number of
      seventeenth-century songs, mostly by Henry Lawes. Hughes's
      style is most successful in pastoral themes, and though his
      lyrics are sometimes lacking in inventiveness, they are
      frequently well suited to musical setting.

James Joyce
(1882-1941)

821. Slocum, John J., and Herbert Cahoon. **A Bibliography of
      James Joyce [1882-1941].** New Haven, Conn.: Yale Univer-
      sity Press, 1953. ix, 195p.

      Includes a list (pp. 161-169) of musical settings, by
      title. Composers may be located by way of the index.
      Publication information and occasionally annotations are
      provided. Supplements by S. Hill in **Long Room** 2 (Autumn/
      Winter 1970) and Alan M. Cohn, **Long Room** 6 (Autumn 1972).

Eduard Mörike
(1804-1875)

822. Heuss, Alfred. "Mörikes 'Das verlassene Mägdlein' in ver-
      schiedenen musikalischen Fassungen." **Zeitschrift für
      Musik** 93 (1926): 140-44.

      Compares the settings of Schumann, Franz, Hermann Goetz,
      and Wolf. Those of Schumann and Franz are held to belong
      to the eighteenth-century tradition of the strophic form
      and unified spirit. That of Goetz is dismissed as too
      disparate and operatic. Wolf's setting combines a gener-
      ally unified impression with expression of details and
      subtle psychological development.

823. Leuwer, Ruth Pirkel. "Mörike-Lyrik in ihren Vertonungen:
      Ein Beitrag zur Interpretation." Ph.D. diss., Friedrich-
      Wilhelms-Universität, Bonn, 1953.

      Critiques the settings of Mörike's poems by various com-
      posers. The composers selected for discussion are Mörike's
      friends Louis Hetsch and Ernst Friedrich Kauffmann, Schu-
      mann, Brahms, Wolf, and Distler. Settings of fifteen dif-
      ferent poems are compared, and aspects of each set of
      analyses are presented in tabular format. Leuwer concludes
      that various different settings of a poem may be valid in
      presenting different but equally viable readings of the
      text. List of settings; bibliography.

824. Kinsey, Barbara. "Mörike Poems Set by Brahms, Schumann and
      Wolf." **The Music Review** 29 (1968): 257-67.

      Compares the rhythmic scansion of parallel settings by
      Wolf and Brahms and by Wolf and Schumann. Brahms's set-
      tings emphasize the meter and have a folk-like, sing-song
      character, as opposed to Wolf's more subtly varied rhythms.
      Schumann's and Wolf's interpretations of the text content
      diverge, as can be shown through their readings of the
      poetic rhythms.

825. Weismann, W. "Probleme vergleichender Liedbetrachtung."
      Studia musicologica Academiae scientiarum hungaricae 11
      (1969): 481-86.

      Departs from the comparison of settings of Mörike's "Das
      verlassene Mägdlein" by Alfred Heuss (see item 823) and
      Heuss's thoughts on such comparative studies. Finds that
      Wolf's setting, like those of Schumann and Franz, fails to

evoke the character of the peasant girl who speaks in the song.

Friedrich Wilhelm Nietzsche
(1844-1900)

826. Thatcher, David S. "Musical Settings of Nietzsche Texts: An Annotated Bibliography, I." **Nietzsche-Studien** 4 (1975): 284-323.

Not examined.

Karl August von Platen-Hallermunde
(1796-1835)

827. Zielinski, Shirley McGaugh. "A Biographical and Critical Sketch of Karl August von Platen-Hallermunde and a Study of the Settings of His Poems by Schubert, Schumann, and Brahms." Ph.D. diss., Washington University, 1981. 215p.

Not examined. According to the abstract in **RILM** (81/3906), begins with a biography and personality study of the poet, based on his diaries. Analyzes eight songs, with emphasis on musical factors related to the texts.

Christian Ludwig Reissig
(1783-?)

828. Deutsch, Otto Erich. "Der Liederdichter Reissig: Bestimmung einer merkwürdigen Persönlichkeit." **Neues Beethoven-Jahrbuch** 6 (1936): 59-65.

Unearths some biographical information about Christian Ludwig Reissig, the poet of a number of Beethoven's Lieder. From the dedications of his poems, Deutsch discovers that Reissig traveled in some of the same Viennese circles as Beethoven. Military records reveal his birth year, 1783, and other details of his career.

Johann Gaudenz von Salis-Seewis
(1762-1834)

829. Weinmann, Alexander. "'Das Grab': Ein Literarisch-Musikalischer Bestseller." **Oesterreichische Musik-**

zeitschrift 28 (1973): 125-32.

Lists twenty settings of the poem "Das Grab" by Salis-
Seewis, composed between 1797 (by Zumsteeg) and 1872 (by
Jacob Dont). Schubert made four settings.

830.   ———. "'Das Grab' von Salis--und kein Ende." **Oesterreichische Musikzeitschrift** 28 (1973): 523-24.

Supplements the author's earlier list (see item 830
above) by adding to the names of composers who set "Das
Grab" that of Franz Friedrich Siegmund August von Boeklin.
Since this setting was published in 1789, it constitutes
the earliest known composition of the text.

Friedrich von Schiller
(1759-1805)

831. Longyear, R.M. **Schiller and Music.** University of North
Carolina Studies in the Germanic Languages and Litera-
tures 54. Chapel Hill: University of North Carolina
Press, 1966. 201p.

Devotes only part of a chapter to art song settings in
the period of Zumsteeg, the Second Berlin School, and
Schubert.   Composers of Schiller texts were more inclined
to set them as choral works than as songs. Bibliographical
essay.   Index.

Christian Friedrich Daniel Schubart
(1739-1791)

832. Weinmann, Alexander. "Zwei unechte Mozart-Lieder." **Die
Musikforschung** 20 (1967): 167-75.

Discusses the two spurious songs "Ehelicher guter Morgen"
and "Eheliche gute Nacht" (K. Anh. C 8.11 and C 8.10) on
texts by Daniel Schubart. The texts were actually set by
other composers, and the songs exist in a number of
sources, but they do not permit a definite attribution of
the versions wrongly attributed to Mozart. Although the
songs have been assigned to Johann Friedrich Hugo Freiherr
von Dalberg in later editions of the Köchel catalogue,
Dalberg's settings, recently discovered, do not correspond
to those once attributed to Mozart.

833.   ———. "Zwei unechte Mozart-Lieder: Ein Nachtrag." **Die**
        Musikforschung 21 (1968): 323-24.

        Cites additional sources for the author's earlier article
        (item 833 above) on the two Schubart songs misattributed to
        Mozart "Ehelicher guter Morgen" and "Eheliche gute Nacht"
        (K. Anh. C 8.11 and C 8.10). It remains impossible to
        determine the actual composer of these songs.

                            Alfred Tennyson
                             (1809-1892)

834.   Bouchelle, Joan Hoiness, ed. **With Tennyson at the Keyboard:**
        A Victorian Songbook. New York: Garland, 1985.   xxv,
        236p.

        Compiles 34 songs on Tennyson texts by 20 composers as
        well as one poem to an anonymous hymn tune. For each
        composer brief historical and descriptive notes are pro-
        vided.

835.   Copley, Ian Alfred. "Tennyson and the Composers." **Musical**
        Opinion 101 (1978): 504-12.

        Quoting extensively from letters to Tennyson, provides
        insight into Tennyson's relationships with the English
        composers Sterndale Bennett, Arthur Sullivan (who set the
        cycle "The Window"), Hubert Parry, and Charles Villiers
        Stanford (who composed several songs on Tennyson texts).

                            Paul Verlaine
                             (1844-1896)

836.   Riessauw, Anne-Marie. **Catalogue des œuvres vocales écrites**
        par des compositeurs européens sur des poémes de
        Verlaine. Ghent: Rijksuniversiteit, 1980.   446p.

        Lists settings of Verlaine's texts in alphabetical order
        by composers. Also provides statistical summaries of var-
        ious observed trends in these settings.

837.   Riessauw, Anne-Marie, and Rodolf Riessauw. "Verbe et mélo-
        die: étude sur les rapports entre le matériel phonétique
        et mélodique dans la composition musicale sur un poème de
        Verlaine." **Jaarboek I.P.E.M.** 1967: 127-62.

Not examined. The authors report in **RILM** (69/3999) that analysis of twelve settings of "Il pleure dans mon coeur" revealed little effect of vowel elements on melodic design.

Walt Whitman
(1819-1892)

838. Wannamaker, John Samuel. "The Musical Settings of the Poetry of Walt Whitman: A Study of Theme, Structure, and Prosody." Ph.D. diss., University of Minnesota, 1972. 636p.

Not examined. According to the author's entry in **RILM** (72/2567), identifies the themes of death and American democracy as the favorites of composers. Links Whitman's organic literary structure to parallel techniques in music in the late Romantic period. Covers 360 works of 177 composers. Bibliography; work-list.

Miscellaneous

839. Otto, Eberhard. "Dichter in Bayern und ihre Komponisten." **Musik in Bayern** 18-19 (1979): 95-109.

Not examined. The author indicates in the **RILM** abstract of the article (79/1912) that the poets discussed include Rückert, Daumer, and Heyse, each of whose texts were set by major Lied composers.

IV

AESTHETICS, ANALYSIS, CRITICISM

840. Abert, Hermann. "Wort und Ton in der Musik des 18. Jahrhunderts." **Archiv für Musikwissenschaft** 5 (1923): 31-70. Reprinted in **Gesammelte Schriften und Vorträge**, edited by Friedrich Blume. Halle: Max Niemeyer, 1929. Reprint. Tutzing: Hans Schneider, 1968.

Discusses the relationships between words and music in thought and practice in the eighteenth and early nineteenth centuries in general. Both poets and musicians, as well as a variety of genres--song, opera, sacred music--are considered. Abert concludes that it was not the issues in the relations between words and music that changed from the seventeenth to the nineteenth centuries, but the nature of the attempts to resolve them.

841. Baron, John H. "First Report on the Use of Computer Programming to Study the Secular Solo Songs in France from 1600 to 1660." **International Musicological Society Congress Report, Bonn 1970**, 333-36. Kassel: Bärenreiter, 1971.

Not examined. The **RILM** abstract (73/3272) states that the project was intended to make computer comparisons of all French **chansons pour boire, chansons pour danser**, and **airs de cour** from 1600 to 1660. Scorings included those for solo voice, voice and lute, voice and basso continuo, and two voices.

842. Baum, Günther. "Wort und Ton im romantischen Kunstlied." **Das Musikleben** 3 (1950): 136-40.

Gives a general overview of the attitudes of Schubert, Schumann, Brahms, and Wolf toward poetry, and of the effect those attitudes had on the relationship between text and music in each composer's Lied style. Quotations from the composers are cited.

843. Booth, Mark W. **The Experience of Songs.** New Haven: Yale University Press, 1981. ix, 226p.

Analyzes the nature of song verse from the point of view of literary criticism. The introduction offers an aesthetic for song verse and singing, based on the nature of oral communication, the listener's identification with the singer, and especially the function of song as a means of achieving self-transcendence. A variety of examples of song verse in English, from medieval lyric to commercial jingle, are analyzed. Chapter 4, "Art Song," centers on a detailed discussion of Campion's "I care not for these ladies."

844. Bunke, Heinrich. "Die Barform im romantischen Kunstlied bei Franz Schubert, Robert Schumann, Johannes Brahms, Hugo Wolf und Felix Mendelssohn-Bartholdy." Ph.D. diss., University of Bonn, 1955. 136p.

Demonstrates how the structural concept of the Bar, passed on to nineteenth-century Lied composers primarily through the chorale and folksong, is reflected in the forms of their songs. The Bar form is discovered in about six per cent of the repertoire, appearing most frequently in the Lieder of Brahms and least in those of Wolf. It sometimes contributes an element of antiquarianism to the songs in which it is used. An appendix summarizes the types of treatment of the Bar principle for each composer. Diagrams, tables. Bibliography.

845. Cadman, Charles Wakefield. "On Writing a Successful Concert Song." **Etude** 50 (1932): 167-68, 221.

Provides a composer's first-hand evaluation of what makes a good song, with advice to aspiring composers, including the selection of poetry, originality, good diction. Also deals with the marketing aspects of song: the help of good singers, saleable style, choice of appropriate publishers, preparation of manuscripts.

846. Castelnuovo-Tedesco, Mario. "Problems of a Song-Writer." **The Musical Quarterly** 30 (1944): 102-11. Reprinted in **Reflections on Art**, edited by Suzanne K. Langer, 301-11. New York: Oxford University Press, 1968.

Considers the composition of songs, primarily from the relationship of the composer to the text. Suggests criteria for a suitable song text: strength and focus of expression, proper dimensions, and flexible form. Discusses the characteristics of major western European languages from the point of view of the medium of song. Describes Castelnuovo-Tedesco's experience of the process of songwriting, from study of the poem, through construction of the vocal melody, to the discovery of the necessary "symbolic" material for the instrumental part.

847. Clinton-Baddeley, V.C. **Words for Music.** Cambridge: Cambridge University Press, 1941. xi, 168p.

Examines the relationship between words and music in song. The author describes, explains, and laments the estrangement of poetry from music in the English language. He suggests the necessary characteristic of a poem for a successful song--that it should be to some extent incomplete--and offers some positive suggestions to poets. A final chapter is devoted to the work of W.B. Yeats. Index.

848. Cone, Edward T. **The Composer's Voice.** Berkeley: University of California Press, 1974. ix, 184p.

Undertakes a philosophical examination of the nature of musical communication, taking vocal music as the point of departure. Examples are drawn from various songs, especially the better-known ones of Schubert, on several of which Cone offers insightful analytical and critical comments. Index.

849. ————. "Words into Music: The Composer's Approach to the Text." In **Sound and Poetry: English Institute Essays 1956,** edited by Northrop Frye, 3-15. New York: Columbia University Press, 1957.

Argues that a musical setting selects and defines a form for a poem, presenting a "unique interpretation of the poem's meaning." Cone also discusses two classic areas of criticism of song composers: the use of text repetitions and rearrangements, and unusual verbal accentuations.

850. Crist, Bainbridge. **The Art of Setting Words to Music.** New York: Carl Fischer, 1944. 95p.

Explains from the perspective of a song composer how musical settings respond to their texts. Sample texts are

set in a variety of ways to illustrate principles involved.
Settings by composers from Debussy and Strauss to the
author himself are discussed.

851. Dent, Edward J. "On the Composition of English Songs."
      Music and Letters 6 (1925): 224-35.

Discusses principles for song writing. Particularly
important is a successful musical form. In English, composers are urged to cultivate a rhythmic style suited to
the subtleties of stress and duration and to the problem of
rapid speech rhythm versus the slower rhythm of singing.

852. Doughtie, Edward. "Words for Music: Simplicity and Complex-
      ity in the Elizabethan Air." **Rice University Studies** 51
      (1965): 1-12.

By examining several representative texts and contem-
plating their settings, illustrates how a song text must
have a certain kind of simplicity or conventionality, as
well as ways in which music can enhance the words. Refers
to the use of standard rhetorical types and devices.

853. Duke, John. "The Significance of Song." **Ars lyrica** 1
      (Winter-Spring 1981): 9-21. Reprinted (without attribu-
      tion to **Ars lyrica**) in **The NATS Bulletin** 40/3 (January-
      February 1984): 19-22.

Defines song as heightened speech and argues that its
value lies in its intrinsic affirmation of human life.
Laments the instrumentalization of the vocal genre after
the late nineteenth century and proposes that a revitaliza-
tion of song should be found between popular music and the
"effete sophistication" of serious music in the present.

854. Eggebrecht, Hans Heinrich. "Vertontes Gedicht: Ueber das
      Verstehen von Kunst durch Kunst." In **Dichtung und Musik:
      Kaleidoskop ihrer Beziehungen,** edited by Günther Schnitz-
      ler, 36-69. Stuttgart: Klett-Cotta, 1979.

Examines ways in which the music of a song contributes to
the understanding of a poem and to the listener's compre-
hension of the composer's reading of the text. Discusses
as examples "Die Nebensonnen" and "Der Leiermann" from
Schubert's **Winterreise** and "Oft denk' ich, sie sind nur
ausgegangen" from Mahler's **Kindertotenlieder.** Bibliography.

855. Fischer-Dieskau, Dietrich. **Töne sprechen, Worte klingen.**
      Stuttgart: Deutsche Verlags-Anstalt; Munich: Piper, 1985.
      500p.

      Discusses the varying relationships between words and
      music in all Western solo vocal repertoires. The opening
      section is devoted to the song; later parts take up other
      genres. In dealing with songs, the author adopts a partly
      historical and partly topical approach and concentrates
      almost exclusively on the German Lied. Glossary. Index.

856. Greene, Harry Plunket. "The Future of English Song." **Music
      and Letters** 1 (1920): 19-26, 123-34.

      A two-part article. The first section, "The Singer and
      the Public," discusses the position of songs and singers
      under the commercial system and argues for public-sector
      support of music and the independence of the artist from
      commercial constraints. The second part, "The Singer and
      the Composer," emphasizes to composers the limitations and
      special needs of the voice and gives a variety of advice on
      considerations in writing an effective song.

857. Günther, Siegfried. "Lied in der Zeit--Zeit im Lied."
      Schweizerische Musikzeitung 107 (1967): 152-58.

      Not examined. According to the **RILM** abstract (67/2012),
      reflects on the sociological position of the art song,
      based on its propagation in modern life in Germany via
      broadcasts and recordings.

858. Hennenberg, Fritz. "Streiflichter auf die Funktionen des
      Liedes." In **Forum: Musik in der DDR.** Deutsche Akademie
      der Künste, Arbeitshefte 9, vol. 2, 70-77. Berlin:
      Henschelverlag, 1972.

      Not examined. The abstract in **RILM** (73/2054) states that
      the paper discusses the music and texts of modern art songs
      as indexes of social change, as well as identifying influ-
      ences of different styles on the art song.

859. Joubert, John. "Composing Music for Poetry." **Composer**
      (Great Britain) 72 (Spring 1981): 6-10.

      Not examined. The **RILM** abstract (81/3887) reports that
      in an interview Joubert discusses what criteria make a text
      appropriate for setting to music, including that it be
      "suitable for reading aloud" and that it affect the com-

poser emotionally. Discusses the problem of song in the
twentieth century.

860. Kramer, A. Walter. "The Things We Set to Music." **The
      Musical Quarterly** 7 (1921): 309-13.

      Takes issue with a statement by Louis Untermeyer that
      American composers are not as productive as their com-
      patriots in poetry. Kramer complains that too many poor
      songs are written, and he attributes this to the lack of
      culture in singers, to commercialism, and to doggerel
      lyrics.

861. Kramer, Lawrence. **Music and Poetry: The Nineteenth Century
      and After.** Berkeley: University of California Press,
      1984. xiii, 251p.

      Considers the relationships between the two arts in gen-
      eral, including song. Chapter 5, "Song," argues that in
      this genre music "adopts the poetry as an origin, and then
      treats it the way all origins are treated, by departing
      from it" (p. 169). Kramer seeks to demonstrate that this
      departure deconstructs the text, as it tends to violate
      speech declamation and to rewrite poetry, in particular by
      "expressive revision, imitation, and structural dissonance"
      (p. 146). Chapter 7, "Song as Insight," consists of a
      detailed analysis and critique of Elliott Carter's handling
      of John Ashbery's "Syringa."

862. LaMotte-Haber, Helga de. "'Es flüstern und sprechen die
      Blumen ...': Zum Widerspruch zwischen Lied als roman-
      tischer Kategorie und musikalischer Gattung." **Zeitschrift
      für Literaturwissenschaft und Linguistik** 9 (1979): 70-79.
      Reprinted in **Musica** 35 (1981): 237-40.

      Distinguishes between literary and musical meanings of
      the term "Lied." The poetry of Eichendorff and Heine and
      the songs of Schumann are taken as examples. In litera-
      ture, the genre is defined by poetic content and the sound-
      value of the verbal composition. This is not paralleled in
      music, where the genre is determined by form and the key-
      board part takes a major expressive role.

863. Lausberg, Heinrich. "Vertonung zweier französischer
      Gedichte." In **Serta romantica: Festschrift für G. Rohlfs
      zum 75. Geburtstag,** edited by R. Baehr and K. Wais, 269-
      89. Tübingen: Max Niemeyer, 1968.

Not examined. The author indicates in **RILM** (69/4937)
that the study, based on Maeterlinck's "Chanson" and
Valéry's "Les Grenades," investigates the "excess meaning"
that a song setting imposes on a text.

864. Lord, Harvey George. "Toward a Theory of the Relationship
between Words and Music in Songs: Emphasis on Thomas
Campion." Ph.D. diss., University of Connecticut, 1978.
188p.

Not examined. According to the author's abstract in
Dissertation Abstracts (39A [1978]: 899-900A), a theory of
the expressive force of songs is developed, based on the
coordination of musical patterns of expectation and fulfillment with the patterns of the poetic content. Illustrative analyses are taken from a number of songs by seven-
teenth- and early eighteenth-century composers, particularly Campion.

865. Müller-Blattau, Joseph. **Das Verhältnis von Wort und Ton in
der Geschichte der Musik: Grundzüge und Probleme.** Stuttgart: Metzler, 1952. 44, [8]p.

Discusses in broad, general terms the changing relationships between text and music in Western music in five major
periods: Antiquity, the Middle Ages, the Renaissance and
Baroque, the Classic-Romantic era, and the twentieth century. Müller-Blattau conceives the situation in the middle
of the twentieth century as having two opposite possibilities, one oriented toward abstract musical principles
(represented by Hindemith) and the other toward the domina-
tion of music by words (represented by Orff). Appendix of
music examples.

866. Racek, Jan. "Zum Wort-Ton-Problem in der geschichtlichen
Entwicklung der abendländischen Musik, unter besonderer
Berücksichtigung der Italienischen begleiteten Monodie."
Die Musikforschung 24 (1971): 121-35.

Proposes that the history of western music can be regarded as a cyclic alternation between periods in which
composers allowed texts to control the structure and expression of their works and periods in which musical procedures operated more autonomously. The Italian monody is
taken as the central example of music guided by text.

867. Reutter, Hermann. "Wort und Ton in der zeitgenössischen
Musik." **Musica** 4 (1950): 121-24. Reprinted as "Wort und

Ton im neuen Lied." In **Kontrapunkte**. Vol. 2, **Die Stimme der Komponisten,** edited by Heinrich Lindlar, 74-78. Rodenkirchen am Rhein: Tonger, 1958.

Stresses the variety of approaches to the treatment of texts by major song composers of the first half of the twentieth century. Reutter suggests that there are many ways to reach a satisfactory interaction of words and music.

868. Schneider, Anneliese. "Tendenzen der Lyriktheorie: Ihre Bedeutung für eine 'Liedtheorie.'" **Beiträge zur Musik-wissenschaft** 19 (1977): 23-50.

Not examined. According to the author's **RILM** abstract (77/1830), applies research on lyric poetry to a theory of song.

869. Schoenberg, Arnold. "The Relationship to the Text." In **Style and Idea,** edited by Leonard Stein, translations by Leo Black, 141-45. New York: St. Martin's, 1975.

Argues that the understanding of a song is different from and independent of an analytical study of the poem on which the song is based. Claims that the composer's own songs were sometimes inspired by the sound of the poem's opening words.

870. Stein, Jack M. "Was Goethe Wrong about the Nineteenth-Century Lied? An Examination of the Relation of Poem and Music." **Publications of the Modern Language Association of America** 77 (1962): 232-39.

Contemplates the problem of the relationship between poem and music in the Lied. The genre began to be more oriented toward musical values than poetic ones and as a result is open to objection on aesthetic grounds. By asserting their interpretations of texts, composers expose their songs to literary criticism, as well as to the charge that the music overwhelms the poetry. Few Lieder meet with Stein's approval as literary readings.

871. Thürmer, Helmut. "Zum Deklamationsproblem im deutschen Sololied." **Colloquium amicorum: Joseph Schmidt-Görg zum 70. Geburtstag,** edited by Siegfried Kross and Hans Schmidt, 386-93. Bonn: Beethovenhaus, 1967.

Investigates melodic rather than rhythmic treatment of

text declamation. A number of melodies are cited in which
high tones approached and left by leap are applied on weak
syllables. This generally occurs because other considerations take precedence over those of good declamation as
regards pitch accents.

872.   Upton, William Treat. "Aspects of the Modern Art Song." **The
       Musical Quarterly** 24 (1938): 11-30.

Compiles statements from a large number of composers in a
representative variety of styles on principles of song
composition. Three songs--by Israel Citkowitz, Vivian
Fine, and Carl Ruggles--are given as examples of stylistic
possibilities. Upton takes the position that true song
must be vocal in melodic style, dominated by the singer's
part, and lyrical; he favors the Citkowitz work, on James
Joyce's "Strings in Earth and Air," as suggesting most
promise for the future of the genre. The composers with
whom Upton corresponded offer little in the way of prophe-
cies as to the style of the art song of the future, but
they seem to agree that the song itself will survive in
some form.

873.   Wells, Robin Headlam. "The Ladder of Love: Verbal and
       Musical Rhetoric in the Elizabethan Lute-Song." **Early
       Music** 12 (1984): 173-89.

Demonstrates that the standard rhetorical image of a
ladder in seventeenth-century literature appears commonly
in song texts. It evokes, of course, a pictorial musical
treatment in the vocal melody.

874.   Williams, C.F. Abdy. **The Rhythm of Song.** London: Methuen,
       1925. 151p.

Examines systematically the problems of rhythm and good
declamation in setting poetry. The text is addressed to
student-composers, with "rules" (pp. 31-35) and exercises.
The principles are thoroughly illustrated by a wide variety
of examples, most taken from art songs.

V

SONG TEXTS AND TRANSLATIONS

Anthologies of Texts in Original Languages

875. Bernhardi, Wilhelm, comp. **Allgemeine deutsches Lieder-Lexicon oder vollständige Sammlung aller bekannten deutschen Lieder und Volksgesänge in alphabetischer Folge.** Leipzig: n.p., 1844. Reprint. 4 vols. Hildesheim: Olms, 1968. 371; 365; 252; viii, 298p.

Consists of texts of 2479 folk songs and art songs in German, in alphabetical order by first line. A few texts in other languages are also included, e.g., the Marseillaise and "Gaudeamus igitur." The poems do not show correct lineation. In some cases where texts are intended for melodies of other, more familiar songs, this is indicated (number 48, for example, employing the melody of "Rule Brittania"). Poets and, in rare cases, composers are indicated. Index by genre--children's songs, drinking songs, etc.

876. Doughtie, Edward. **Lyrics from English Airs 1596-1622.** Cambridge, Mass.: Harvard University Press, 1970. xxi, 657p.

Presents a critical edition of the ayre texts, excluding those of Campion. There is a fine general introduction, as well as brief biographies of the composers. Indexes.

877. Douliez, Paul, and Harmann Engelhard, eds. **Das Buch der Lieder und Arien: Ein Texthandbuch für Rundfunkhörer und Schallplattenfreunde.** Munich: Winkler, 1968. 861p.

Not examined. The **RILM** abstract (69/3359) reports that

the book contains original texts for the available recorded
repertoire, including sacred texts (Latin texts are translated into German) and opera arias, as well as songs.

878. Fischer-Dieskau, Dietrich, ed. **Texte deutscher Lieder: Ein
      Handbuch.** Munich: Deutscher Taschenbuch Verlag, 1968.

      Contains texts of many songs of the repertoire from the
      eighteenth to the twentieth century, presented in alpha-
      betical order by title. A substantial introduction out-
      lines some principles and the history of text setting in
      the Lied since the eighteenth century. Indexes by com-
      posers, poets, titles and first lines.

879. Lerche, Julius. **Das Wort zum Lied: 2000 der beliebsten
      Konzertlieder im Texte.** Berlin: Bote & Bock, n.d.

      Prints complete texts of Lieder, arranged alphabetically
      by composers, with indications of poets and publishers.
      Key to selected poets citing important texts and composers;
      list of songs by occasional topics; list of composers.
      Brief essay on text setting. Index of songs by title and
      first line.

                              Translations

880. **Word by Word Translations of Songs and Arias.**
      Part I. **German and French.** Translations by Berton
      Coffin, Werner Singer, and Pierre Delattre. New York:
      Scarecrow, 1966. 620p.
      Part II. **Italian.** Translations by Arthur Schoep and
      Daniel Harris. Metuchen, New Jersey: Scarecrow, 1972.
      xiii, 563p.

      Gives literal translations interlineated with original
      texts. In cases where the meaning is not clear from a
      strict word-by-word translation, indications of more idiom-
      atic readings are provided. The translations are organized
      alphabetically by composers. Index of songs by titles and
      first lines.

881. Fischer-Dieskau, Dietrich, ed. **The Fischer-Dieskau Book of
      Lieder.** Translated by George Bird and Richard Stokes.
      New York: Knopf, 1977. 435p.

      Provides an English edition of Fischer-Dieskau's **Texte**

deutscher Lieder (see item 883 above). Gives idiomatic translations of more than 750 texts of Lieder and a few poems in other languages set as songs by German-speaking composers. The translations are printed in parallel columns with the original texts. Indexes by composers, authors and translators, poems.

882. Miller, Philip L., comp. and trans. **The Ring of Words: An Anthology of Song Texts.** New York: Norton, 1973. xxviii, 518p.

Offers parallel-column translations of song texts for a large core of the art-song repertoire in German, French, Italian, Russian, Scandinavian languages, and Spanish. The texts are organized by poets, with a brief comment on each author. For each text the major settings are listed. Indexes are provided by composer and by titles and first lines.

883. Paquin, Marie-Thérèse, trans. **Dix cycles de Lieder/Ten cycles of Lieder.** Montreal: Les Presses de l'Université de Montréal, 1977. 277p.

Gives word-for-word and idiomatic translations of ten major German cycles into both French and English. The works translated are Beethoven, **An die ferne Geliebte;** Brahms, **Vier ernste Gesänge;** Mahler, **Kindertotenlieder** and **Lieder eines fahrenden Gesellen;** Schubert, **Die schöne Müllerin, Winterreise,** and **Schwanengesang;** Schumann, **Frauenliebe und -leben, Dichterliebe,** and **Der arme Peter.**

884. Phillips, Lois, trans. **Lieder Line by Line and Word for Word.** New York: Charles Scribner's Sons, 1979. x, 365p.

Gives absolutely literal English translations, interlined with the German texts, as well as free translations in parallel columns. The book is organized by composers and includes texts for songs of Beethoven, Schubert, Schumann, Wagner, Brahms, Wolf, Mahler, and Strauss. Index of titles and first lines.

885. Prawer, S.S., ed. and trans. **The Penguin Book of Lieder.** Harmondsworth, Middlesex: Penguin, 1964. 208p.

Provides German texts and English translations in parallel columns for many songs in the standard repertoire. The body of the text is organized chronologically by composers, for each of whom a brief biographical and stylistic note is

provided.   There are also notes on poets.   Bibliography;
discography.   Index of songs.

Singing Translations

The performance of art songs in languages other than that in
which they were composed is not common practice, for both literary and musical reasons.   Nevertheless, there is a recurring and
reasonable argument that because songs were written in the language of their composers and their intended auditors, and because
the listener's understanding of interactions between words and
music is all-important, singing translations ought to be made and
used.   It is regrettable but nevertheless true that audiences are
rarely literate in a variety of languages.   Moreover, even well-
trained singers are rarely fluent in peripheral languages,   such
as those of eastern Europe.   For student singers whose language
study may not have progressed as far as their vocal technique and
musicality, translations might be appropriate.   All the sets of
translations here are included with the caveat that each translation they offer should be subjected to stringent criticism and
never allowed to substitute for a true translation of the original text.

886.   Schoep, Arthur, et al. **English Singing Translations of
        Foreign Language Art Songs.** New York: NATS Publications,
        1976.   44p.

        Offers singing translations of major songs in French,
        German, Italian, and Spanish.   Besides single songs, the
        following cycles are included: Schubert, **Die schöne
        Müllerin** and **Winterreise;** Schumann, **Dichterliebe** and
        Frauenliebe und -leben; Mahler, **Lieder eines fahrenden
        Gesellen.**   Perhaps the main value of this collection is to
        illustrate the problems of singing translations--strained
        rhymes, impossible accentuations, false readings, and pure
        nonsense are all in evidence.

An indefatigable translator, Henry S. Drinker produced numerous
collections.   The following list is organized alphabetically by
the composers.   In each case the translations are presented
interlined with the original poems; where rhythms do not match
precisely, musical notation indicates how the English is to be
fit to the music.   Annotations indicate only the peculiarities of
the different sets.

887.   Drinker, Henry S., trans. **Texts of the Vocal Works of**

> **Brahms in English Translation.** New York: Association of
> American Colleges Arts Program, 1945. xi, 210p.
>
> Organizes the translations by opus number, and includes
> indications of poet, key and meter, range, and tempo for
> each song.

888.   ———. **English Texts for the Songs of Nicholas Medtner.**
       Merion, Pennsylvania: By the translator, 1946.

> Incorporates 103 songs, up to op. 59, in order by opus
> numbers.   Includes a brief introduction on Medtner by
> Alfred J. Swan.

889.   ———. **English Texts for the Songs of Modeste Moussorgsky
       (1835[sic]-1881).** Merion, Pennsylvania: By the trans-
       lator, 1950. 22p.

> Provides sixty-five translations, arranged in chronolog-
> ical order of the composition of the songs and keyed to the
> 1931 edition by Paul Lamm.

890.   ———. **Texts of the Solo Songs of Franz Schubert in
       English Translation.** 2 vols. New York: Association of
       American Colleges Arts Program, 1951, 1954. 380p.

> Volume 1 includes the songs in the seven-volume Peters
> edition; Volume 2 contains the additional songs in the
> Breitkopf & Härtel edition and part songs.   Indexes to
> poets and to German titles and first lines.

891.   ———. **Texts of the Vocal Works of Robert Schumann in
       English Translation.** New York: Association of American
       Colleges Arts Program, 1947. 145p.

> An extensive preface describes the problems in making the
> translations.   The songs are given in order of opus num-
> bers.   Index issued separately.

892.   ———. **Texts of the Solo Songs of Hugo Wolf in English
       Translation.** New York: Association of American Colleges
       Arts Program, 1949. xv, 128p.

> Includes indexes to both German and English titles.

One of the champions of singing translations, and a respectable
literary talent in this area was A.H. Fox Strangways. His translations sometimes appeared in conjunction with his writings on

the song literature. The following items stand independently.

893. Fox Strangways, A.H. "Translations." **Music and Letters** 9
      (1928): 381-85.

      Presents English translations of twenty Schubert song
      texts, keyed to the Peters and the Breitkopf & Härtel
      editions.

894. ————. "The Songs in 'Wilhelm Meister'." **Music and Letters**
      23 (1942): 290-97.

      Gives translations of the texts of all of the songs in
      Goethe's novel, suitable to the settings by Wolf. Linking
      prose narrative fills in the story between the songs.

The following is a discussion specifically of the problem of
making singing translations.

895. Benn, Maurice. "Traduttori—Traditori: English Translations
      of Lieder." **Studies in Music** (Australia) 4 (1978): 81-85.

      Criticizes currently available performing translations of
      texts of Lieder. Suggests that translators would be wise
      to forgo rhyming translations and calls for more attention
      to this endeavor.

VI

PERFORMANCE

General

896. Barthes, Roland. "La musica, la voce, il linguaggio." **Nuova rivista musicale italiana** 12 (1978): 362-66.

Originally a conference paper for the Accademia Filar-monica Romana, discusses the singing style of baritone Charles Panzéra. Treats the nature of diction in singing, which, Barthes maintains, should not be "articulation," which destroys the verbal and musical line, but "pronuncia-tion," which conveys the sense of the linguistic and musical phrase.

897. Bernac, Pierre. **The Interpretation of French Song.** Transla-tions of song texts by Winifred Radford. New York: Praeger, 1970. Reprint. New York: Norton, 1978. xvi, 327p.

Gives detailed suggestions for performance of many of the major works in the mélodie repertoire from Berlioz to Poulenc. Bernac was a major performer of this material and is able to write with considerable authority. Introductory chapters discuss vocal performance in general and of the French repertoire in particular. The body of the text treats individual songs, providing line-by-line transla-tions, indications of elisions, and notes regarding tempo, dynamics, and other nuances of interpretation. A final chapter lists composers and works not otherwise included. Indexes.

898. Emmons, Shirlee, and Stanley Sonntag. **The Art of the Song Recital.** New York: Schirmer, 1979. xx, 571p.

Makes practical suggestions to vocal recitalists and accompanists on such matters as programming (with numerous sample programs), study and preparation, and performance. The authors are concerned about the possibility that the recital may become obsolete and offer ways to revive it. Particularly useful is a very extensive repertoire list. There is also a list of song publishers. Very limited bibliography.

899. Greene, Harry Plunket. **Interpretation in Song.** New York: Macmillan, 1921. xii, 307p.

Advises singers on topics ranging from general principles of musicality such as maintaining rhythmic motion, and vocal matters such as diction, breathing, and vocal color, to practical suggestions on program-building and how to study a song.

900. Lehmann, Lotte. **Eighteen Song Cycles: Studies in Their Interpretation.** London: Cassell, 1971. xii, 185p.

Gives song-by-song discussions of major sets and cycles, offering detailed suggestions for interpretive nuances and subtexting. General introductory chapters and biographical notes on composers and poets are included. Index of songs by titles and first lines.

901. ————. **More than Singing: The Interpretation of Songs.** Translated by Frances Holden. New York: Boosey & Hawkes, 1945. 192p.

Makes suggestions for the interpretation and performance of many standard works. The bulk of the repertoire included is nineteenth-century Lieder, but a few songs from earlier periods and in other languages are included as well. The discussions describe the emotional content of the songs and the feelings the singer should convey, as well as giving specific instructions on such matters as dynamics, tone color, use of rubato, breathing, and body movements.

902. Moore, Gerald. **Singer and Accompanist: The Performance of Fifty Songs.** New York: Macmillan, 1954. xi, 232p.

Offers detailed recommendations to both singers and pianists for the performance of a miscellany of songs. The poetic and musical character of each song is summarized, followed by the discussion of the song from beginning to end. Such matters as breathing, rhythmic and dynamic subtleties, articulation, and pedaling are treated. Index.

903. Panzéra, Charles. **50 Mélodies françaises: Leçons de style et d'interpretation.** Translations by William Pirie with Julian Griffin, Jill Humble, Keith Humble. Brussels: Schott, 1964. 157p.

Gives practical and interpretive suggestions for the performance of selected songs. The remarks range from evocative characterizations of mood to simple instructions on when to breathe. The text is given in French and English in double columns.

904. Schiøtz, Aksel. **The Singer and His Art.** New York: Harper and Row, 1970. xxi, 214p.

A general book on singing, contains a substantial section of the art song. The repertoire is discussed by language, with hints on the interpretation of specific, representative songs. Other sections deal with vocal technique; oratorio; opera; teachers, coaches, and accompanists; and recital singing. Appendix of international phonetic symbols. Discography; bibliography. Index.

Performance Practice in Early Song

905. Amstad, Marietta. "Die vokale Ornamentik in der Musik des 17. und 18. Jahrhunderts." **Musica** 22/1 (1968): 67-73.

Presents a concise overview of the main ornaments used in seventeenth- and eighteenth-century vocal music, relying principally on Tosi's, Agricola's, and Mancini's treatises. Emphasizes three principles: (1) that the ornaments must suit the character of the music; (2) that the ornaments are generally to be incorporated into the duration of the immediately following note; (3) that the beat must remain steady. The ornaments discussed include appoggiaturas, trills, mordents, passaggi.

906. Bacilly, Bénigne de. **Remarques curieuses sur l'art de bien chanter.** Paris: C. Blageart, 1668. Reissued in an English edition by Austin B. Caswell as **A Commentary upon the Art of Proper Singing.** Musical Theorists in Translation 7. Brooklyn: Institute of Medieval Music, 1968. xxiv, 224p.

Constitutes a valuable discussion of the techniques and principles of singing in the French Baroque style. Important for performers is the detailed discussion of ornaments, but the treatise also demonstrates how the long and short syllables of French texts affect the composition and singing of the air. The English edition includes a helpful translator's preface.

907. Cohen, Albert. "L'Art de bien chanter (1666) of Jean Millet." **The Musical Quarterly** 55 (1969): 170-79.

Outlines the discussion of vocal ornamentation found in Millet's treatise. The performance practice described applies to the lute-accompanied **airs de cour** of the first half of the seventeenth century. Millet classifies ornaments according to their position in relation to the main notes and illustrates them. Facsimile.

908. Cyr, Mary. "A Seventeenth-Century Source of Ornamentation for Voice and Viol: British Museum MS Egerton 2971." **R.M.A. Research Chronicle** 9 (1971): 53-72.

Not examined. The author's abstract for **RILM** (71/4400) states that the manuscript preserves thirteen songs, some unique and some in uniquely ornamented versions. The study provides various reference materials.

909. Duckles, Vincent. "Florid Embellishment in English Song of the Late 16th and Early 17th Centuries." **Annales musicologiques** 5 (1957): 329-45.

Illustrates the application of vocal ornamentation in the English songs of the late Renaissance and early Baroque, especially by court singers. The tradition is preserved in performers' and teachers' manuscript copies of the repertoire, providing fifty examples of decorated songs. The English practice was affected by both the Italian expressive manner of interpretation and the French use of ornamented **doubles**, the latter especially in the early seventeenth century.

910. Jones, Edward Huws. "'To Sing and Play to the Base-Violl Alone': The Bass Viol in English Seventeenth Century Song." **Lute Society Journal** 17 (1975): 17-23.

Not examined. According to the **RILM** entry (76/1584), discusses the performance of songs with accompaniment by viol without lute or theorbo or keyboard. The bass part

would include improvisatory filling-out, including realization of harmonies in basso continuo songs.

911. Spencer, Robert. "Performance Style of the English Lute
      Ayre c. 1600." **The Lute Society Journal** 24 (1984): 55-68.
      Also in **The NATS Bulletin** 41/3 (January-February 1985):
      13-19.

      Espouses a more highly expressive style of singing in
      this repertoire than is current, supporting the argument
      with quotations from contemporary writers on music. Offers
      practical suggestions for performance. Suggests further
      resources.

912. Spink, Ian. "Playford's 'Directions for Singing after the
      Italian Manner'." **Monthly Musical Record** 89 (1959): 130-
      35.

      Deals with performance practice in the solo song in
      seventeenth-century England, based on the translation in
      Playford's **Introduction to the Skill of Musick** (4th ed.,
      1664) of Caccini's preface to **Le nuove musiche**. Spink
      concludes that florid ornamentation was practiced in
      England throughout the middle of the century.

Accompanying and Coaching

913. Adler, Kurt. **The Art of Accompanying and Coaching.** Minne-
      apolis: University of Minnesota Press, 1965. 260p.

      Covers all aspects of the accompanist's and coach's work,
      from vocal physiology and diction and the construction of
      instruments to fingering and ornamentation. The later
      chapters, on "Elements of Musical Style," "Program-Build-
      ing," and "The Art of Accompanying and Coaching," are the
      ones of most direct importance to the art song, though they
      also consider opera and instrumental music. Bibliography.
      Index.

914. Bos, Coenraad V., with Ashley Pettis. **The Well-Tempered
      Accompanist.** Bryn Mawr, Pennsylvania: Presser, 1949.

      Offers observations and advice on some of the subtleties
      of accompanying, particularly in songs, illustrated by
      specific examples and interspersed with personal anecdotes.
      Portraits of the author and several of the art-song singers

he accompanied are included, as well as a discography of
his recordings.

915. Libbert, Jürgen. "Lieder und Gesänge mit Gitarre." **Musica**
      35 (1981): 250.

      Recommends the performance of songs with guitar as an
      alternative to the piano. The practice was common from the
      seventeenth to the early nineteenth centuries, and the
      repertoire for this combination has grown in the twentieth
      century. The literature includes a number of songs origi-
      nally for guitar accompaniment, of which some composers are
      listed. The publication of Schubert songs in guitar ver-
      sions is also mentioned.

916. Noll, Günther. **Liedbegleitung: Improvisierte Spielformen
      und Begleitmodelle am Klavier.** Mainz: Schott, 1970.
      169p.

      Not examined. According to the abstract in **RILM** (71/
      1472), classifies styles of accompaniment.

917. Werba, Erik. "Der Liedbegleiter: Zwölf Gebote--zwölf
      Verbote." **Oesterreichische Musikzeitschrift** 17 (1962):
      78-83.

      Lists "dos and don'ts" for song accompanists. Areas
      covered include the player's relation to the songs and to
      the singer.

VII

BIBLIOGRAPHIES

Literature

918. "Bibliographie: Sololied." **Musik und Bildung** 4 (1972): 132-
      36.

      A substantial bibliography on the Lied, listing almost
      entirely references in German. The bibliography is divided
      into the following categories: surveys, monographs,
      articles, didactic essays, and a rather cursory discography
      of twentieth-century works. No commentary or annotations
      are offered.

919. Swanekamp, Joan. **English Ayres: A Selectively Annotated
      Bibliography and Discography.** Westport, Connecticut:
      Greenwood, 1984. xii, 141p.

      Begins with a section of general sources, then lists
      material by composers. In each case the material is di-
      vided into literature, music, and recordings. Annotations
      are light. Collections of music and recordings are re-
      listed under each composer whose works appear in them, and
      the annotations list which songs appear. Indexes of
      authors, songs.

Lists of Songs and Collections

920. Albrecht, Otto E. "English Pre-Romantic Poetry in Settings
      by German Composers." In **Studies in Eighteenth-Century
      Music: A Tribute to Karl Geiringer on His Seventieth
      Birthday,** edited by H.C. Robbins Landon in collaboration

241

with Roger E. Chapman, 23-36. London: Allen and Unwin,
1970.

Gives an extensive list of the repertoire of German songs
based on English poems from before 1800 (excluding texts by
Shakespeare and Burns as well as the MacPherson Ossianic
poems). The article is valuable because it provides the
first identifications of the originals of some poems that
were set only in German (often from the translated collections of Johann Gottfried Herder). The composers surveyed
range from the time of the First Berlin School to the
twentieth century.

921. American Academy of Teachers of Singing. **Song Lists.** New
York: American Academy of Teachers of Singing.

Tabulate information on the songs including composer,
title, author of text, dates, range, availability, and
characterizations of songs. The following lists are rele-
vant to art song:
1-3 (in one). Three Hundred Songs by American Composers
5. One Hundred Songs by Modern English Composers
6. One Hundred Songs by Modern British Composers
8. Translations of Classic and Semi-Classic Songs
9 (three parts). Songs for the First Two Years of Study
10. Recital Songs by American Composers
12. Contemporary American and British Composers.

922. BBC Music Library. **Song Catalogue.** 4 vols. British Broadcasting Corporation, 1966.

Comprises a massive alphabetical listing. Volumes 1-2
list composers alphabetically, then songs alphabetically
together with information on keys, languages, and publishers. Volumes 3-4 list titles alphabetically, then
composers and publishers. The catalogue is not restricted
to art songs but also includes popular and show songs,
folksongs, arias, etc.

923. Böhme, Franz Magnus. **Volksthümliche Lieder der Deutschen im
18. und 19. Jahrhundert.** Leipzig: Breitkopf und Härtel,
1895. Reprint. Hildesheim: Georg Olms, 1970. xxii, 628p.

Arranges by categories 780 song melodies and texts from
the German folk-style song repertoire. The pieces include
those by major and minor composers and poets, as well as
anonymous works. Informative notes are provided on poets,
publication history, textual variants. Appendices include

an index of song collections, biographical notes on poets and composers. Index of songs.

924. Boytim, Joan Frey, ed. **Solo Vocal Repertoire for Young Singers: An Annotated Bibliography.** New York: National Association of Teachers of Singing, 1980, 1982. xi, 114p.

Lists repertoire appropriate for singers from junior high school to college ages. The items are grouped according to secular and sacred content (with a special section for Christmas songs) and by individual songs and collections. Each section is organized alphabetically by composers. Entries include titles (with translations), publishers, difficulty, ranges, languages, appropriateness to particular age levels, and cursory annotations. List of publishers.

925. Buckley, Wendell Dean. "The Solo Song Cycle: An Annotated Bibliography of Selected Published Editions with an Historical Survey." Ph.D. diss., University of Iowa, 1965. iii, 235p.

Lists cycles published since 1800 in English, French, German, and Italian. Works are listed alphabetically by composer, and each entry gives the cycle's title, the source of the text, publication data, a list of individual songs within the cycle. Annotations include performance forces, vocal range, language, duration, a description of texture and the nature of the cyclical unity of the work, and other evaluative comments. The historical introduction discusses cycles beginning in the Renaissance, with some critical treatment of major works. Appendices list cycles by accompaniment medium, composers by nationality, and poets. Bibliography.

926. Carman, Judith, et al. **Art-Song in the United States, 1801– 1976: An Annotated Bibliography.** N.p.: National Association of Teachers of Singing, 1976. xx, 308p.

Lists songs alphabetically by composers and titles. The annotations include title, poet, publication information, date of composition, dedication, key, range and tessitura, meter and tempo, length, level of difficulty, voice type, mood, descriptions of both vocal and piano parts, and comments about special problems or uses. A supplement incorporates songs from 1759 to 1819. Appendices give additional listings, a list of publishers included, and

sample programs. Bibliography. Indexes by subjects and
poets, composers, and song titles.

927. Challier, Ernst. **Grosser Lieder-Katalog.** Berlin: Ernst
      Challier, 1885; supplements, 1888-1914. 1053p.

      Consists of a very large listing of songs for solo voice
      and piano, including those with additional instruments.
      The repertoire includes all types of songs in all languages
      published in Germany, as well as many songs published in
      other countries. The songs are listed in alphabetical
      order by title and first line (with German translation
      where necessary), followed by the composers who set each
      text, opus numbers, publishers, and prices.

928. Coffin, Berton. **Singer's Repertoire.** 2nd ed. 5 vols. New
      York: Scarecrow, 1960, 1962.

      Catalogues vocal repertoire. Each of the first four
      volumes is devoted to a particular vocal range and sub-
      divided by voice type. Works are grouped by type and
      style. For each piece, available general and specific
      ranges are listed, as well as publishers. Volume 5, sub-
      titled "Program Notes for the Singer's Repertoire," gives
      brief paragraphs on composers and synopses of texts, and
      has indexes by title and composer. (Werner Singer is
      listed as co-author of the fifth volume but to judge from
      the preface seems to be principally responsible for its
      contents.)

929. Day, Cyrus Lawrence, and Eleanor Boswell Murrie. **English
      Song Books, 1651-1702.** London: Oxford University Press,
      1940. xxi, 439p.

      Lists 252 printed books of songs or books containing
      songs from the second half of the seventeenth century.
      Transcriptions of title pages, bibliographic data, location
      of extant copies, and notes are given for each book. An
      index of the 4150 songs included in the books gives refer-
      ences to the collections in which they appear and other
      information. Indexes to composers, authors, singers and
      actors, tunes, sources, songbooks, and printers, pub-
      lishers, and booksellers. Plates.

930. deCharms, Desiree, and Paul F. Breed. **Songs in Collections:
      An Index.** Detroit: Information Service, 1966. xxxix,
      588p.

Locates songs in 411 collections; scholarly editions are
not included. Songs are listed alphabetically by composer
or, in the case of anonymous songs, by nationality and
title. Brief annotations are provided for individual
songs. Indexes of titles and first lines, text authors.

931. Espina, Noni. **Repertoire for the Solo Voice.** 2 vols.
Metuchen, N.J.: Scarecrow, 1977. 1290p.

A massive list of pieces for voice, including repertoire
other than art song. The book is organized by nationality,
with sections subdivided by chronology, then alphabetically
by composer. Each piece is well annotated. The book can
be helpful in locating songs in collections, but the collections referred to are primarily performing, not scholarly, editions. Indexes of text sources, composers.

932. Fortune, Nigel. "A Handlist of Printed Italian Secular
Monody Books, 1602-1635." **R.M.A. Research Chronicle** 3
(1963; repr. 1970): 27-50.

Compiles a comprehensive list of books including secular
monodies from Caccini's **Le nuove musiche** to 1635. The
items are listed chronologically by year of publication and
alphabetically by composer or compiler. For each collection the number of secular monodic songs it includes is
given, as well as brief notes on editions, locations of
rare exemplars, and various miscellaneous details.

933. Gilbert, Dale, comp. **British and American Art Songs Published since 1967.** Elmhurst, Ill.: Chicago Singing
Teachers Guild, 1974. iii, 36p.

Lists songs alphabetically by composers. For each work
the publisher, title, text author, vocal range and tessitura, accompaniment, voice type, and other comments, including characterization of style, are given. The list is
intended as a supplement to Sergius Kagen's **Music for the
Voice** (see item 943 below), whose format it follows.

934. Goleeke, Thomas. **Literature for Voice: An Index of Songs in
Collections and Source Book for Teachers of Singing.**
Metuchen, N.J.: Scarecrow, 1984. [ix], 223p.

Lists the contents of standard practical collections and
indicates the range of each song. Bibliography; list of
audio material. Indexes of songs, composers.

935. Gooch, Bryan N.S., and David S. Thatcher. **Musical Settings
      of Late Victorian and Modern British Literature: A Cata-
      logue.** Garland Reference Library of the Humanities 31.
      New York: Garland, 1976. xxiii, 1112p.

      Lists works according to authors, giving for each title
      the composers who have set the text, publication informa-
      tion, genre (not only songs are listed), and performers
      required. Index by composers. Backnotes, keys to abbre-
      viations.

936. Hovland, Michael. **Musical Settings of American Poetry: A
      Bibliography.** Music Reference Collection 8. Westport,
      Conn.: Greenwood, 1986. xli, 531p.

      Comprises a listing of 5640 works (not exclusively songs)
      by over 2000 composers. The music is listed alphabetically
      by poets and texts, in entries giving titles, publication
      information, genre, and performing forces.

937. Huls, Helen Steen, et al. **Repertoire for Young Voices.** New
      York: National Association of Teachers of Singing, 1969.
      iii, 22p.

      Gives a list of appropriate songs for high school and
      college singers. Not only art songs are listed, and some
      collections are included. Entries, listed alphabetically
      by composer, include difficulty level, appropriate voice
      types, keys, ranges, very brief annotations indicating
      authors of texts, and publishers.

938. Kagen, Sergius. **Music for the Voice: A Descriptive List of
      Concert and Teaching Material.** Revised edition. Blooming-
      ton, Ind.: Indiana University Press, 1968. xx, 780p.

      Lists vocal repertoire selectively but extensively, in-
      cluding cantatas, arias, and folksongs, as well as art
      songs. The art songs will be found in the first two sec-
      tions of the book, grouped into pre-1800 and post-1800
      songs. The sections are further divided by languages and
      by composers. For each composer there is a brief note on
      the character of his oeuvre and a list of editions, fol-
      lowed by an alphabetical list of songs with indications of
      range and tessitura, voice type, and descriptive remarks.
      Index of composers.

939. Nardone, Thomas R., ed. **Classical Vocal Music in Print.**
      Philadelphia: Musicdata, 1976. x, 650p.

Uses a very broad definition of "classical," including sacred music, folk music, and semi-popular songs, as well as art songs and arias. Composers and titles (including translations) are interfiled alphabetically. Entries include indications of performers required and publishers. List of publishers.

940. Sears, Minnie Earl, et al. **Song Index: An Index to More than 12000 Songs in 177 Song Collections Comprising 262 Volumes.** New York: H.W. Wilson, 1926. xvii, 648p. Supplement. 1934. xxx, 366p. Reprint. Hamden, Conn.: Shoe String Press, 1966.

Lists individual song titles with keys to collections; composers, authors, and first lines with cross references to title entries. Not restricted to art song.

941. Stein, Franz A. **Verzeichnis deutscher Lieder seit Haydn.** Berne: Francke, 1967. 209p.

Lists composers alphabetically and songs by date under each. Song entries indicate title and first line, author, key, range, date, opus or thematic-catalogue number or both, publisher. Indexes of composer, poets, songs.

942. Thein, Anthony P. **American Art Songs for Tenor, Baritone, and Bass Voices from 1850-1920.** Ph.D. diss., University of Minnesota, 1978. 309p.

Not examined. According to **RILM** (78/4569), the entries include publication information, voice type, and range and tessitura. Analyses deal with harmony, melody, rhythm, and form.

943. Vogel, Emil; Alfred Einstein; François Lesure; Claudio Sartori. **Bibliografia della musica italiana vocale profana pubblicata dal 1500 al 1700.** 3 vols. Pomezia: Staderini-Minkoff, 1977. Vol. 1-2, xxii, 1888p.; Vol. 3, 615p.

Brings up to date Vogel's classic work, originally published in 1893, and a variety of supplementary efforts. Lists publications alphabetically by composer, running to 3030 entries. Each entry gives complete title page information, notes, contents, and locations of known exemplars. The third volume indexes names of composers, authors, singers, dedicatees etc., and text incipits.

Discography

944.   Stahl, Dorothy. **A Selected Discography of Solo Song.**
        Detroit Studies in Music Bibliography 13. Detroit: Infor-
        mation Coordinators, 1968.   xi, 90p.
        Supplement, 1968-1969. 1970.   xi, 95p.
        Cumulation through 1971. Detroit Studies in Music Biblio-
              graphy 24. 1972.   137p.
        Supplement, 1971-1974. Detroit Studies in Music Biblio-
              graphy 34. 1976.   99p.
        Supplement, 1975-1982. Detroit Studies in Music Biblio-
              graphy 52. 1984.   236p.

        Lists recorded art songs by composer.   Index by song
        titles and first lines.   Lists of recordings.

VIII

SOURCES

945. Baron, John H. "Secular Spanish Solo Song in Non-Spanish Sources, 1599-1640." **Journal of the American Musicological Society** 30 (1977): 20-42.

    Examines a number of collections of guitar songs that exist in sources without texts. A number of these are reconstructed by combining the guitar versions with vocal lines from concordant solo or polyphonic settings. These works do not show the influence of the Italian monodic repertoire, but are more nearly related to the chansons and airs of France.

946. Béhague, Gerard. "Biblioteca da Ajuda (Lisbon) Mss 1595/1596: Two Eighteenth-Century Anonymous Collections of Modinhas." **The Yearbook (Anuario) of the Inter-American Institute for Musical Research** 4 (1968): 44-81.

    Places two manuscript collections of songs in historical perspective. MS 1596 provides early examples of the Brazilian influence in the Portuguese songs of the last quarter of the eighteenth century, including several works of Domingos Caldas Barbosa unknown from other sources. The pieces in MS 1595 illustrate the accomodation of the modinhas to mainstream European (operatic) music. Facsimiles.

947. Brito, Manuel Carlos de. "A Little Known Collection of Portuguese Baroque Villancicos and Romances." **R.M.A. Research Chronicle** 15 (1979): 17-37.

    Not examined. The **RILM** abstract (79/358) by the author reports that the collection is of pieces preserved for the most part in sixteen manuscripts in the Biblioteca Geral da

Universidade in Coimbra, of which three are discussed in
detail. Style and performance are dealt with. Facsimiles.
Bibliography; work-list.

948.   Chan, Mary. "Edward Lowe's Manuscript British Library Add.
        MS 29396: The Case for Redating." **Music and Letters** 59
        (1978): 440-54.

        Makes the case for a new view of the collection of 106
        songs compiled by the seventeenth-century Oxford musician
        and teacher. Chan believes that the manuscript was assem-
        bled over a long period, from 1636 to the late 1670s, and
        thus that it represents one influential musician's record
        of changing musical tastes spanning the period of the
        Restoration. A complete list of contents of the manuscript
        is provided, including poets and composers for many of the
        songs.

949.   Cutts, John P. "A Bodleian Song-Book: Don. C.57." **Music and
        Letters** 34 (1953): 192-211.

        The manuscript in question is a substantial source for a
        large repertoire of ayres from the first half of the seven-
        teenth century. Most of the settings are for melody and
        bass, but several include tablature for theorbo. A com-
        plete table of the manuscript's contents is given, as well
        as notes on many of the individual songs.

950.   ————. "Drexel Manuscript 4041." **Musica disciplina** 18
        (1964): 151-202.

        Gives a detailed description of the manuscript, which is
        in the New York Public Library collection, as well as an
        outline of its provenance. A complete list of the contents
        is provided, and commentary on the individual songs is
        appended.

951.   ————. "Early Seventeenth-Century Lyrics at St. Michael's
        College." **Music and Letters** 37 (1956): 221-33.

        Describes the two manuscript collections MS 1018 and MS
        1019. In addition to Italian and Latin songs, there are
        thirty-four English songs with either lute or bass accompa-
        niments. Each English song is discussed, and the texts of
        several are printed for the first time.

952.   ————. "'Mris Elizabeth Davenant 1624': Christ Church MS.
        Mus. 87." **Review of English Studies,** new ser., 10 (1959):

26-37.

Sketches the background of the manuscript collection of songs, describes the volume, and lists the twenty-five songs it contains, with notes on each item.

953. ————. "A Reconsideration of the **Willow Song.**" **Journal of the American Musicological Society** 10 (1957): 14-24.

Discusses the seventeenth-century setting of the song used in Shakespeare's **Othello.** The text that is included in the Folio of 1623 appears to be a corrupt adaptation. The complete music and text of the authentic version are printed. Also discussed is the similar adaptation in **Twelfth Night** of Robert Jones's "Farewell, dear love," which is also printed with this article.

954. ————. "Seventeenth-Century Lyrics: Oxford, Bodleian, Ms. Mus. b.1." **Musica disciplina** 10 (1956): 142-209.

Describes the manuscript and outlines the history of its treatment in the literature. A table of contents and commentaries on individual songs form the bulk of the article. A number of texts are printed for the first time.

955. ————. "Seventeenth-Century Songs and Lyrics in Edinburgh University Library Music MS. Dc.1.69." **Musica disciplina** 13 (1959): 169-94.

Describes the history and present state of the manuscript, and connects three separate pages now in Birmingham City Library (MS. 57316) to the Edinburgh book. Gives table of contents and commentary on individual pieces. Texts and music are given for several songs.

956. ————. "Seventeenth-Century Songs and Lyrics in Paris Conservatoire MS. Rés. 2489." **Musica disciplina** 23 (1969): 117-39.

Describes a large fragment of an earlier, larger volume of songs set for treble and bass. Lists and comments on all the songs, including printing a number of the texts.

957. ————. "'Songs unto the Violl and Lute'--Drexel MS. 4175." **Musica disciplina** 16 (1962): 73-92.

Describes and surveys the provenance of this manuscript in the New York Public Library Music Collection. Lists the contents and provides commentary on each piece.

958. Duckles, Vincent. "The Gamble Manuscript as a Source of
      Continuo Song in England." **Journal of the American Musi-
      cological Society** 1/2 (Summer 1948): 23-40.

      Discusses several songs in this large manuscript book,
      which is in the New York Public Library. The English
      continuo song of the first half of the seventeenth century
      represented in the Gamble collection did not derive from
      the Italian monody but grew up independently. The continuo
      song developed a more declamatory melodic style and more
      chromatic and tonal harmony than its predecessor the lute
      song during this period.

959. Einstein, A. "Ein unbekannter Druck aus der Frühzeit der
      deutschen Monodie." **Sammelbände der Internationalen
      Musikgesellschaft** 13 (1911-12): 286-96.

      Discusses Johann Nauwach's 1623 collection of Italian
      monodic songs. The source was important for the transmis-
      sion of the monody from Italy to Germany, and it shows
      Nauwach's familiarity with the use of ornamental diminu-
      tions.

960. Fischer, Kurt von. "Ein schweizerisches 'Gegenstück' zur
      Marseillaise." **Schweizerische Musikzeitung** 118 (1978):
      10-14.

      Presents the little-known song "Friedensreigen," pub-
      lished in 1796, with a text by Johann Heinrich Voss and
      music apparently by Hans Georg Nägeli, who published it.
      The song is purely a celebration of peace and adopts no
      political stance. Despite its march-like rhythm, which
      resembles that of the "Marseillaise," "Friedensreigen" does
      not have a militaristic musical style. The complete music
      and text are given.

961. Fogle, James Charles Baruch. "Seventeenth-Century English
      Vocal Music as Reflected in British Library Additional
      Manuscript 11608." Ph.D. diss., University of North
      Carolina, 1979. 2 vols., 587p.

      Not examined. According to the author's abstract in **RILM**
      (79/376), the issues addressed include the contrast between
      lyrical and declamatory vocal style, and embellishment.
      Besides solo songs the manuscript contains dialogues. An
      annotated edition of the collection is included. Fac-

similes. Bibliography; work-list.   Index.

962. Fortune, Nigel. "A Florentine Manuscript and Its Place in
      Italian Song." **Acta musicologica** 23 (1951): 124-36.

      Discusses a manuscript collection, shelf-mark Q49 in the
      Liceo Musicale in Bologna, entitled "Raccolta di Arie à
      voce sola e Madrigale à più voci." Its repertoire dates
      from the second quarter of the seventeenth century and
      consists mostly of strophic songs. A complete list of
      contents is provided. A postscript discusses a number of
      other Florentine manuscripts.

963. Ghisi, Federico. "An Early Seventeenth-Century Ms. with
      Unpublished Italian Monodic Music by Peri, Giulio Romano
      and Marco da Gagliano." **Acta musicologica** 20 (1948): 46-
      60.

      Describes the source, in the private Barbera collection
      in Florence, and its contents. The manuscript includes
      monodic madrigals and canzonette, **arie spirituali,** and some
      fragments of dramatic works. A complete catalogue is
      given, including several incipits.

964. Harley, John. "Two Jacobean Songs." **Early Music** 6 (1978):
      385-89.

      Prints the only two songs of the period actually set for
      voice and keyboard. The pieces, Briant Ladlawe's "In
      Sorrowe Drown'd" and Thomas Campion's "Shall I Come, Sweet
      Love, to Thee?" are found in the John Bull manuscript MS 52
      D.25 in the Fitzwilliam Museum.

965. Hart, E.F. "Caroline Lyrics and Contemporary Song-books."
      The Library, 5th series, 8 (1953): 89-110.

      Reviews the extant sources, including manuscripts and
      printed editions. Points out that the musical sources
      sometimes provide more authoritative readings of the lyrics
      than do the publications of the texts by themselves, or may
      represent early drafts of the poems.

966. Nettl, Paul. "Ueber ein handschriftliches Sammelwerk von
      Gesängen italienischer Frühmonodie." **Zeitschrift für
      Musikwissenschaft** 2 (1919-20): 83-93.

      Describes and lists the contents of a manuscript collec-
      tion in the Lobkowitz collection in Raudnitz, of sixty-

seven one-, two-, and three-voice pieces with instrumental accompaniment. The collection represents the first third of the seventeenth century. The monodic songs include both madrigal and aria types.

967.   Niessen, Wilhelm. "Das Liederbuch des Leipziger Studenten Clodius." **Vierteljahrsschrift für Musikwissenschaft** 7 (1891): 579-658.

Discusses a manuscript of 109 songs, dated 1669. The texts represent a wide variety of types, from student songs to religious poems. The melodic sources include seventeenth-century published collections and actual folk tunes. Niessen regards the manuscript as important for its witness to a period of transition in the development of musical style. Index of the manuscript. Supplement of representative songs.

968.   Oboussier, Philippe. "Turpyn's Book of Lute Songs." **Music and Letters** 34 (1953): 145-49.

Describes the collection of twelve lute songs in the manuscript of Francis and Elizabeth Turpyn, in the Rowe Library at King's College, Cambridge. The book dates from 1610-1615 and contains some songs and versions of songs that are unique.

969.   Spink, Ian. "Sources of English Song, 1620-1660: A Survey." **Miscellanea musicologia** 1 (1966): 117-36.

Groups the published song books into three categories: miscellanies, collections of songs by single composers, and catch books. These did not appear in the years preceding and during the civil war. Manuscript sources, however, do provide songs from the period from 1622 to 1652. These manuscript books also give a fuller picture of the details of actual performance than the simpler and regularized printed books. List of song books published from 1651 to 1669; annotated list of twenty-one principal manuscripts.

970.   Willetts, Pamela J. "A Neglected Source of Monody and Madrigal." **Music and Letters** 43 (1962): 329-39.

Examines a collection of early seventeenth-century Italian music including a number of monodic songs, British Library Add. 31,440. Willetts speculates that the music may have been compiled by Walter Porter. A complete list of the contents of the manuscript is given.

INDEX OF AUTHORS, EDITORS, TRANSLATORS, COMPILERS

255

SUBJECT INDEX

Aesthetics 2, 3, 54, 55, 57, 65, 90, 99, 107, 111, 241, 249, 262, 399, 756, 806. See also Ch. IV.
Agricola, Johann Friedrich 905
Albéniz, Isaac 134
Albert, Heinrich 50, 77, 106, 135
Alberti, Rafael 788
Alison, Richard 232
Alnaes, Eyvind 129
Altenberg, Peter 167, 168, 169, 170
Ammann, Heinrich 509
Anacreon 297
Antoni 120
Apollinaire, Guillaume 456
Argento, Dominick 136
Ariosto, Ludovico 118
Arne, Michael 137
Arne, Thomas Augustine 137, 138
Arnim, Achim von 789
Arnold, Friedrich Wilhelm 187
Ashbery, John 861
Austria 51, 83, 84, 85, 86, 94, 95, 104, 115
Bach, Carl Philipp Emanuel 139
Bach, J.S. 359, 369
Bacon, Ernst 31, 140
Ballad 5, 18, 71, 85, 89, 101, 138, 319, 387, 388, 389, 390, 391, 419, 538,

554, 608, 692, 784, 785, 787, 802
Ballard 38, 43
Banville, Théodore de 272
Bar form 410, 412, 844
Bartók, Béla 141, 142, 143, 157
Bataille, Gabriel 144
Baudelaire, Charles 267, 272
Baudron, Antoine Laurent 483
Baumberg, Gabriele von 637
Bavaria 839
Bax, Sir Arnold 145
Beaumarchais, Pierre Augustin Caron de 483
Becker, Nikolaus 87
Becker, Reinhard 142, 157
Beethoven, Ludwig van 57, 66, 104, 113, 142, 146, 147, 148, 149, 150, 151, 152, 153, 154, 155, 156, 157, 158, 159, 160, 161, 162, 446, 609, 681, 800, 806, 811, 828, 883, 884
Bélanger 644
Benda, Georg 163, 785
Bennett, William Sterndale 164, 835
Berg, Alban 165, 166, 167, 168, 169, 170, 171, 395
Berg, Helene 165
Berger, Ludwig 172
Berkeley, Lennox 791
Berlin 65, 77, 91, 139, 172, 244, 474, 553, 647, 780,

265

CHOICE

NOV '87

Reference

SEATON, Douglass. The art song: a research and information guide. Garland, 1987. 273p (Music research and information guides, 6) (Garland reference library of the humanities, 673) bibl indexes 86-33553. 43.00 ISBN 0-8240-8554-X. ML 128. CIP

Seaton's guide represents the first attempt to provide an annotated bibliography of literature concerning art songs written between 17th century and the present. The bibliography was compiled with both musicologist and performer in mind. Included are historical surveys, books, articles, and dissertations that treat individual composers and poets, aesthetics and analytical principles, manuscript and printed sources, guides to song interpretation and performance practice, and lists of songs and collections. Since the scope of the art song is broad, Seaton excludes encyclopedia articles, composer biographies, and articles from pedagogical periodicals. Studies concerning the German lied account for nearly 60% of the bibliographic entries, but one should not regard this as evidence of bias on Seaton's part; an examination of the literature on art song reveals the unfortunate fact that art songs of other countries have received inadequate attention from researchers. Seaton has provided an excellent compilation; his bibliography will be used as a major research tool by both musicologists and performers. Academic libraries, all levels.—*D. Ossenkop, SUNY College at Potsdam*